THE TELEWORKING HANDBOOK

New ways to work in the information society

Sponsored by:

Lloyds TSB Group plc
Hewlett Packard
BT
European Commission (DGXIII/B)
Tolson Messenger

Get your money back!

If you are not already a member of the TCA, Europe's leading teleworking organisation, join today and get the price of this book back off your membership. Membership is open to all with an interest in teleworking. Benefits include subscription to Teleworker magazine, the handbook, group discounts, reductions on seminars, access to local groups, information on the telecottage network and a lobbying force that highlights issues affecting teleworking. Simply ring 0800 616008 to arrange payment details and we will send you membership information.

THE TELEWORKING HANDBOOK
Working from home in the information society

Written by Imogen Bertin and Alan Denbigh
Designed by Imogen Bertin and Sara Roberts at Cork Teleworking Centre
Cartoons by Colin Wheeler
Indexed and proofed by Stephanie Dagg, Virtual Editing Services
Published by TCA, the Telework, Telecottage and Telecentre Association

Copyright © TCA 1996

Apart from any fair dealing for the purposes of research or private study, or criticism or review, as permitted under the UK Copyright Designs and Patents Act 1988, this publication may not be reproduced, stored, or transmitted, in any form or by any means, without the prior permission in writing of the publishers, or in the case of reprographic reproduction, only in accordance with the terms of the licences issued by the Copyright Licensing Association in the UK, or in accordance with the terms of licences issued by the appropriate Reproduction Rights Organization outside the UK. Enquiries concerning reproduction outside the terms stated here should be sent to the TCA at the address printed on this page.

For further information on activities undertaken by the TCA, contact:
TCA
Freepost CV2312
WREN Telecottage
Kenilworth
Warwickshire CV8 2RR
Tel: +44 1203 696986 or 0800 616008
Fax: +44 1203 696538
Email: 100272.3137@compuserve.com
WWW: http://www.tca.org.uk

ISBN 0 9528492 0 8

British Library Cataloguing in Publication Data.
A catalogue for this book is available from the British Library.

Printed on paper made from 100% recycled fibres.

Contents

Introduction i
Acknowledgements. ii
Chapter 1: Overview 1
Chapter 2: Implementing Teleworking. 34
Chapter 3: Survival Guide 58
Chapter 4: Getting work 75
Chapter 5: Telecottages and telecentres 99
Chapter 6: Ideas for teleservices 123
Chapter 7: Staying safe and legal. 134
Chapter 8: Email and online services 160
Chapter 9: Quality for teleworkers 180
Chapter 10: Disability and teleworking. 194
Chapter 11: Teleworking equipment 204
Chapter 12: Training for teleworkers 231
Glossary: 264
Index: 267

Disclaimer

While every effort is taken to ensure the accuracy of the information given in this book, no liability can be accepted by the author or publishers for any loss, damage or injury caused by errors in, or omissions from, the information given. Readers are expected to check all essential information and to seek professional or expert advice as appropriate to specific circumstances.

Foreword

By Francis Kinsman, author of The Telecommuters

We probably all know the story of the beginnings of teleworking; or telecommuting, as it is called in the US. How a few far-sighted and intrepid pioneers, like their Professor Jack Nilles of the University of Southern California and our own Norman Macrae of *The Economist,* insisted that this was the way of future work. How the baton was picked up by others such as Steve Shirley, founder of computer software group FI, and Philip Judkins, mastermind of Rank Xerox's Xanadu downsizing/re-contracting experiment in independent and location-free working practice.

Teleworking has almost become an automatic fact of life since then, with hundreds of thousands of people in the UK and millions in the US making a living at it, in a myriad of different occupations. Add to that the vast drive among managers to be able to work remotely part-time, and you have a revolution on your hands – one in which the UK and Ireland are leading pioneers in Europe.

The degree of sophistication in the flexible working mode is more evident here than anywhere else in the world, with the possible exception of Scandinavia, where amazing things are going on. On the other hand, the volume per head of flexible working is greatest in the US, thanks to both Vice President Al Gore's "information superhighway" initiative, and to the recognition of the value of flexible working techniques in coping with California's post-earthquake damage limitation exercise, as well as with its stringent regulations on vehicle emissions caused by commuter traffic.

The advantages to the individual – of freedom, of control of personal fulfilment – are so immense that it is amazing more people haven't cottoned onto them yet. Admittedly, there is the fear of isolation, although that has been largely countered by the burgeoning telecottage and telecentre movement. The advantages to the organisation are likewise manifest in terms of cost-effectiveness, but are similarly unexplored due to management fears. The advantages are enormous. Thus, benefits are enormous and utterly unappreciated to date. It is to be hoped this book will help to bridge these gaps.

Yet some movement is discernible. The EU is getting its act together, as is the DTI in the UK and Forbairt in Ireland. The movement is painfully slow, however, with many obstacles such as unclear income tax laws, waiting to trip up the novice teleworker. The main thrust of activitiy is still in the networking and proselytizing efforts of individuals and associations such as the TCA, the Henley Future Work Forum and the UK Telework Platform.

The motto is for us all to keep networking and comparing notes. I am sure this book will inspire us to do so.

Introduction

by Alan Denbigh, Executive Director of the TCA

In the 18th and 19th centuries, the industrial revolution altered society entirely by mechanising physical work, and changing its method and location – people moved into towns in order to work in the factories where the expensive new machines were situated. As we approach the 21st century, the "mechanisation" of information work will constitute an equally drastic revolution.

Teleworking is just one of the changes which will make up the new information society. The word teleworker means simply working at a distance, but it indicates the freedom which information workers now have, by virtue of the technology they use, to determine the how and where of their work. People are moving back to their homes to work, rather than spending up to half a day in travel to an office which may only be in active use for as little as one fifth of the day.

This book is intended to provide a comprehensive guide to teleworking. It addresses issues facing a wide range of teleworkers – the corporate telecommuter, the self-employed freelancer, managers of teleworker projects and those involved in telecottages and telecentres. It is a reference book, and not intended as a "cover to cover" read. We have cross-referenced sections and provided an index so there is no need to start at the beginning!

The information presented here began life as a set of documents provided by the ACRE teleworking project, which was then updated over a period of years to form the TCA's factsheets, and sent out to members of the Association. It has been substantially updated and expanded to provide this handbook.

Acknowledgements

We are very grateful to our sponsors, all of whom are involved in their own sphere with teleworking as you can read in the sponsorship pages – Lloyds Bank, BT, Hewlett Packard, Tolson Messenger and DGXIII/B of the European Commission.

Information and assistance in preparing this handbook has been received from many different sources and in many cases from information available over the Internet. The TCA wishes to thank all those who have contributed their time and knowledge, in particular:

Andrew Bibby, journalist
Monica Blake, Information Consultant
Lesley Carr of People, Processes and Systems
Patrick Cotter, Waterstones Bookshop, Cork
Ian Culpin, DGXIIIB of the European Commission
Freddie Dawkins of the Telework Europa Forum
Ashley Dobbs, former Chair of the TCA
Brian Goggin of Wordwrights
Roy Guthrie, Chairperson, Scottish Teleworking Association and TCA Chair
Malcolm Lake of Effective Quality Management
Deborah Lowe, co-editor of *Teleworker*, the journal of the TCA
Sheila McCaffrey, Chairperson, Telework Ireland
Paddy Moindrot, Development Officer, Telecottages Wales
Barnaby Page, former co-editor of *Teleworker*, the journal of the TCA
Stephen Simmons of Cornix
Rhys Taylor of ACRE
Kevin Tea of the Telework Europa forum
Richard Warren of SteppingStones
Colin Wheeler, cartoonist
The staff of the WREN telecottage

Overview

What is teleworking?

Teleworking is working at a distance from your employer, either at home, on the road, or at a locally-based centre. Teleworkers use computers, telephones and faxes to keep in contact with their employers or customers.

In 1985, the Institute for the Future predicted 40% of employees in the US would be teleworkers by the year 2000 – yet the teleworking revolution hasn't happened yet. According to the 1993 BT manual *Teleworking Explained* "Teleworking is not a new idea. Nearly 25 years ago, during the 1970s oil crisis, it struck American academic Jack Nilles that instead of people commuting to work, the work could commute to them by telephone – telecommuting. But teleworking has failed to live up to the grand, expansive predictions made in the 1970s. AT&T predicted then that "all Americans could be homeworkers by 1990...

"What is more likely is an evolutionary change in working practices... Teleworking will increasingly be absorbed into the mainstream of normal working practice... the distinctions will begin to blur and it will become accepted practice for people to spend part of their time working outside the traditional office" The recession of the late 1980s and early 1990s didn't help, dampening all economic activity and removing one of the main drivers for teleworking – the need to expand organisations without crippling increases in overheads.

The 1996 *TeleFutures* report takes up the story: "Despite the slow take-off, in 1994 the European Union placed the adoption of telework at the top of the Bangemann Report list of actions to make Europe more competitive. The EU even set a target of 10 million teleworkers in Europe by the year 2000. Meanwhile, our screens and magazines are full of lifestyle articles on how to convert your spare bedroom into a home office, which Internet provider gives the best service, comparisons of mobile phone costs and announcements of high technology job creation."

A variety of interchangeable terms are used to describe the new forms of work, including teleworking (the catch-all term for workers who use tele-technology), telecommuting (often used to describe those who work for just one employer and who spend only part of their time working from home), distance working, and remote working.

There is wide variation between different researchers regarding what constitutes teleworking, which explains the disparity between different estimates of the uptake of teleworking, according to Ursula Huws writing in the UK Employment Department report *Teleworking in Britain*. These variations include:

- the **location** of work – is teleworking just home-based work or should it include other forms of remote working such as branch or satellite offices, neighbourhood work centres or mobile work?
- the **proportion** of working time involved in the remote working arrangement – should it apply only to workers who spend the majority of time away from the office base or include people who work off-site only on rare occasions?
- the degree of **dependence** of the teleworker on the employer – should it cover just permanent employees or freelances as well?
- the use of **information technology** – should "teleworking" apply only to those working arrangements where direct online electronic links form an essential part of the working arrangement, or be extended to cover workers who have traditionally been based away from the office but who now make use of information technology.
- the amount of **working time**: should this include people only spending the majority of time working away from the office or as little as one day per week ? What about part-time workers?
- the **contractual arrangement:** are only full employees of the organisation included or should it include self-employed freelancers?
- the **degree of use** of information technology: should the terms only apply where online computer links are used, or at the opposite extreme, where the worker mainly uses mainly postal systems?

Probably all that can be said about the widely varying figures given in different research studies is that they are useful in sketching out trends and giving some kind of guidance on how differing legal and social conditions in a variety of countries are affecting the trend towards teleworking.

The *Teleworking Explained* estimate of 1.27 million teleworkers in the UK consisted of the following:

1. Teleworkers spending majority of time at established home offices	
Self-employed/small business	570,000
Employed in major organisations	60,000
2. Teleworkers employed by major organisations who spend a minority of time at home offices	140,000
3. Mobile teleworkers on the road or in hotels	500,000
Total teleworkers	**1,270,000**

The UK Department of Employment Labour Force Survey estimates nearly 500,000 non-manual workers working at home but excludes part-time workers. Ursula Huws estimated in 1993 that approximately 6% of UK employers used teleworkers (*Teleworking in Britain*, Analytica), while the Henley Centre predicted in mid-1994 that there could be as many as 3.3

million teleworkers, or 4.6% of the workforce, in the UK by the end of 1995. The Institute of Marketing came up with a figure of 20% of employers using teleworkers or other homeworkers in autumn 1994.

The UK Employment Department's *Employment Gazette* re-analysed the 1991 census data in 1995 to estimate homeworking. According to authors Alan Felstead and Nick Jewson, around 1.2 million people in Britain (about 5% of the working population) work mainly at home or live at their place of work. The figure is constant between England, Wales, Scotland and Northern Ireland with few regional differences, although some rural areas, particularly tourist areas, reported higher figures. There was little difference between the figures for men and women. These figures include non-teleworkers such as farmers, but likely teleworkers scored quite highly – around 454,000 people where working from home in managerial, professional, technical, clerical and secretarial occupations. Around 224,000 were self-employed, with 71,000 working for an outside firm:

- 7.3% of employers and managers worked from home in 1991
- 6.0% of professional workers worked from home in 1991.

However, these figures are based on an ambiguous census question and have been queried by other researchers. The perennial UK Labour Force surveys suggest a figure closer to 2 million homeworkers. The situation in Europe and the US is also confused by problems with definitions and samples surveyed, but the 1996 *TeleFutures* report attempted to make a comparison making use of the 1994 TELDET EU survey and other sources:

Country	Labour force	Teleworkers	Percent teleworking	Phone lines per 100 population (ITU, 1994-5)
US	121,600,000	5,518,860	4.54%	57.38
Germany	36,528,000	149,013	0.48%	45.69
France	22,021,000	215,143	0.98%	53.60
UK	25,630,000	563,182	2.20%	49.42
Italy	21,015,000	96,722	0.46%	41.75
Canada	14,907,000	521,745	3.50%	57.5
Spain	12,458,000	101,571	0.82%	36.43
Netherlands*	6,561,000	27,203	0.41%	49.94
Portugal*	4,509,000	25,107	0.56%	31.13
Belgium*	3,770,000	18,044	0.48%	43.66
Greece*	3,680,000	16,830	0.46%	27.57
Sweden	3,316,000	125,000	3.77%	66.96
Denmark	2,584,000	9,800	0.37%	58.88
Ireland	824,000	15,000	1.40%	32.78
Luxembourg	165,000	832	0.50%	54.11

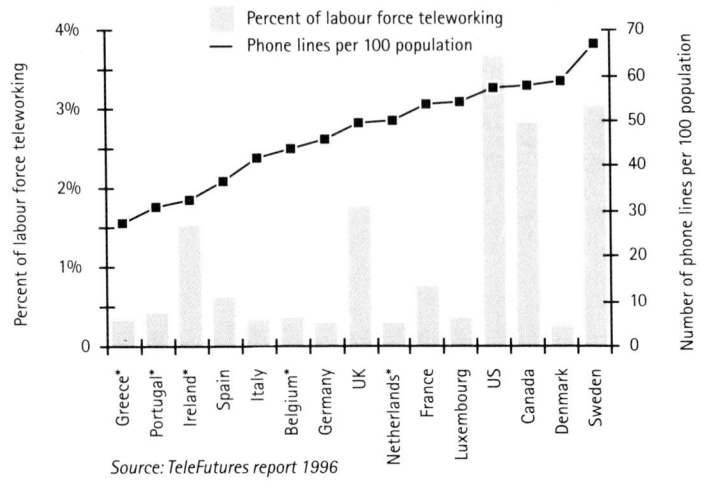

Percentage of labour force teleworking

Country	% labour force teleworking	Phone lines per 100 population
Greece*		
Portugal*		
Ireland*		
Spain		
Italy		
Belgium*		
Germany		
UK		
Netherlands*		
France		
Luxembourg		
US		
Canada		
Denmark		
Sweden		

Source: TeleFutures report 1996

*All the asterisked figures are extrapolated by the TELDET EU project. The numbers for Sweden are taken from a June 1994 report for the Swedish communications ministry, "A study of Sweden's Information Technology Infrastructure" by PA Consulting, and from information provided by Cobalt Trading Relations AB of Gotland. The Danish figures are supplied by TeleDanmark Consult and also relate to 1994. The Canadian figures are by courtesy of The Enterprise Network, Newfoundland.

These figures by definition do not include the wide range of workers who "tacitly" telework – spending odd days working from home, or persuading IT departments to supply them with portable PCs rather than desktops. Tacit corporate teleworking is probably the area of fastest growth in 1996.

Reasons for implementing telework

There are a wide variety of different reasons for adopting teleworking, many of which are listed below, but overall the drivers for increased teleworking fall into four main categories:

- improved competitiveness – large companies can keep down costs and overheads in comparison to non-teleworking competitors. Small companies that are growing fast can expand without major capital investments.
- better lifestyles for workers – more flexibility, less commuting stress, better balance between home and work lives.
- environmental considerations – reduced commuting means less pollution, better use of office space, less traffic congestion.
- improved technologies – developments in the use of ISDN

(videoconferencing, fast file transfer), the Internet (email and World Wide Web) as well as increased interoperability of IT systems make teleworking a practical alternative.

Teleworkers work in a wide range of fields. As a general guide, all jobs that do not involve physical production, extensive face to face customer contact and expensive specialist equipment can be teleworked. Other tasks suitable for teleworkers include those where the work that can be easily measured, those that involve mental rather than physical effort, and those that do not require extensive hands-on management or a large degree of team work.

Typical teleworker categories listed in John and Celia Stanworth's *Telework: The Human Resource Implications* include:

- professionals and management specialists: architects, accountants, management, marketing, public relations, human resources, finance, financial analysts and brokers.
- professional support workers: bookkeepers, translators, proofreaders, indexers, researchers.
- 'itinerant' field workers: company representatives, surveyors, inspectors, property negotiators, auditors, journalists, insurance brokers.
- information technology specialists: systems analysts, software programmers and engineers.
- clerical support workers: data entry staff, word processor operators, directory enquiry staff, telesales staff.

Other categories who often telework include technical support staff, quality managers and software localisation experts.

Teleworking advantages

(with thanks to *A Manager's Guide to Teleworking* and *TeleFutures*)

For the employer

■ **obtaining greater productivity**

Productivity gains quoted in published research due to teleworking range from 10–60%. The improvements can be attributed to a number of different factors:

- reduction of distractions, office gossip, interruptions of colleagues, noise in open plan offices etc.
- reduced commuting means that staff can be available for work at a given time irrespective of traffic conditions, weather, breakdowns etc.
- fewer people to mingle with means fewer bugs to spread, no sick building syndrome and less sick leave.

BT's Inverness Directory Enquiries experiment which included 12 people working from home found that the teleworkers were able to provide a service even when their office based colleagues were unable to come to the office in bad weather. Staff were not constrained by transport considerations – needing to catch public transport, get a lift home, car breakdowns etc.

- reduced sickness - studies have shown that teleworkers have lower absenteeism.

Travelling to work puts up a barrier which may encourage the decision to stay away, anticipating a worsening condition. Removing the effort of strain and commuting means teleworkers may consider themselves fit to work. An improvement in their condition during the day may also mean they put in half a day's telework, but would not have turned up for work if commuting was involved. Lombard North Central bank found their average sick leave halved from 6 days to 3 days per annum.

- increased flexibility

Staff working from home show greater flexibility. Teleworking may assist a company to provide a service out of hours – a rota of teleworkers could more easily provide this than getting people into a centre at times when travel might be considered unsociable or even dangerous.

■ **retaining valued staff**

Individual staff training costs can sometimes amount to tens of thousands of pounds per annum, and skills updates are estimated to take up 10–20% of managerial time, so losing valued and skilled staff is a drain on resources. If staff need to move in order to fit in with a partner's career, teleworking may provide a solution whereby the employee could continue to work for the company.

■ **accessing a wider pool of skills, or skills only needed on occasion**

A teleworking policy allows Helensburgh based publishers Crossaig to trawl more widely for staff – quite simply the number of people they need with medical and specific technical knowledge do not live within commuting distance of their office. Without a teleworking policy the company might have to relocate, be restricted in its growth or provide extensive staff training. Employees live up to 80 miles away and may visit the office only once or twice per year.

Brian Goggin of Wordwrights designs and develops courses for large organisations ranging from Aer Lingus to IMI – mostly Dublin based – from a spare bedroom in his home. "If you are good at what you do, most companies don't care how or where you do it," he says. Goggin believes companies will streamline their organisations further and make more use of services like his. "Companies know they can hire us for a particular project without having to commit to taking us on forever."

■ **reducing office overheads or avoiding moves to larger premises**

Research by Digital's Stockholm office in 1993 indicated that the average overhead costs for a European office worker amount to £6,000 per head per year. The average office space used per employee is 11 square meters. It has been independently estimated by Noel Hodson of SW2000 that, taking into account holidays, weekends, and daytime-only use, office premises are unused for 86% of the time. A flexible working policy introduced by Digital and supported by computer integrated telephony allows staff to occupy any desk space and have calls routed to them whatever their location. The new approach has enabled 650 people to work from one building in Stockholm which previously accommodated 450 and allowed two buildings to be closed at an annual saving of £2 million.

In the year to November 1995, IBM Ireland added 100 people to its workforce thanks to the ability of many of its workers to telework from home. Personnel manager Anne Keenan says: "of our 350 full-time staff, at least 150 have the necessary equipment to work from home. We also have a number of staff who do a lot of work abroad, and for them we have created what we call a "smart office", work space that different people use at different times. The company has made definite savings in this area because we are fitting 80 people into a space where we previously fitted 40."

■ **reducing the time mobile workers have to spend "in the office"**
Salespeople working for IBM in the US have cut out trips to the office between calls. Using laptops and wireless modems they can interrogate stock and price databases from the customer's office and print out quotations immediately. (BBC Radio 4 *In Business*, October 1995)

Field staff are an obvious occupational category to consider teleworking. Teleworking allows staff more time to complete the work and allows more time between jobs hence reducing stress. One such scheme has been the use of the Antur Teifi telematics centre in Newcastle Emlyn, Wales as a "neighbourhood office" for Dyfed County Council social workers. Twenty-five staff, whose headquarters is either Lampeter or Cardigan, can link up to the HQ word processing and database facilities through the telecentre. Staff were previously returning to base between each case visit, involving them in additional travel.

■ **maintaining competitiveness – faster services and lower costs**
At Instant Search, a small teleworking business based in Lancashire, customers phone in their requests for information on companies held at Britain's Companies House. Staff take down details and credit card numbers and then perform expert online searches of the Companies House databases. The information is swiftly faxed or emailed to the customer, providing savings in time and money over paper or in-person searches made directly by the customer.

■ **facilitating the management of a regionally-based service**
Burger King introduced teleworking for 600 of its regional managers. The company invested $5m in IT infrastructure and reported savings of $20m a year in reduced office costs. They shut down 12 out of 13 regional offices in the US and 50% of their office space outside the US. Managers reported

> **Conclusions to the confused state of teleworking research**
>
> Perhaps only three clear points emerge. The first is that teleworking is spreading as a trend. The second is that most people who telework like it. The third is that almost all pieces of academic research into telework should be treated with suspicion unless you have access to details of the questions asked and survey samples used.

preferring the freedom to choose when and where they worked and said they could manage their time better, but one said the downside was "You are never offline."

- **taking advantage of of labour in a different locality or timezone**

Cigna Benefits Processing, based in Loughrea, Co. Galway, handles health insurance claims for the American market. The claims are posted to a PO box at JFK airport in New York and sent by courier to Loughrea, where the Irish workforce is in constant contact with Cigna computers in the US via a leased line telephone link. The results of the claims are logged on the American computers for printout and dispatch of cheques by mail. The Loughrea location allows the US company to operate extra processing "overnight" and has the advantage of far lower staff turnover and training overheads compared to the American operation.

In Silicon Valley, the computer workers nod off after a a hard day's work while the day is just beginning at the rain-spattered KITE telecottage near Enniskillen run by Sheila McCaffrey. Handwritten CVs for that day's Silicon Valley job vacancies arrive by fax from San Francisco, are formatted neatly and sent back ready for immediate dispatch to clients of a job placement agency. Another recent KITE contract involves filing and preparing medical reports for a hospital in Boston. "They sometimes need us to do reports when it is the middle of the night over there and it would be hard to get anybody to do the job. We get a spoken report, put it into the computer and send it back down the line," explains Managing Director Sheila McCaffrey.

- **facilitating relocation or disaster recovery**

When Digital's office in Basingstoke, UK, burned down, the company decided to restructure the 110 workers based there. All except 11 now telework. The remaining 11 are the core staff operating a virtual office with "hotdesking" facilities for the other workers when they need to use the office. When in the office, teleworkers pick an empty "hotdesk", plug in their laptops and notify the receptionist which telephone extension they are using. The company is said to be saving round £330,000 a year on premises costs.

For the employee or self-employed teleworker

- **job satisfaction**

Teleworkers are actually more satisfied with their work than non-teleworkers according to a study by M.H. Olson (1989). In 1990 Ursula

Huws and others surveyed 118 teleworkers and found that they were rarely dissatisfied with their tasks, their place of work, or life as a whole. They were mildly dissatisfied with their financial situation, relations with friends and neighbours, equipment and leisure time available.

A European research study (PATRA, 1993) suggested that teleworkers can in fact suffer more stress than office based workers, but they are happier with their lot, and the stress symptoms decline the longer a person has been teleworking. The PATRA report also noted that teleworkers suffer fewer problems, such as repetitive strain injury, probably due to their freedom to take breaks and move around when they wish. Teleworking can allow time spent in traffic jams and on crowded suburban trains to be exchanged for more leisure, greater involvement in the local community, and a better family life. Teleworking can also satisfy the desire for autonomy and escape from office politics that a number of workers express.

■ **freeing up commuting time and expense related to office work**
According to the 1994 UK Department of Transport National Travel Survey commuters take an average of 27 minutes to complete their journey to work (in London this rises to 57 minutes). The average weekly journey time therefore accounts for five hours per week – over half a working day simply to get to work and back. The time and the cost is usually borne by the employee.

Aside from costs of cars or public transport season tickets, there are a number of costs which, taken together, mount up for the employee. These include: clothing (the need to maintain a business outfit including several changes of suits, shirts and shoes and the associated cleaning bills), lunch and drink costs. Those who commute often do not realise that for perhaps a 13 hour day out of the house, they are being paid for a little over half of their hours.

■ **retaining work after relocation**
Nicola Sheridan teleworks for Ireland's semi-state Voluntary Health Insurance company from her home in Castlebar, Co. Mayo. Nicola had 11 years experience as a systems analyst with VHI in Dublin when she married and moved to the west. "I was lucky to have a progressive boss who figured I could still do the job from home, put forward the idea of an "Electronic Cottage", as he called it, and arranged the whole set up." Nicola converted some space over her garage and VHI supplied the office equipment. She visits Head Office on average once per month and her boss visits her at least once a year.

■ **balancing work and caring for families**
Deirdre Talbot of Canada Life is an experienced underwriter who formerly worked from the company's Dublin office, but found that she was unable to spend the time she needed with her five year old son. Six months ago she decided it had to stop and planned to move back to her hometown of Nenagh, commuting 25 miles into Canada Life's Limerick office. Her boss

had a bettter idea: "Deirdre was a very valued member of staff and we didn't want to lose her. We banged a few heads together and decided that there was absolutely no reason why we could't set up an office and have her continue to work from home".

Although some jobs require the teleworker's presence during a core of hours in order to communicate with colleagues, many tasks may not require this core presence, giving the teleworker the opportunity to work at times convenient to them – which can sometimes be early in the morning or late at night. Teleworking does not solve the issues of child care, but the additional flexibility and lack of wasted commuting time make it easier to deal with the problems raised. In emergencies it is possible to work with children around, particularly very young children who spend most of the time asleep. Teleworking can help women returners to combine work with child-rearing, and allow fathers greater involvement with their children.

■ **providing jobs in remote areas**

Grampian Regional Council joined forces with IT experts Hoskyns to create a telework centre in the remote Forres region near Aberdeen in Scotland. Here 200 jobs have been created in 12 months, with up to 2000 planned by the end of 1996. The centre uses document image processing and workflow management to process council tax forms quickly and economically. Each form is scanned into the computer system; once scanned, different parts of the form can be processed by different operators, speeding the entire process. The Forres centre works not only for Grampian but also for a number of councils based in the south-east of England where wage rates are substantially higher than in Scotland, as well as processing two contracts from the US.

■ **providing jobs for staff with disabilities**

Cathy Cumberbatch is a trilingual PA with 20 years experience. Five years ago a car crash and subsequent stroke left her with reduced use of one arm and a number of other health problems that preclude full-time office work. Through a scheme organised by the Disabled Drivers Association as part of the EU funded HYPIT project, Cathy now works processing claims from her home office for an insurance company based in Dublin, work which leaves her some time free to freelance her secretarial skills to other local businesses. Even if she were able to work full-time, insurance rules in Ireland, which impose heavy premiums to cover workers with impaired mobility, would probably preclude an employer taking her on for a conventional office job.

Teleworking disadvantages

For the employer

■ **management resistance to the change**

In many surveys the main barrier to teleworking appears to be management attitudes. BT's 1993 study of 115 senior personnel managers reported in

Teleworking Explained also found many personnel managers resistant to teleworking:

Corporate obstacles to teleworking	(%)
Corporate structure and identity threatened	35.3
Face-to-face customer interface needed	21.0
Difficulty in managing teleworkers	
(adapting from eyeball management to management by results)	12.5
Access to communications equipment	14.2
Cost of setting up teleworking	11.7
Isolation of teleworkers	2.5
Security (data, confidentiality)	0.9
Selection of teleworkers	0.9

BT itself, when it experimented with its teleworking directory enquiries operators in Inverness, found that middle management resistance to change was a far greater obstacle than the technical issues which had to be overcome.

■ **monitoring teleworkers' productivity**

Some work tasks, such as answering directory enquiries calls, are very easily measured and unlikely to create much of an issue. Others, where work measurement is less easy, need to be piloted on a longer term basis until comparative statistics reveal whether value for money is being achieved. In all approaches a degree of trust is involved, and managers need to bear in mind that even in the existing office-based situation where they can "see" if someone is working, there is actually no guarantee that the work is being done, or being done efficiently. Conversely, not being able to see the employee does not alter this reality. This involves a change from "eyeball" management to management by results to see whether the work done represents good value to the employer, is completed to the correct quality and is delivered on time.

■ **motivation of teleworkers**

Contrary to expectations, research shows that motivation may not be a major issue. However, the results need to be treated with caution because many teleworking pilot studies have involved volunteers, anxious to make the system work, who may well have regarded working from home as a privilege that they were keen to retain. Implementing teleworking on a trial basis is advised (see Chapter 2, *Implementing Teleworking*). In the case of long-term teleworking employees, research by ICL/CPS specifies motivation and loyalty as two of the corporate benefits of their teleworking scheme since staff appreciate the flexibility afforded by teleworking.

■ **isolation and consequent damage to corporate culture**

The BT directory enquiries project in fact found that although they had designed voluntary opportunities for team members to socialise, some preferred to use the time for hobbies or home activities. Some of the distractions that make up "normal" office life also provide an important informal communications system which is not available to teleworkers. However, where teleworkers are linked by the corporate email system, it is often used for social contact and informal communication as well as to send and deliver work. The necessity for a team to be in the same place in order to work effectively may also be overstated, as many group projects are in effect broken up into different modules carried out by individual team members. The development of a range of software applications loosely called Computer Supported Co-operative Working (CSCW) can provide tools which enable a design team to remotely input alterations to one object viewed by all the group at their own location.

■ **security**

Security is often perceived as a risk because it is assumed that the existing arrangement is automatically more secure than a distributed working method. While there may indeed be security risks, usually the process of trialling telework will allow risks to be identified, and appropriate measures taken depending on the value and sensitivity of the information concerned (see Chapter 2, *Implementing Teleworking*). An increasing number of companies are adopting teleworking but maintain that trust and confidentiality are key issues. Therefore teleworking projects commonly involve existing company employees of long standing, rather than new recruits.

For the employee

■ keeping 'office' and family separate

The opposite side of the coin from management concerns about motivation is the need for teleworkers to be able to "switch off". Despite the rosy picture, working from home can cause family stress, particularly if the teleworker does not have a separate room or office for work. Typical strategies include ensuring there is a separate "home office", use of answerphones on the work telephone line to "buffer" after hours calls, and clear understandings about work duties between the teleworker and their family on issues such as interruptions and working hours.

Children often find it difficult to understand that a parent can be physically present in the home, but inaccessible to them while teleworking. Partners may find irregular working hours in the evening and weekends difficult to cope with, and computers frequently don't take kindly to pet hair.

Teleworkers sometimes find that their work is not taken seriously by family, neighbours and colleagues when they first start working at home. However, the initial scepticism usually wears off. Fletcher (1992) found that 27% of teleworkers thought that others perceived them not to be working when at home, but the same report noted that 57% of teleworkers thought that friends and neigbours looked upon their work situation favourably.

■ adversely affecting career prospects

"Out of sight out of mind" is a real fear for many teleworkers. Employed teleworkers may worry that they will receive less pay than office employees for the same work, or that they will not get the same opportunities for promotion because they may not be informed when vacancies occur (Murray, 1992).They may feel that they have to continually remind their employer that they are there, what work they are performing, that they are serious about their career and that teleworking is not a soft option. In particular, teleworkers need to ensure that their skills are kept up to date and that they are not left out of training opportunities.

■ isolation

The disadvantage most frequently reported by teleworkers is isolation from the companionship of the workplace. A 1992 survey by the National Computer Centre found that 75% of respondents cited loss of face-to-face contact as a significant problem. Solutions include ensuring regular managerial contact, supplemented with face-to-face meetings for the work team on a regular basis, and the use of available communications technologies, ranging from collaborative software tools such as Lotus Notes, email, videoconferencing and audioconferencing where appropriate to involve the teleworkers in decisions and developments.

Telecottages, or telecentres (see Chapter 5) can also help to overcome isolation by providing a place for teleworkers to meet and discuss common problems. Some telecottages operate a jobs or skills agency and act as a source of work. Telecottages can also supply equipment which can be used on a bureau basis, or hired, but which cannot be justified for home purchase on grounds of high cost and low usage levels. Examples are colour photocopiers, the provision of meeting rooms and access to videoconferencing units

■ **collective bargaining and trade unions**

Some trade unions have strong reservations about teleworking which were summed up in a 1991 TUC report ; "Overall the relevance of the union to the membership would almost certainly suffer as they (teleworkers) become one step removed from direct contact with the union through its representatives. The likelihood is that there will be a diminution in meetings and less contact with union representatives. Members will also be less likely to participate in any of the activities of the union which may become so distant the teleworkers will see union membership as an irrelevance."

However, Bill Walsh of MSF Union takes an opposing view: "The alternative to taking a positive stance on these potential developments is to try to sustain the unsatisfactory and unpopular employment status-quo for many people who want to opt for change... For these reasons, MSF is campaigning to ensure that home based working is a genuine extension of freedom for people at work.... The union wants to see a wide range of employment opportunities being made available to the home based worker." MSF's guidelines for teleworkers are given in the *Implementing Teleworking* chapter.

Other unions including the the Communication Workers Union have stressed that teleworking must be voluntary and that all pay, leave, pension and other contractual entitlements should remain unchanged. CWU also requested, in its pioneering teleworking agreement with BT, that it should also have access to the technology linking teleworkers to management in order to provide member services on an equal basis.

The National Union of Journalists provides members with subsidised email and online information services, and is moving into providing relevant training in software skills for members.

■ **the move to self-employment**

Sometimes a move to teleworking is accompanied by a move to self-employment. These teleworkers take on the usual risks of self-employment – they need to earn adequate income for their needs, insure themselves against sickness and incapacity, contribute to a pension fund, and buy new equipment periodically. Teleworking will not prop up a business idea that is fundamentally unsound, and those moving to self employment must satisfy themselves on the viability of their service. Potential self-employed teleworkers should seriously consider the risks involved in giving up a conventional job, such as loss of social welfare benefits, as well as examining the many opportunities that teleworking can offer.

Environmental considerations

Teleworking is good for the environment because it reduces traffic pollution, uses less energy than conventional office work and encourages rural development. In the US, clean air legislation, particularly in California, has led a number of large companies to introduce telecommuting programmes in order to reduce environmental damage caused by their employees commuting to work. The legislation requires that by 1996, in nine major US cities, companies with over 100 employees must cut the number of car journeys made by their employees commuting by 25%. While there has been no major attempt as yet to reduce commuting into city centres in Europe, concern for public health issues related to car use is increasing. City-by-city transport legislation may result in the creation of toll fees for those who drive in to metropolitan areas, as has been established in Norway. Increasing use of toll roads (road pricing) is planned by the UK Department of Transport, and studies indicate that two thirds of commuters use a private car to travel to work.

Conventional employees with company cars and petrol benefits often use them mainly to get to work and back and may also have parking costs paid for. Whilst a teleworker may still need the company car, the use and associated costs are usually greatly reduced. In some cases the need for the company car may disappear and an alternative arrangement may be to the benefit of employer, employee and environment. In two-income households, where one person works from home, it is likely that the need for a second car will be reduced.

A 1994 study of transport/telecommunications substitution by Horace Mitchell of Management Technology Associates examined Department of Transport statistics and found that 30 miles is the average travel-to-work distance avoided by teleworking. The national average figure of seven or eight miles is true if applied to all car journeys to work, but only because large numbers of people travel just three or four miles to work by car – these people are unlikely to look at the teleworking option. Only 4% of all car users travel over 50 miles to work, but they account for 22% of the total mileage of car commuters. Mitchell's argument is that the further the distance travelled, the more likely telecommuting is to become an attractive option. According to his analysis, if the top 15% of car commuters travelling the most miles switched to telework, it would halve the UK's total car commuting miles, petrol use and congestion.

Mitchell summarises that more miles on the data highway as opposed to the physical road means:

- fossil fuels conserved
- emissions reduced and thus damage to the ozone layer reduced
- revitalisation of rural areas.

The EU SAVE project, operated by EA Technology in Sheffield, has estimated that working at home consumes up to 80% less energy than working in an office. Similar reductions in carbon dioxide emissions are also achieved. The project surveyed 106 Sheffield officer workers and 22 homeworkers. Andrew Wright of EA Technology comments: "The average energy consumption for offices is much greater than for domestic use because it's a lot less controlled – corridors need heating, lights are left on for cleaners, PCs are left on in the evening and so on. A shift to teleworking would also create a much flatter electricity load profile – currently domestic and office supplies impose peaks on the system in their different areas, requiring additional system capacity and the starting up of less efficient generators at peak times." Home offices are also occupied full-time, in contrast to wasted office space. Cornell University estimated that over 40% of all desks are unoccupied on any given work day, the equivalent of 3 million empty desks in the UK.

In rural areas, where the decline of agriculture, let alone recent food scares, continue to cause growing unemployment, teleworking allows job creation without sacrificing greenfield sites to manufacturing industry. Geographically isolated areas which suffer disadvantage through increased transport costs can also benefit from teleworking jobs.

Technology trends and telework

Technology developments such as the World Wide Web and widely available, affordable PCs have made teleworking feasible. The current spread of teleworking could be described as a "limited contagion". Almost everyone has heard of it, and at conferences the questions have moved on from the naive to the detailed "how to" and "what if". A number of developments are likely to enhance teleworking possibilities over the next two years.

PCs spread into the home

According to market research specialists Romtec, the installed UK PC user base at end of January 96 was 26% (based on a total of 23 million households). Intel and Mac platforms make up 19% (the remaining 7% will include games machines, minority architectures such as Atari, and semi-obsolete machines such as the Amstrad PCW). Computers in the home are on an upward trend, making up the following percentages of the total PC market over the past few years:

Year	Home PCs as a percentage of total PC sales
1993	15%
1994	18%
1995	34%
1996 forecast	36%
1997 forecast	42%

This growth is partly due to the increased numbers of outlets on the high street and mail order chains, including Comet, Dixons, ESCOM, Currys, Dell Direct and Gateway. Home buyers tend to buy higher specification machines, going for safer purchases and looking at the longer term usefulness of the machine.

ISDN

ISDN lines provide teleworkers with fast file transfer and access to collaborative working tools such as videoconferencing. To date only a few teleworkers have been able to justify the cost of ISDN lines, but tariffs are falling fast, and developments may well follow tariff structures in the States, where telecoms companies are offering cheap ISDN access to teleworkers who "pre-purchase" blocks of usage. One company is even offering unlimited ISDN access for $129 per month. Widespread uptake of ISDN will lead to much more teamwork among teleworkers, as tasks which would normally require a physical meeting become possible at a distance through collaborative working software, speedy transfer of large files and videoconferencing.

Internet phones

Video and voice compression techniques have made the infamous Internet phones possible by compressing voice data into digital signals which can be transmitted across the Internet. Although the quality is not as good as that from standard lines, it is acceptable and substantially cheaper. Major telephone companies such as AT&T are trying to persuade the US authorities to ban Internet phones, but it appears they are unlikely to succeed, and the European regulatory attitude so far is to encourage competition and reductions in price through these new technologies.

Taking email and the Web to the limits

Dynamic links within email messages are changing the nature of information that is transmitted over the Internet. A number of software companies are converging email reading software with Web browsers so that instead of attaching a file to an email, the sender simply includes its URL (uniform resource locater). The reader then clicks on the URL and is immediately switched across the Internet to the source of the document, which he or she can read or download as they please.

"HotJava applets" are small application programmes which can be

ISDN connections and teleworking

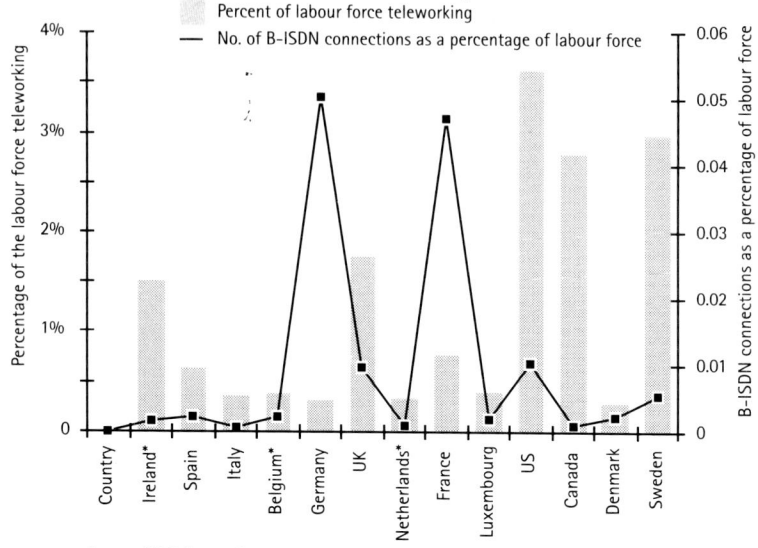

■ Percent of labour force teleworking
— No. of B-ISDN connections as a percentage of labour force

Countries (x-axis): Country, Ireland*, Spain, Italy, Belgium*, Germany, UK, Netherlands*, France, Luxembourg, US, Canada, Denmark, Sweden

Source: ISDN figures for end 1994 from Tarifica Omnicom
* indicates TELDET project extrapolations

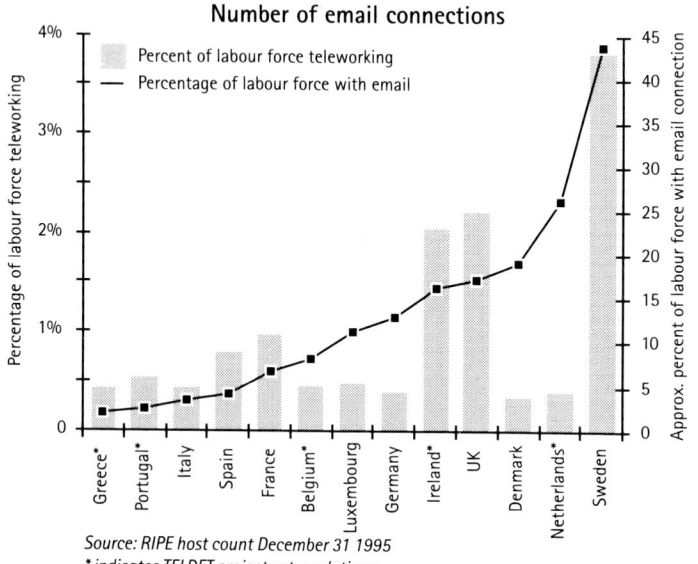

Number of email connections

■ Percent of labour force teleworking
— Percentage of labour force with email

Countries (x-axis): Greece*, Portugal*, Italy, Spain, France, Belgium*, Luxembourg, Germany, Ireland*, UK, Denmark, Netherlands*, Sweden

Source: RIPE host count December 31 1995
* indicates TELDET project extrapolations
NOTE: the RIPE host count only indicates the number of Internet hosts per country and should not be taken as a good measure of the absolute number of email connections; it is used here as a comparative measure of Internet development.

downloaded across the Internet, and carry out tasks for the person browsing the site on demand. However, a lawsuit between Sun and AOL is temporarily restricting the previously rapid development of this technology.

Electronic publishing is taking a leap forward with the widespread adoption of Adobe's portable document format (PDF). This format allows a document to be transmitted electronically and read remotely, including all formatting, typefaces, graphics etc. without any problems of compatibility. The reader does not have to have the same software, computer system or fonts as the sender. In conjunction with the proliferation of CD-ROMs and World Wide Web servers, and developments in HTML authoring software (the programming language used to produce World Wide Web documents), this is likely to lead to companies holding their customer documents on the World Wide Web, where they can be easily updated and accessed on demand by customers, rather than producing paper documentation.

Providing the right support for teleworkers

Remote technical support is a service that many experienced teleworkers need, as the complexity of modern computer systems and the plethora of add-on devices which often accompany the basic PC multiplies the possibilities for problems. Until recently, most people either relied on their company IT department or local computer dealer for help – very frustrating when your system has crashed and a deadline is imminent. Now a number of computer dealers and specialists are offering premium rate telephone helplines, or remote diagnosis assistance using modems. In the Far East, one company is offering a 24-hour helpline to business people staying in hotels who may have a problem with their PCs.

Training: reducing the overheads

Distance learning courses are now available from a number of suppliers, including the Open University. Both the range and the availability of these courses are likely to improve as course materials are developed for new tele-technologies such as World Wide Web. In conjunction with the spread of telework practices, and the need for constant updating of software and other work skills, it seems unlikely that conventional training courses involving travel to a training centre can continue to be the major form of training on cost and convenience grounds alone, though classwork will remain an important element of many training courses.

Social trends and telework

Telework is maturing as a profession – though many might argue it is not a profession but just a way of working that covers a number of different disciplines. The problems and advantages are remarkably consistent, whatever the area of work, however, and reveal a series of paradoxes.

Many of the initial technical problems, such as compatibility of software, reliability of electronic mail, credibility of homeworkers with clients, measurement of increased productivity and so on have been solved, but a new set of problems are appearing. These include the difficulties self-employed teleworkers find in getting training to maintain their skills, and anomalies of social welfare systems which can operate to the detriment of teleworkers who become ill or otherwise unemployed, when compared to traditional, office-based PAYE employees.

Research has been carried out to look at whether teleworkers become casualised, or suffer from low pay and poor conditions due to their isolation from processes of collective bargaining. In particular, some reports have claimed teleworking is bad for women, causing problems with the boundary between home and work, exploitation, interference with housekeeping duties and so on, often assuming a domestic role for women as the status quo. These reports conflict with the strong enthusiasm of female workers for teleworking because it provides increased flexibility to combine home and work duties.

To examine whether this problem is widespread, DGV, the Social Affairs directorate of the EU, commissioned Ursula Huws of Analytica to carry out a survey (in press) using a properly controlled sample across Europe. Some previous research studies had compared high-level professional male teleworkers against low-level clerical female workers, leading to the predictable conclusion that the women fare worse than the men. Huws selected some of her sample through a translation agency with workers in all European countries and discovered that differences in conditions, problems experienced and other factors were much smaller than had been previously found.

In fact, although previously women teleworkers had been reported to have greater difficulty with interruptions from family, Huws found that they tended to opt for clearer boundaries and working hours than their male counterparts, suggesting that they prefer and instigate a more rigid work structure.

Huws also found quite a few of the male teleworkers were "new men" who had chosen to telework in order to be with their children or partners, and to adopt a less stressful rural lifestyle. Men who made these choices were "feminised" in labour market terms, often adopting less secure and lower paid work in exchange for their lifestyle choice.

Overall, current changes in patterns of employment seem likely to lead to more teleworking, with trends to more part-time workers, more service and IT-based jobs, and more women at work, who require flexible employment patterns. A separate survey of female professionals found that 80% are in favour of teleworking, preferring to work at home one to three days a week where possible.

European governments seem to be convinced that a move to flexible working practices is crucial to maintaining competitiveness in comparison to other world regions. This trend, which implies a greater number of self-employed people, has perhaps moved too fast for existing member state structures, since in many European countries workers have a vested interest in not becoming self-employed, as they then lose many health and welfare benefits.

For example, in the UK if you have been self-employed for more than a year, you are only entitled to minimal, means-tested welfare benefits should you become unemployed or suffer disability or illness. Although self-employed people in Britain pay national insurance, their contributions only cover the National Health Service and Old Age Pension, not the wider range of benefits available to PAYE employees.

Some trade unions have opposed the introduction of teleworking and flexible work on the grounds that it leads to casualisation, low pay and loss of employment rights, while others see it as a way forward and an opportunity to increase their membership and services to the new breed of workers. Teleworking was initially held up as a job creation tool which would allow long-term unemployed, and those in rural areas, to access work formerly restricted to cities, but the technologies developed to allow teleworking, such as call centre software, are reaching levels of sophistication that require fewer, more highly skilled operatives, and major employment creation through teleworking seems unlikely. Indeed, teleworking may be contributing to the phenomenon of "jobless growth" currently being experienced in Ireland.

A further split seems to be appearing between those trained as low skilled teleworkers equipped to handle clerical work, (who may have difficulty in finding work unless a former employer wants to take them on, and whose jobs are often threatened by technology developments), and the professionals who telework. The professionals, in contrast, are complaining of excessive demand for their services, overwork and stress, and the difficulties of keeping up their skills in an ever-changing work environment.

Add to this welfare benefits systems which, because they take into account the earnings of spouses or cohabitees, encourage either double income households with no leisure, or no income households with no work, and it becomes clear that we may be heading for increased social division as a result of the move to flexible working.

Although telework undoubtedly offers opportunities to rural dwellers, it seems as though it is the city dwellers who are gaining the advantage because of their greater skills and higher levels of telecoms infrastructure and physical communications. The statistics taken from censuses show relatively low levels of teleworkers in cities, yet most urban dwellers will be able to think of a couple of teleworkers in their street – architects, designers, financial advisors – the attraction of doing without office overheads is luring increasing numbers to work from home. Conversely, the number of successful rural telework businesses appears to be lower than the census statistics suggest – Ursula Huws thinks this may be due to retired professionals in rural areas putting down a homeworking profession on census returns and surveys when in fact they are not active in business.

The global village is also some way away despite the handful of high profile examples of rural dwellers working for European and American clients featured in newspaper articles. The recent *TeleFutures* survey in Ireland confirmed that although 26% of the sampled companies allow their employees to telework, and 28% want to outsource certain tasks to teleworkers within a year, 81% would prefer to use a teleworker within a radius of 25 miles who would be available for face-to-face meetings.

The response of DGV of the EU, which develops social policy, to these paradoxes is as yet unclear, and there is considerable difficulty in coming to an agreement between European countries in this area as national law varies wildly (for example, homeworking except for family businesses is strictly speaking illegal in Italy). Currently proposals to create a third category of worker apart from the employed and self-employed, to cover teleworkers working on contract from home, are floating around. This move may put extra burdens onto employers using contractors, which will have a severely negative impact on the spread of teleworking and is likely to meet strong resistance from certain countries, particularly the UK.

Many of the often-quoted pieces of research have been extrapolated from tiny, statistically insignificant samples of as few as 20 actual teleworkers, or have selected their teleworkers in ways which bias their results. Others have asked confusing or ambiguous questions of their sample which lead to inaccurate conclusions. A large number of the research projects have been funded, designed or driven by companies which sell teleworking technology and have a vested interest in presenting teleworking in a postitive light, or from academic disciplines which have an axe to grind (such as women's studies PhD students looking into conflicts between telework and housework). No-one knows exactly how many people are teleworking, how, where and when they telework, or whether it is better for them than traditional office work. Base your actions on your own research, trials and experiences – it's your life, your family and your money.

The Information Society Initiative (ISI)

The DTI has launched a four year £35 million 'Information Society Initiative' designed to encourage British business 'take up tools' in the emerging information-based economy. There is also a European information society programme.

The comprehensive package of measures include a help line, research programmes, local support centres, case study information, and a number of innovation stimulating awards and competitions. Companies will also be encouraged to run their own technology awareness campaigns in the communities in which they are employers.

For more information on the ISI :

ISI info line 0345 15 2000
email info@isi.gov.uk
http://www.isi.gov.uk

The EU's telework programmes

This section has been provided by Richard Warren of Stepping Stones, a consultancy involved in a number of European projects.

Europe receives revenue through VAT and other levies. These resources are then redistributed into specific funds and budget lines which support actions to promote economic growth and social cohesion in all Member States. It is important to understand that these funds and budget lines are agreed upon by representatives from each Member State at a European level, and are designed to supplement, not replace, any existing provision that a particular State may have already established.

The structural funds

The structural funds consist of Regional (ERDF), Social (ESF), Agriculture (EAGGF) and Fisheries (FIFG). The European Social Fund (ESF) is the third largest item of Community expenditure and includes action lines to combat youth and long-term unemployment and the integration of the workforce into the changing job market. The structural funds have six priority objectives:

1. development of poorer regions (those with a GDP less than 75% of average)
2. support for regions and urban communities affected by industrial decline
3. combating long-term and youth unemployment and exclusion from employment of disadvantaged groups
4. facilitate adaptation of the work-force to meet new employment challenges
5. support for rural development
6. support areas with extremely low population densities

The level of funding for activities varies depending upon the level of priority, thus projects in Objective 1 regions (poor areas) can receive funding equal to 80% of the project's costs whereas only 45% is provided for projects combating unemployment in the better off areas.

Mainstream ESF programmes mainly cover local vocational training initiatives. Sub-sections of ESF include the following strands which normally require some form of trans-national partnership.

1. The Community Initiative which has three strands (women, disabled and elderly, youth)
2. ADAPT which targets adapting the skills of workers

3. INTERREG which supports cross-border co-operation and certain isolated coastal areas
4. RECHAR, RESIDER, RETEX, and KONVER which support areas involved in coal, steel, textiles and defence industries respectively
5. URBAN which supports depressed urban areas (population 100,000 plus)
6. Special support programme for peace in Northern Ireland and border counties of Ireland which supports a wide range of training and business measures to aid reconciliation between communities.

The structural funds are all managed by national state bodies or agencies. For an individual or a telecottage to make use of these funds they would need to apply through an agency such as a college, enterprise council or charity through whom the funds would be channelled, to the relevant national state body.

The European Social Fund has been used to assist a number of telework training programmes, especially for women returners, through programmes such as NOW (New Opportunities for Women).

Research and development

There are a large variety of research and development funds available through Europe, but nearly all of them require pan-European co-operation – you have to create a consortium with people from other member states, and write a proposal which covers your plans and stresses how the European aspect of the research is important. Many of the current funding lines address the needs of new technology and so hold potential for telecentres which are well established and interested in research. The first step is to become involved at a European level by registering with the Community Research database (CORDIS Partners) to build up working links. There are approximately 92 current research strands the details of which are available through the CORDIS Projects database.

The best known programmes are ACTS (Advanced Communications and Technology Services) and TAP (Telematics Applications) programmes. ACTS covers fundamental research into new technologies, while TAP looks at effective implementation of existing technologies.

ACTS supports telework projects through its "general" chain of research, which covers telework, computer supported collaborative software, actions to help SMEs use telework, and work to develop global networks for teleworked services.

TAP is an extremely wide-ranging programme organised into 9 sectors, which include: urban and rural areas, healthcare, training and education, libraries, disabled and elderly people, administration, transport, research, environment and engineering. Both research programmes are operated by DGXIII, which covers telecommunications and information research.

The ESPRIT programme is mainly involved in developing software, but some of its applications fall into the telework area, especially with regard to software that promotes flexible working and business reengineering.

The trans-European networks (TEN) programme, also run by DGXIII, contains some actions to encourage EU connections between teleworkers and telecentres in its TEN telework programme.

As a result of the Bangemann Report and the G7 summits relating to the Information Society, a number of research projects are underway. Some of these are highly technical, involving testing and setting standards for broadband telecoms technologies, but one strand involves helping small companies to reach a global marketplace through teleworking, amongst other techniques.

DGV, Social Affairs, is involved in looking at changes to laws on work practices, health and safety and benefits which may be needed to accommodate the move to teleworking.

DGXXII is working on an interesting concept of teleplacement, or teleapprenticeship, under which trainees would not go on placements to employers physically, but would work for them from training centres, under the supervision of their trainers.

Other Community Actions

There are a number of actions designed to help European businesses compete on the world market and provide employment opportunities. The programmes listed below are most likely to be of use to small operations such as telecentres and teleworkers. Details of all these programmes should be available through local business centres or National Awareness Partners. Details are also available from your national European Office.

1. The SME INITIATIVE is intended to help small and medium sized enterprises strengthen their competitiveness. Companies with at least 10 employees located in regions eligible for ESF Objectives 1 and 2 funds can apply.

2. SEED CAPITAL provides interest free loans (up to 50%) for entrepeneurs

3. IMPACT (run by DGXIII section E) supports the information services market through grants to SMEs in less favoured regions (Objective 1, 2 and 5 regions, particularly for the development of multimedia and electronic publishing research, and thus involves some telework-related projects.

4. CRAFT helps SMEs conduct research by contributing up to 50% of the research costs

5. LEI supports women, alone or in partnership, in creating their enterprise. Grants of 2,000 ECU can used to confirm the viability of a business, test its market or draw up a business plan.

Employment and Vocational Training

Most of the initiatives for Education and training involve the active participation of Universities or ESF institutions. There is, however, a major new programme that addresses SMEs including telecottages, telecentres and individuals called LEONARDO.

This programme started in 1995 to cover vocational training. It is a transnational programme which includes:

1. transnational pilot projects aimed at improving vocational training systems
2. transnational training or work-placements
3. exchanges for trainers
4. innovative actions in training such as tele-learning
5. demonstration projects using the new technologies for training and job creation
6. language training
7. surveys and studies related to vocational training

Any organisation involved in vocational training (including companies providing employment opportunities) is eligible to apply for funding. The process is through published calls for proposals from the Commission in Brussels. Details of the current Leonardo, and other, calls are available on the World Wide Web (http://www.cec.lu/en/comm/dg22/progr.html), or through your local enterprise council or European Office.

Other funding possibilities

There are many other European funding opportunities for a wide variety of social, cultural and political ventures. If you have a clear project, with European benefits, and are unable to access sufficient local funds, it is worth enquiring whether Europe can help. Funds may be simple grants of up to 30,000 ECU to conduct a study or pilot experiment, or larger grants to protect the European environment or heritage. Always remember that these funds are not free handouts but designed to help make Europe a better place to live and work in.

The LEADER II rural development programme contains as one of its objectives the support of projects which use innovation and technology to assist in rural development, and thus can assist with some telework projects in rural areas.

Bibliography

Each chapter has a separate bibliography and contacts list. Because of the fast-changing nature of teleworking, the bibliographies are arranged in reverse date order, and subordered by alphabetical title. Prices are omitted due to the difficulty of maintaining accurate price information updates.

Periodicals

Distans
Editor: Marta Sanden
Source: Titel-Data AB, Stockholm, Tel: +46 8 652 4300, Email: distans@ett.se
Comment: Swedish teleworking magazine

Flexibility
Editors: Edna Murphy, Andy Lake
Source: Home Office Partnership (HOP), Jeffreys Building, St John's Innovation Park, Cambridge
Comment: Periodical

Flexible Working
Source: The Eclipse Group, 18-20 Highbury Place, London, N5 1QP, Tel: 0171 354 5858
Ref: ISSN 1360-9505.
Comment: Periodical

European Journal of Teleworking
Source: Addico Cornix Publications, 64 Morrab Road, Penzance, TR18 2QT.

Telecommuting Review
Editor: Gil Gordon
Source: Gil Gordon Associates, 11 Donner Crt, Monmouth Jn, Tel: + 1 818 797 5482, Email: 74375.1667@compuserve.com
Comment: US periodical publication

Teletravail
Editor: Alain Maurice
Source: Sarl Teletravail,14 Rue Yvonne le Tac, 75081 Paris, Fax: +33 142522501, Email: 101572.527@compuserve.com
Comment: French teleworking magazine

Telewerken
Editor: Th Snijders
Source: Kommunikatie Service Nederland, Tel: +31 8850 18008, Fax: 08850 13234
Comment: Dutch teleworking magazine

Teleworker Magazine
Editor: Alan Denbigh Tel: 01453 834874 Fax: 01453 836174 Email: 100272.3137@compuserve.com
Source: TCA Tel: 0800 616008 or +44 1203 696986 Fax: +44 123 696538
Comment: Bi-monthly magazine for TCA members

XIII Magazine
Author: CEC DGXIIIF
Source: Commission of the EC DGXIIIF,TR61 2/1, Rue de la Loi 200, B-1049 Brussels, Belgium
Comments: Magazine of Directorate General XIII – concerned with European Community policy for IT industries and telecommunications. Includes strong interest in teleworking.

Publications

TeleFutures – a study on teleworking in Ireland *Date:* 1996
Authors: Imogen Bertin and Gerard O'Neill
Source: International Services, Forbairt, Wilton Park House, Wilton Place, Dublin 2
Tel: +353 1 660 2244 Contact: International Services – Declan Murphy

Teleworking - A Director's Guide *Date:* 1996
Authors: Various
Source: BT, IoD, Tel: Director Publications, 0171 730 6060

Teleworking: Thirteen Journeys to the Future of Work *Date:* 1996
Author: Andrew Bibby
Contact: Turnaround Distribution, 27 Horsell Road, London N5 1X2 Tel: 0171 609 7836

The Social Implications of Teleworking *Date:* 1996
Source: The European Foundation for the Improvement of Living and Working Conditions, Loughlinstown House, Shankill, Co. Dublin TeL; +353 1 282 6888
Comment: A series of three informative papers covering the legal situation in a number of European countries 1) The legal and contractual situation of teleworkers 2) The social security postiion of teleworkers 3) Teleworking health and safety issues

Europe and the Information Society *Date:* 1995
Authors: Spikes Cavell & Co on behalf of 3Com Europe
Source: Spikes Cavell & Co, Benham Valence, Newbury, Berkshire, RG20 8LU, UK

European Guide to Teleworking *Date:* 1995
Source: The European Foundation for the Improvement of Living and Working Conditions, Loughlinstown House, Shankill, Co. Dublin TeL; +353 1 282 6888
Comment: General guide from a social issues perspective.

Communicating Britain's Future *Date:* 1995
Source: Labour Party HQ Tel: 0171 277 3389
Comment: A Labour Party pre-policy document advocating greater employment protection for teleworkers.

Flexispace/Mobility of work *Date:* 1995
Source: The European Foundation for the Improvement of Living and Working Conditions, Loughlinstown House, Shankill, Co. Dublin TeL; +353 1 282 6888

Employment and economic impacts of advanced communications, and social trends in use of communications services *Date:* 1995
Source: DGXIIIB, European Commission Tel: +322 296 3460
Comment: findings of several EU research programmes, AD-EMPLOY, ACCORDE, SOCIAL TRENDS, METIER

How Vehicle Pollution Affects our Health *Date:* 1995
Source: Ashden Trust, 9 Red Lion Court, London EC4A 3EB

Legal, organizational and management issues in telework *Date:* 1995
Source: DGXIIIB, European Commission Tel: +322 296 3460
Comment: findings of several EU research programmes, COBRA, PRACTICE and ATTICA

Rural England: A Nation Committed to a Living Countryside *Date:* 1995
Authors: Dept. of Environment, Ministry of Agriculture, Fisheries & Food
Source: HMSO Publications Centre, PO Box 276, London, SW8 5DT Ref: White Paper, ISBN 0-10-130162-6

Review of Telework in Britain: Implications for Public Policy *Date:* 1995
Authors: Andrew Gillespie, Ronald Richardson & James Cornford
Source: University of Newcastle upon Tyne, NE1 7RU

Telehomework Case Study *Date:* 1995
Source: The European Foundation for the Improvement of Living and Working Conditions, Loughlinstown House, Shankill, Co. Dublin TeL; +353 1 282 6888
Comment: Empirical study on conditions and effects carried out in conjunction with IBM.

Telework and small business networking *Date:* 1995
Source: DGXIIIB, European Commission Tel: +322 296 3460
Comment: findings of several EU research programmes, WORKNET, EXPERTS UNLIMITED, TELEURBA

Teleworking in Ireland conference proceedings *Date:* 1995
Authors: Imogen Bertin and Brian Goggin
Source: Telework Ireland, Reagrove, Minane Bridge, Co. Cork Tel: +353 21 887300

Telework, Telecommuting and Decentralisation Date: 1995
Source: DGXIIIB, European Commission Tel: +322 296 3460
Comment: findings of four EU research programmes, OFFNET, EVONET, TWIN and HRM TC

Transnational collaboration from local telework centres *Date:* 1995
Source: DGXIIIB, European Commission Tel: +322 296 3460
Comment: findings of four EU research programmes, OFFNET, EVONET, TWIN and HRM TC

Transport Statistics Report *Date:* 1995
Source: Department of Transport, HMSO, Publications Centre, PO Box 276, London, SW8 5DT

Working at a Distance - UK Teleworking and its Implications *Date:* 1995
Source: Parliamentary Office of Science & Technology, Houses of Parliament, Millbank, London Ref: ISBN 1 897941 85 4

Work at Home: Estimates from the 1991 Census *Date:* 1995
Authors: Alan Felstead and Nick Jewson
Source: Employment Gazette, Department of Employment

1994 Survey of Rural Services *Date:* 1994
Authors: BMRB Int Ltd
Source: Rural Development Commisssion (RDC), Communications Dept., 141 Castle Street, Salisbury, Wiltshire Ref: ISBN 1 869964 44 6

Telematics Applications for Urban & Rural Areas *Date:* 1994
Source: European Commission DG XIII - C2, Rue de la Loi 200, B-1049 Brussels, Belgium
Comment: EC publication giving overview of use of telecoms and IT.

Teleworking: Right for your Business, Right for your People *Date:* 1994
Author: BT
Source: BT, Tel: 0800 800 600

DTI Teleworking Study 1992–1993 *Date:* 1993
Author: Horace Mitchell
Source: Brameur Ltd, 237 High Street, Aldershot, Hants GU11 1TJ

Flexible Work in Europe 1993: Survey and Analysis *Date:* 1993
Author: Home Office Partnership
Source: HOP, The Jeffreys Building, St John's Innovation Park, Cambridge CB4 4WS

Psychological Aspects of Teleworking in Rural Areas   *Date:* 1993
Author: PATRA deliverable report
Source: Available from Professor David Oborne, Psychology Department, University of Swansea.
Comment: This report is a literature review. Other reports from the PATRA project may also be available from Professor Oborne.

Teleworking - BT's Inverness Experience   *Date:* 1993
Author: BT
Source: BT, Tel: 0800 800 600
Comment: Much of the information from all pre-1994 BT booklets is summarised in the Teleworking Explained book, listed below.

Teleworking Explained   *Date:* 1993
Authors: Mike Gray, Noel Hodson, Gil Gordon
Source: John Wiley & Sons, Baffins Lane, Chichester Ref: ISBN 0 471 93975 7
Comments: Extremely comprehensive teleworking guide.

Teleworking in Britain – A report to the Employment Dept   *Date:* 1993
Author: Ursula Huws
Source: Research Strategy Branch, Employment Dept, Moorfoot, Sheffield, S1 4PQ, or Tel: 0171 273 6969. Ref: ISBN PP51/16304/494/52
Comments: Thorough national survey. Ref: Research Series No. 18

Analysis of a Major (UK) Teleworking Survey   *Date:* 1992
Author: W. Murray
Source: The National Computing Centre, Oxford Road, Manchester M1 7ED

Flexible Working   *Date:* 1992
Author: Trend Monitor
Source: Trend Monitor, 3 Tower Street, Portsmouth, Hants PO1 2JR.
Tel: 01705 864714

Review of Current Experiences and Prospects for Teleworking   *Date:* 1992
Author: Synthesis/Protocol Communications
Source: Commission of the EC DGXIII, Rue de la Loi 200, B-1049 Brussels, Belgium
Comments: This is one of a series of publications produced as part of the ORA project (Rural Areas project).

Strategic Briefing on the Tele-Economy   *Date:* 1992
Author: Trend Monitor
Source: Trend Monitor, 3 Tower Street, Portsmouth, Hants PO1 2JR Tel: 0705 864714

Telework – The Human Resource Implications   *Date:* 1991
Author: John and Celia Stanworth
Source: Institute of Personnel Management, IPM House, Camp Rd, Wimbledon, London, SW19 4UX. Ref: ISBN 085292 465 8
Comment: Very clear and comprehensive guide to issues affecting employed teleworkers and personnel management.

The Best of Both Worlds   *Date:* 1992
Author: Department of Employment
Source: Department of Employment, Caxton House, Tothill Street, London SW1H 9NF
Tel: 0171 273 4985
Comments: Small section on teleworking in pamphlet on flexible working, particularly for women employees.

The Economics of Teleworking   *Date:* 1992
Author: Noel Hodson, SW 2000, for BT
Source: BT, Tel: 0800 800 600

Comment: A shorter version of this report is available free as part of the BT Teleworking Programme listed above.

The Home Office Partnership Survey of Chief Executives *Date:* 1992
Author: Home Office Partnership
Source: HOP, The Jeffreys Building, St John's Innovation Park, Cambridge CB4 4WS
Comments: HOP worked on the Marketing Implementation of Teleworking in Rural Environments (MITRE) project funded by the EC.

Marketing Telecottages and Teleworking *Date:* 1992
Author: Various
Source: TCA/ACRE, Somerford Court, Somerford Road, Cirencester Glos GL7 1TW

Telecottages: the UK Experience *Date:* 1992
Author: Various
Source: TCA/ACRE, Somerford Court, Somerford Road, Cirencester Glos GL7 1TW

The Teleworker Portfolio *Date:* 1992
Author: Mercury Communications
Source: 0800 424 194
Comments: Free publication.

Clerical Teleworking - How it Affects Family Life Date: 1991
Authors: Leslie Haddon, Dave Tucknutt
Source: BT, Tel: 0800 800 600
Comment: A shorter version of this report is available free as part of the BT Teleworking Programme listed above.

A Study of the Environmental Impact of Teleworking *Date:* 1990
Author: D J Tucknutt
Source: BT, Tel: 0800 800 600
Comment: A shorter version of this report is available free as part of the BT Teleworking Programme listed above.

Conditions of Work Digest Volume 9,2/1990 *Date:* 1990
Author: Various – International Labour Office
Source: From Chater Associates, Wantage, Oxon
Comments: International telework case studies.

Telework: Towards the Elusive Office *Date:* 1990
Author: Huws, Korte, Robinson
Source: John Wiley, Baffins Lane, Chichester Ref: ISBN 0 471 92284 6

Rural America in the Information Age *Date:* 1989
Author: Edwin Parker
Source: Aspen Institute, 1333 New Hampshire Avenue N.W., Suite 1070, Washington DC 20036

Telecommunications in Rural England *Date:* 1989
Author: Various [NB scheduled to be updated during 1996]
Source: Rural Development Commission, Castle St, Salisbury. Ref: ISBN 1 869964 08 5

Tomorrow's Workplace – Harnessing the Challenge of Teleworking
Date: 1989
Author: The Henley Centre for Forecasting, for British Telecom and CBI conferences.
Source: Henley Centre

Work at Home for Computer Professionals: Current Attitudes and Future Prospects *Date:* 1989
Author: M.H. Olson
Source: ACM Transactions on Office Information Systems 7 Oct. 317–338

Telework: Present Situation and Future Development of a New Form of Work Organization. *Date:* 1988
Source: North-Holland Elsevier Science Publishers B.V. Amsterdam.

The Dilemma of Telework: Technology vs Tradition *Date:* 1988
Author: Gordon, G.E. In Korte, W.B., Steinle W.J. and Robinson, S. (eds)

The Telecommuters *Date:* 1987
Author: Francis Kinsman
Source: John Wiley & Sons, Baffins Lane, Chichester. Ref: ISBN 0 471 91789 3

Contacts and URLs

European Commission DGXIII, Directorate B, Advanced Communications, Technologies and Services, Rue de la Loi 200, B-1049 Brussels, Belgium Tel: +32 2 296 3460 Fax: +32 2 296 2980.

The Telework Special Interest Group was set up by a group of volunteers at the request of the DTI. It does not provide services to teleworkers but runs events such as seminars and workshops. 212 Piccadilly, London W1V 9LD Tel: 0171 917 2920 Fax: 0171 917 2836 Email: telework-request@mailbase.ac.uk

The UK Telework Platform is an association of the leading UK telework organisations and exists to promote teleworking. It runs a promotion programme funded by commercial sponsorship and organises seminars and conferences to spread understanding of telework, focussing on employers. It coordinates national activities and is the focus for European Telework Week in the UK. Warbrook Mead, Warbrook Lane, Eversley, Hants RG27 0PL Tel: 0118 973 1919 Fax: 0118 932 8650 Email: optima@cix.compulink.co.uk

Management Technology Associates, Clark House, King's Road, Fleet, Hampshire GU13 9AD Tel: 01252 812 252 Fax: 01252 815 702, Email: 100142.31@compuserve.com. Some of MTA's teleworking reports are available at http://mtanet.co.uk

Stepping Stones (Europe) Ltd, 194 Southcroft Road, Tooting London SW17 9TW Fax: +44 181 767 8030 Email: 100270.2407@compuserve.com. Services to small businesses including online searches, business training and community training.

EA Technology (EU SAVE programme). Contact Andrew Wright, tel 0151 347 2364

http://www.agora.stm.it/ectf ECTF is a network of academics and consultants whose discussions have been supported by the European Commission.

http://allserv.rug.ac.be/~dducheyn/telework/telework.html is a Belgian teleworking/distributed working site with information on telework in Belgium and on Belgian servers.

http://www.att.com/Telecommute_America is Telecommute America!

Some French teleworking information from Club de l'Arche is at http://www.atelier.fr/Galaxie/Arche/SemaineTeletravail.html

Teleworker editor Barnaby Page has a series of articles on teleworking available at http://www.compulink.co.uk/~ludlow/ including topics such as environmental impacts, urban planning and the developing world, and the impact of flexible working on equal opportunities issues.

http://www.dnai.com/~isdw The Institute for the Study of Distributed Work has a number of academic resources available.

http://www.echo.lu/teleforum/dg/13 - European Teleforum

http://www2.echo.lu/ie/en/iehome.html" is the European Commission's site giving details of projects in the Telematics applications programme.

http://www.eclipse.co.uk/pens/bibby/telework.html is journalist Andrew Bibby's home pages which contain a number of articles on telework.

http://www.fedworld.gov - Telecommuting evaluation information also available by telnetting to fedworld.gov (IP address 192.239.92.203)

The Telefutures report is available online at http://www.forbairt.ie/telefutures

The Foundation for Development of http://www.fundesco.es:80 Social Function of Telecommunications (Spain)

http://www.gilgordon.com Gil Gordon's website is a mine of useful information.

http://www.ghbg.org.uk gives pointers on how to take advantage of the ISI initiative.

http://www.icbl.hw.ac.uk:80/bill/telework/conts.html - A useful site from Heriott Watt University in Scotland including http://www.icbl.hw.ac.uk Community Teleservices International

http://www.isi.gov.uk is the address for the UK's Dept of Trade and Industry's new "Information Society Initiative", targeted at raising business awareness and use of Internet, open electronic networking etc.

http://www.ispo.cec.be gives access to a listserv which contains information about information highways and electronic democracy, including the EU's information society initiative. http://www.eto.org.uk will feature telework-specific elements of the ISI through the European Telework Online site. This site also contains information on the pre-arrangements for European Telework Week 1996 (4-11 November 1996)

UK management consultants MTA have a site with information about their teleworking reports called http://mtanet.co.ukMtanet which also includes information about a number of activities.

Scottish http://nsa.bt.co.uk:80/menu.html distance working information

http://ourworld.compuserve.com/homepages/Teleworker is some information from the Teleworker magazine

http://www.RACE.analysys.co.uk This is the excellent server operated by British telecoms consultancy Analysys. It contains information on the EU's RACE and ACTS programmes. Do not miss the SONAH section which gives succinct, practical useful summaries of the findings of several EU projects.

http://www.tca.org.uk is the location for the TCA web pages.

http://www.tweuro.com gives access to the Telework Europa pages, which contain a catalogue of other hypertext references related to telework and the EU's TAP programme.

The International Flexwork Forum in Tokyo is accessible at iff-info@apic.or.jp

The WELL (Whole Earth 'Lectronic Link) has information about a number of US community programmes at their gopher site gopher://gopher.well.sf.ca.us - look in the section marked civic, community and freenets for information by city.

Implementing teleworking

There are four main routes by which teleworking is implemented, which depend on the existing organisation structure. (Your organisation may be a "hybrid" suitable for more than one route which you should identify.)

1. In conventional organisations, **planned introduction of teleworking** usually involves three identifiable stages – the idea, the trial and the "contagion" by which the practice spreads out from the trial to widespread usage within the organisation. In this scenario, teleworking is no different from other changes that are introduced within organisations – it has to be justified, planned, and carried out with the consent of the people it will affect.

2. **Tacit teleworking** describes another method by which teleworking spreads in conventional organisations, usually through the practices of a management elite (who perhaps insist on being given laptops and modems so they can telework after hours or on the road). The elite may consist of individuals or groups who have high visibility and influence in the organisation. Elites sometimes include external figures such as consultants, academics or interest groups. They may not have formal authority, but they do have the attention of those in authority.

3. In flexible organisations, such as practices of professionals and some academic organisations, **teleworking is often endemic**. For example, at the Open University, which as its core business deals with remotely located students using teletechnology, there is an established tradition of email use and flexible work arrangements which has grown up on an ad hoc basis. Small virtual organisations sometimes begin from a distributed, flexible working basis. In these types of organisations, a review of the implementation of "endemic" telework arrangements covering issues such as software standardisation and training can be very productive.

> Gil Gordon's US-based *Telecommuting Review* is one of the best known periodicals for teleworkers. His upbeat resolutions for 1996 were:
>
> - **stop dabbling, start doing** – all the evidence from telework trials is that they work, so don't be tentative and feed the fears or the sceptics but "just do it".
>
> - **stop trying, start testing** – teleworking isn't technology dependent, but whatever technology you do use, test it properly for suitability – don't just try it out tentatively
>
> - **stop grovelling, start grabbing** – stop scraping and bowing for permission to give teleworking a trial – be assertive.

The stages involved in assessing a change to teleworking are:

- *feasibility study*
- *identifying suitable jobs for teleworking*
- *setting up a pilot project*
- *selecting suitable staff members*
- *drafting and agreeing changes to contracts and agreements*
- *arranging training*
- *installing the home office, mobile office or hotdesking system*
- *providing continuing support to teleworkers*
- *monitoring and evaluating the pilot*

4. For some, the introduction of teleworking may accompany a **move to self-employment,** or be a method of reducing overheads and improving productivity for an existing small business.

This chapter looks at the steps involved in introducing teleworking to a conventional organisation, but many of the points made are relevant to flexible or virtual organisations, and to the self-employed.

Stages of implementation

Feasibility studies

It is well worthwhile to assess the existing level of tacit teleworking at the beginning of any attempt to trial teleworking. Many personnel and human resource departments have no idea of the extent of tacit teleworking going on in their organisations – a celebrated exercise at the World Bank indicated that there were no teleworkers according to the human resources department, but a different story was told by the IT department – over 1,000 telecoms links being used for around 240,000 man days per year.

The feasibility study should outline the business case – including the operational, strategic, cost or employee advantages to be gained. If there are no gains to be made, don't proceed! The study should give an implementation plan covering the stages given above, and identify the main problems likely to be encountered and suggest solutions. This handbook does not cover cost benefit evaluations and methods in detail because they are admirably handled in BT's manual *Teleworking Explained* – the one book every manager implementing teleworking should buy.

Identifying suitable teleworking jobs

In order to select appropriate departments, some consideration needs to be given to the jobs that are encompassed. Some categories were listed in the previous chapter on page 5.

A classic example where teleworking has been practised for a number of years is journalism. Many journalists work remotely from their employer processing information from one form to another. The output is easily measured (pay rates for freelances are per thousand words) and the work is delivered by electronic means (fax, email or telephone). Technology has made it increasingly easy for journalists to deliver both text and images from remote locations, and many journalists prefer the peace of a home office to the hectic clatter of a newsroom, though most also like to visit the publication offices for social contact, feedback and ideas. In its extreme form the editorial office can simply be an administrative centre co-ordinating the various journalistic inputs.

It is also worth remembering that in the long term, introducing teleworking may give the company access to the skills of former staff members who have left due to early retirement, family reasons, travel difficulties and so on.

Setting up a pilot project

The first step is to establish a team for the teleworking pilot. You will need a project manager, clear responsibilities and reporting arrangements, and links to a sponsoring board member. The person driving the pilot project should have a neutral outlook on teleworking – neither a champion for teleworking nor a total sceptic – to ensure a measured and reasoned approach to the study. A number of organisations offer consultancy in telework trials and feasibility studies. You may not need to use a consultancy at all, but it is worth while talking to consultants to get an idea of the areas they cover – and you may find you go back to them at a later stage for specialist help with a particular area of the project.

The second step is to identify the parameters that will be used to assess the success of the pilot – without a clear measure of success or failure it will be hard to spread teleworking beyond the pilot study to other areas. In looking at how to evaluate the pilot project, the team needs to bear in mind whether the function chosen for the project is limited to that unit, or whether it is representative of the wider activities of the company.

A common error is to attempt the pilot project too quickly – a realistic timetable will allow time for problems to develop and be resolved without constant "firefighting", and anxieties among those involved. The project should also build in opportunities for individual and group meetings to review progress at an early stage in order to quickly identify and resolve teething problems which may otherwise become major difficulties.

The problem most widely encountered in teleworking trials is "middle

Case study: Britannia Building Society

Britannia Building society is using digital dictation technology to overcome an impending space problem at its 1300-strong headquarters in Leek, Staffordshire.

Each night, documents dictated during the day by headquarters staff are automatically downloaded to the PCs of home-based audio typists, who process the work the following day, returning it by modem for printing.

Britannia's teleworking initiative began with a pilot study in April 1995, involving 12 volunteers from three departments, and is now to be widened. As well as attacking the space problem, Britannia's move was motivated by the availability of cost-effective technology and the opportunity to offer staff more flexible working practices.

The Britannia system, unlike many voice-based systems, does not use ISDN lines. Diane Winkle, manager of the Central Document Processing Department, explains: "The only supplier offering equipment that would allow us to dial up the existing system, copy work from it and batch-download the audio to the girls at night was VDI UK". The system chosen supports five teleworkers and 500 authors. It containeds a two-port central processing unit, as well as voicecards, footpedals and headset controls for the teleworkers. Non-urgent jobs are downloaded via the system to the teleworkers as audio files, which are played back by the teleworkers in the same way as a standard audio casette – except that there's no tape because the dictation is held within the computer and played through the voice card.

The system provided good monitoring for the trial, as Diane Winkle explains: "I can access any information I need, such as time of work allocated, number of letters allocated, length of dictation, author, and how long it took to type. The home workers keep a record of their total hours worked, length of break and any system problems. I found that if the girls were not feeling 100%, instead of calling in sick, they would just ask for less work. During the winter months I believe we will experience even more time savings as staff will not have to brave the elements to struggle into work."

But the proof of the pudding is in the productivity: "My statistics showed an astonishing 40% increase in productivity over three months from the five audio typists working from home, compared to their output in the office. Operating a seven hour day, a homeworker processes an average of 85-90 letters, compared with 55-60 in the office."

---

management syndrome", which describes the difficulties encountered in management cultures where status depends on the number of people reporting to a manager. These managers like to see staff sitting at their desks and find it hard to make the change from eyeball management to managing by results. They can become a major obstacle to an effective trial.

Staff selection

It may be that teleworking is being offered to staff with caring responsibilities or with a particular reason to want to work from home – in which case the staff will be self-selecting. In more broadly based selections, experience has shown that some people are unsuited to the demands that teleworking may place on them. Those who think they are suited and wish to volunteer may not be. In particular, introverted people who are poor communicators are unlikely to adapt easily but may be attracted by the solitary workstyle. Some companies have used psychometric tests and counselling to ensure that applicants are likely to make a success of the change. The crucial personality traits are good decision making, effective problem solving and skills in self and time management – these are the people who will take the opportunity that teleworking offers and run with it.

Some employers may consider that established mature staff are more likely to want to telework and more likely to be successful at it. Staff selection, as with inspection of home premises for health and safety reasons, is a sensitive issue that needs to be handled carefully.

The physical situation in a staff member's home is also important to selection – a visit by a manager prior to beginning a telework trial to assess any problems is recommended, and investigations into the local telecoms infrastructure are vital. Some areas may have old fashioned exchanges which are unsuitable for high speed modem traffic, or else line quality to a teleworker's home can be poor due to long runs of overhead poles. Availability of ISDN services should also be checked (see below). It is also important that any disruption to the home caused by installation of equipment be kept to a minimum and negotiated with the staff member and their family in advance. Issues which need to be borne in mind in designing the home office are covered in Chapter 7, *Staying Safe and Legal* and in the Premises section of the Equipment chapter.

Agreements and contracts

Issues which need to be identified include:

- what is the likely reaction to the introduction of teleworking?
- can a general agreement be reached which deals with concerns or will the trial be handled on a one-by-one basis?
- is there a union to negotiate and plan with?
- who will provide and pay for IT equipment and telephone lines?
- what arrangements will be made for private usage?

Some companies formally draft a variation to the contract of employment of the teleworker (which can be a fairly simple, one-page affair outlining the main issues). Others have been advised by their lawyers to avoid making a specific agreement. Both approaches – contractual and informal – have merit and should be considered by the company's legal advisors. In

> **Case study: Allied Dunbar**
>
> At Allied Dunbar headquarters in Swindon, another financial services sector company, the teleworking trials are more of a "toe in the water" affair, with less than 1% of employees teleworking. Many other staff are salespeople working on the road, who in effect have always teleworked. Martin Wibberly, Director of Personnel says: "It is difficult to claim hard, quantifiable benefits. In terms of soft quantifiables, you hang onto people rather than losing them. It makes work more person-friendly.
>
> "We see an increasing desire on the part of our people to work other than from a corporate office block. What we want is to hang onto their skills whilst allowing people to work from home. Their motivations vary – we have a visually handicapped person who wants to work from home so we have installed all the IT equipment they needed to make that happen – places of work are not necessarily as friendly to disabled people as we would like. We have another who had domestic reasons for working from home – women shoulder the competing burdens of parenting and employment, so homeworking enables more of them to play a part in the labour market."
>
> Allied Dunbar teleworking kit precisely mirrors the norm at head office – a PC, a telephone, a printer and access to their mail accounts. To date, videoconferencing is only used on a trial basis due to the expense. Training is limited to specific technology and communications skills – there is nothing specific or different for the home workers.

creating the contract it is worth considering guidelines provided by the MSF union, which are reproduced in Chapter 7, *Staying Safe and Legal*

Training

Both management and staff will need training in order to adapt to the new circumstances. Much of this will focus on effective communication. Management in particular may need to adapt to a new culture – managing by results – which requires skills in the areas of delegation, co-ordination and orchestration. The common thread to the new management skills is improving interpersonal skills for a work environment involving less authority and more trust.

Specific management training material may be needed to cover:

- specifying aims and criteria clearly
- agreeing and negotiating work tasks
- relating pay to performance (where appropriate).

Colleagues will also need to be informed of the teleworking initiative, including the company reasons for introducing it, who is managing the project and what the outcomes are likely to be, as well as how they will be measured. Open information should dampen speculation about the long term teleworking intentions of the company and also assist the teleworkers in their communications with non-teleworking colleagues.

Other training strategies may include a programme of workshops for new teleworkers, allowing new teleworkers to shadow more experienced teleworkers, and allocating mentors to the teleworkers. Specific IT training modules will probably be required, such as the use of dial-up email via a modem, which will be new to those used to using office LANs.

Providing continuing support

Commonly, those who have been teleworking for some years report that lack of positive feedback becomes an increasing problem. Often teleworkers only receive feedback when there is a problem to be solved or a deadline to be met – they can get left out of team back-slapping when a contract is won or a customer's letter of satisfaction is posted on the office noticeboard. Rank Xerox, veteran of long term widescale use of teleworkers, takes the view that communications are also important to team building. Teleworkers are kept on circulation lists, listed in the company directory, invited to departmental meetings and invited to social functions.

The teleworking organisation is devoid of much of the informal communication that comes from people working in close proximity and needs to find a way of replacing the useful parts of this. However, the introduction of teleworking for part of a department can lead to a "them and us" situation. Management may need to think of measures to discourage this split (one employer encouraged a lottery syndicate to encompass all team members rather than just those "in the office").

Experienced telework managers have also reported the need to develop a "sixth sense" about detecting when teleworkers have a personal problem during telephone conversations. Don't forget that teleworking does not necessarily mean working at home in isolation 5 days per week, 20 days per month. A sensible teleworking programme should include regular face-to-face management meetings as well as opportunities for colleagues to mix at head office.

The pilot project team needs to create a support function which will deal with both technical and managerial issues arising from the project. In the main, these issues will be provision of technical support for computer and other equipment usage, and continuing management contact covering the following areas:

- reviewing performance
- determining pay and bonuses
- agreeing goals and improvements in performance
- individual development – counselling and training
- training (both giving and receiving)
- general gossip and banter that forms part of all working life

- providing space for "brainstorming", feedback and general discussion on the operation of the department.

The fact that the teleworker is now responsible for everything that goes on in the home office, including all supplies, can easily be overlooked. Hence it may also be wise to create a small budget for teleworkers to compensate for the extra burden – this could include paying for office cleaning, taking post, getting office supplies etc. Another solution is to arrange for a local supply of stationery, paid for from the central office.

Keeping in touch

Careful choice has to be made to ensure that the most appropriate communications means are used for the different types of information. The communication needs to be clear and unambiguous and should provide a record of any agreements for action. The overall system should also ensure teleworkers are kept informed, to reduce any feelings of isolation.

A set of communications guidelines could be established to take into account the cost, convenience and practicality of different communication methods, their merits and recommended uses for different applications. The excellent guide *Teleworking Explained* contains a sample table listing types of office communication and how they should be achieved, which can be adapted as the basis of the policy.

For example, an urgent request for administrative work may well be best faxed, including details of when the task needs completing and so on. The fax can be annotated and returned, easily confirming the receipt of the request and highlighting any ambiguities. An electronic mail message in contrast may well go unnoticed for some time, unless there are guidelines for frequency of collecting email.

Telephone

The telephone is a vital way of reinforcing other communications – for example details passed through by fax and email can be followed up with a phone call to talk through and develop a greater comprehension, or to negotiate a problem. But at the end of a phone call, without some kind of written back up it is possible for two different interpretations of the topic to persist. The telephone is a useful way of informally airing problems where fax or electronic mail are too constraining, formal, or unambiguous. The disadvantage of the telephone is that it requires the simultaneous presence of both callers, and the syndrome of "telephone tag" between busy people is all too familiar. Teleworkers may also find continuous calling from the employer causes interruption to their work and is irritating.

Fax

Fax provides a good method of getting short, sometimes urgent, instructions across and delivering copies of documents that may be held in one location but not the other. Because faxes physically appear in the teleworker's office, they are good for urgent documents – in contrast to email which requires the teleworker to actively log on and check whether any mail is waiting. However, fax limits the subsequent processing of the information as it is not delivered in a computer-readable form (even if you use a fax modem, the fax transmitted to the computer is a graphical image, not editable text). Fax also provides a way of transmitting information quickly and more reliably to countries with slow or unreliable postal service.

There can be a temptation to fax everything to save taking it to the post. But faxing large documents is wasteful and if the recipient does not have a plain paper fax, then the document needs recopying from easily-damaged thermal paper in order to preserve it.

Post

Teleworkers usually need to move physical documents around by post. The organisation should instigate a method of ensuring that company mail is regularly delivered to the teleworker – for example pigeon holes can be allocated and regularly swept by the internal system. It will probably also be necessary to make arrangements for urgent deliveries via courier on occasion. The Royal Mail quotes that 92% of first class deliveries arrive next day, but it is reasonable to assume that the 8% that don't are to locations off the beaten track – such as to rurally based teleworkers. Post in rural areas may arrive late and leave early, so specific information on the limits to local postal services is important and may vary for the range of locations where the company's teleworkers are based.

Email

Electronic mail is a good way of transmitting information that needs to be reworked by the recipient, and of keeping tabs on documents involved in a large number of projects, since most email readers provide an electronic "filing system" for messages. All commonly used email networks are "store and forward" systems which means the person at the other end doesn't

---

Case study: Siemens Stockholm

Relocation was the key to a major telecommuting pilot underway in Sweden. Siemens Nixdorf Informationssystem decided to relocate to a new site 30 km north of Stockholm in August 1994. Following agreement with trade union SIF, a teleworking programme was piloted in a trial beginning in December 1994. Formal agreement for teleworking was signed in April 1995, and 50 out of 170 staff are now teleworking, including the managing director and marketing director.

Staff who wish to telework apply first to their manager or supervisor, and that decision is later ratified by the MD. All teleworkers spend at least one day a week at the company's premises. Siemens Nixdorf pays for the cost of equipment (typically including a fax, a PC, a modem and a mobile phone) but employees meet any additional cost of working at home. The company is also opening a neighbourhood office at the town of Nynäshamn, and considering other offices to be located around Stockholm.

have to be online at the same time to receive the message – it is stored on the system until the recipient logs on to collect it. Other applications include documents which need collaborative work, details of progress against a plan, circulating general memos to a large group and maintaining regular background contact. It is also a good way of providing quick technical fixes for software – these can be "zipped" (compacted) and sent to the user very quickly. Many systems now provide "receipts" which return a message to confirm the original document has been picked up by the recipient, which can prove a useful project management tool.

Email is excellent for developing documents and technical specs through the use of different fonts or colours or annotations in a mutually used word processing package. The annotations show the additions and developments in a document passing through a team evaluation. Email is also a highly cost effective communications medium to international locations – a conversation of sorts can be held across thousands of miles and several time zones. Ironically a conversation with, say Australia, works better by email than a local one would, as the time phase difference means that email communications are less likely to cross.

Email generally makes a poor discussion medium and with the absence of intonation can sometimes be misinterpreted when opinions and views are conveyed. The latter has led to an etiquette around its use with various symbols and abbreviations, covered in Chapter 8, *Email and Online Services*.

Many companies now have their own World Wide Web servers and password protected ftp file transfer servers. These can be used to supply teleworkers with a "library" of corporate information and documents which can be browsed from the teleworker's remote site when needed and downloaded onto the teleworker's computer. Web servers are also useful for providing software tools, a general "noticeboard", news and other functions to staff. Where Web servers are not available, widespread distribution of corporate notices can take place by email, and these communications have largely replaced the traditional "office memo" in a number of organisations.

Equipment requirements

More detailed information on teleworker equipment and home offices is given in chapters 7 and 11, including issues of business rates, changes to MIRAS relief for the employee, and selection of hardware. This section specifically covers issues affecting organisations setting up a home office for an employee or telecommuters.

General considerations

In principle all equipment required should be supplied by, and remain the property of, the employer. As a ballpark guide to costs, a recent survey by Bill Murray reported in the Flexible Working magazine gave an estimated average setup cost per teleworker of £2,250–£3,500, with annual costs (heat, lighting, use of home as office) ranging from around £1,000 to £1,500 per employee.

Equipment should be ergonomically sound especially where repetitive movements are likely to occur. Furniture should provide adjustment for correct working heights – a good quality, comfortable, adjustable chair is especially important. Lighting should also be reviewed as home lighting is unlikely on its own to be adequate for office work. As part of the health and safety requirements, the employer should consider inspecting all home office equipment for ergonomics and safety and should organise regular inspections to test for electrical safety as with all other company equipment.

Veteran teleworkers tend to favour a separate building for the home office to give a work environment away from the potential distraction of the home, to assist with "switching off" at the end of the day and to prevent work material becoming distributed around the house. Failing a separate office, the space for the home office should be carefully chosen to take it out of the main family thoroughfare – ideally it should be lockable.

Often home spaces are characterised by lack of space, so good use of available room needs to be made. Both office and home furniture manufacturers are beginning to recognise the home office as a new market and produce special ranges. Typical features incorporated are lock away desks and cabinets where computers can be kept, space saving furniture (e.g. wall beds, high level shelving) and home-friendly office furniture (for example made of pine to match home decor).

Telephone equipment

A separate line is recommended in order to ensure that personal and work calls are distinguishable. This is desirable for both professional and psychological reasons. The phone costs should be paid for directly by the employer so that there is no perceived tax benefit. Additional services now available for standard telephone lines include call diversion, divert on busy, and conference calling, all of which are available at minimal cost and assist the teleworker in handling calls. Where much time is spent on the phone, hands free operation should be available and in some work situations such as technical support, a headset allowing more comfortable operation and less risk of strain injuries can be a boon. A cordless phone may also be useful allowing the teleworker the freedom of the house without missing calls.

Where a fax machine is required, an additional line rather than a line shared between telephone and fax is recommended. This has the advantage of allowing the teleworker to receive and send faxes whilst using the telephone and avoids annoying busy lines due to fax traffic. If significant online work is being performed a separate line for the modem should also be installed. If the use is not significant, sharing with the fax line should be adequate.

Case study: Digital

Digital Equipment Corporation (DEC) has long been seen as a teleworking pioneer. According to DEC's teleworking consultant Stephen Jupp: "we have saved £16m per annum in costs worldwide through teleworking and we have seen a 20–40% growth in productivity". DEC currently has 9,000 out of a worldwide workforce of 65,000 teleworking, and the UK operation has over one-third teleworkers, with 1,500 out of 3,500 home working.

There is no particular selection process, staff just ask if they want to telework, but the company has been keen to encourage teleworking where lease breaks occurred so that by teleworking a workforce they could "get rid of" a building. Once individuals decide to telework, DEC provides two courses, one to help them understand the differences between homeworking and office working, thinking through what work is all about. The other covers the practical side, such as accessing mail from home, handling client calls to home, and recording telephone usage.

Increasingly, transferable personal numbers are being used. A permanent or personal number is rented by the company which can be linked to the teleworker's existing line. This means that if the teleworker relocates or moves back into the central office the number remains the same. When employees leave the company the number is effectively assigned to a company position and can simply be reassigned to the next person taking up that position.

Message taking

Corporate voice mail systems are often used to take messages for teleworkers, but an answering machine is flexible and easily controlled and may well be the simplest solution. Users should be encouraged to provide a message which is dated, states when the teleworker will be next available, and if an alternative number can be called. A number of companies offer message taking services, which use call diversion from the teleworker's home and caller line identification tools to create a customised response.

ISDN (Integrated Services Digital Network) lines

With more sophisticated requirements, and larger amounts of data transfer, a high speed digital ISDN line may be appropriate. This type of line allows faster transfer of data, high quality voice communication and videoconferencing. A number of devices can share the same ISDN line, so only one is likely to be required per teleworker. ISDN is not available on some older exchanges, and enquiries will need to be made with your telephone supplier for specific locations, especially in rural areas.

ISDN lines are increasingly used for personal videoconferencing equipment. The equipment, whose cost is fast reducing, can be installed in a PC, and consists of a camera which is attached to the PC monitor or stands on a separate stalk, an ISDN connector, cards which fit into the PC, and software. The videophone, in addition to providing visual images, can transmit files and allow application sharing between remote users.

Another benefit of ISDN is that it can be used to provide an apparent continuous link to a remote computer whilst in fact disconnecting the line and saving call charges when there is no activity. This enables the line costs for remote staff accessing central databases to be substantially reduced, particularly if the access is intermittent. The technique is known as spoofing (this is also available on standard phone lines but is not as "transparent" in its operation owing to the lower speeds available). Spoofing is so called because it convinces the linked computers that a connection still exists even though the line may well have been "timed out". Algorithms controlling the disconnection point will take into account the tariff system – allowing, for example, for minimum call charges.

ACD (Automated Call Distribution systems)

The degree of technology employed for clerical and administrative staff carrying out "call centre" type duties is quite likely to be greater than that for professional teleworkers. For example, the technology employed for the BT Directory Enquiries project included the ability to distribute calls from a central location with an Automated Call Distribution system as well as links to a central database, electronic mail and videophone support. ACD systems allow incoming calls to be distributed to homebased teleworkers, giving an even loading amongst operators and equalising the caller response time.

The BT system used the two channels available through the ISDN(2) digital phone line connection – on one channel voice and data was combined for transmission using a multiplexor. The other channel was used for videophone transmission. A further BT trial underway in Southampton has dispensed with the video link, but maintained the other equipment.

Case study: Lombard North Central

Lombard undertook a two year teleworking trial for 10 professionals. All changes in working conditions were drafted into existing employment contracts. Managers visited worker's homes to advise on health, safety and security issues. The final results initially showed 20% productivity gains, which settled down to 10% above normal, but the quality of work also improved. Sick leave reduced by 50%, from the company's average of six days a year to three days.

PCs and technical support

The computer, and in particular the software to be used, should be compatible with that available at the head office allowing greater flexibility, compatibility and support. This also eases the teleworkers transition to the home office and, where necessary, back to using the head office base. Technical support mechanisms should prioritise the teleworker, who after all may well be isolated and unable to work without a functioning PC – in contrast to central office based colleagues. For companies without their own means of nationwide equipment support, it may be worth looking at subscribing to a technical support service which can ensure speedy repair, assistance or replacement of equipment at teleworker's homes.

CSCW techniques

The DTI is running a series of projects to develop Computer Supported Co-operative Work (CSCW) techniques, and the following text is taken from their CSCW website:

"The traditional view that IT should emulate existing business processes has been overturned. IT is increasingly seen as an opportunity to change business processes. The concept of (CSCW) is seen as providing some of the answers. It combines computers, telecommunications and software to support new organisational structures. CSCW embraces the theories of business process re-engineering, the technology of client/server networks and software technologies such as electronic mail and "groupware". It is not a "product" in the traditional sense– but a way of thinking about how technology and people can work together more effectively.

CSCW has the following functions:

- providing the effective, efficient support of organisational goals
- adopting a cooperative attitude to work, taking into account interdependency, teamwork and graphical mobility
- shared mediated collaboration
- cooperating in work supported by technology."

Software for CSCW tasks is often known as groupware. The most common application of groupware is customer tracking. For example, where a customer rings up a bank to enquire about a loan, a customer tracking form is automatically created. From that point forward, every telephone call, meeting, piece of correspondence and so on can be documented on the tracking form – gone are the problems of an employee being out sick with crucial documents locked away in their office. Groupware can also allow several people to work on the same document – all the team download the document and make their changes. The groupware software recognises which parts of the document have been changed and copies only those parts back to the central computer, indicating the author of the changes in each instance.

An example of groupware in action is the use of Lotus Notes by the Henley Management College in its global classroom project to overcome the geographical barriers to distance learning. Henley has adopted groupware technology to support its 7,000 distance learning students world-wide, providing interaction with peers, tutors, staff and other information sources. Electronic support for students using PCs and modems started in 1988. This interaction complements the written course materials, workshops, telephone helpline and newsletters. Henley adopted Lotus Notes in early 1994.

The key objectives were to provide students interaction with a peer group of students, a sense of community and the lasting networking opportunities that those offer, interaction with tutors and access to the Henley library. Students are provided with a remote version of Lotus Notes on their PC so that they can work on databases off-line: when convenient, they use a modem to "replicate" their databases with those on Henley's server. Students can send electronic mail, search databases and retrieve and send files, as well as being able to participate in electronic discussions led by Henley faculty. They can read profiles of other Notes users, and network with those with similar interests. The electronic booking of workshops and ordering of papers is in place; electronic submission and marking of assignments and course works has also recently been launched.

A tutor from New Zealand explains: "When I receive a query from a student on Notes, I have time to give a full answer with accurate references, indeed I can give the student a mini tutorial, and it will also be available to other students. The student raising the query gets the benefit of one to one tuition but other students can get involved if they wish."

CSCW software products such as Lotus Notes, Novell Groupwise and Microsoft Exchange are discussed in Chapter 11, *Equipment*, along with technologies such as audioconferencing and videoconferencing. It is important to note that there is considerable academic discussion on the merits of CSCW tools – some companies have claimed large returns on investment, paying back over an average period of two years. Others have had less spectacular results, and a report by PA Consulting estimates that 88% of companies installing CSCW tools fail to implement them properly and achieve few benefits because they do not realise the potential for business restructuring that the tools offer.

Security

Physical security and insurance issues are covered in detail in Chapter 7, *Staying Safe and Legal*. It is worth noting that commercial insurers are developing specific home office policies to reflect the move to teleworking, and the lower risk involved in insuring home offices. Domestic insurance policies will not normally cover home office equipment including PCs, and employees should be instructed to notify their home contents insurers of their intention to work from home.

Case study: Oxfordshire County Council

Oxfordshire County Council employs 16,000 people, 80% of them female, and 57% part-timers, many of whom work flexitime. Recently, the Council introduced a flexiplace scheme, as part of a bottom-up, grass roots initiative to allow working from home where appropriate. Homeworking is always voluntary, and employees can return to conventional arrangements if they wish.

The prime consideration is that there should be no effects on the level and quality of the service provided. To date the scheme has been largely "budget neutral" – costs have to be met from the normal operating budget of the relevant department, and there have been no major workspace savings. The council is now looking at establishing neighbourhood work centres around the county for employees who, for example, need to send the occasional fax but whose work does not justify purchase of an individual fax machine.

A survey of travel costs showed that the council was spending around £3 million on car allowances and other costs. Journeys ranged from 290 miles a month for a social worker to 1,135 miles a month for an engineering works manager – teleworking is helping to reduce these costs and their associated environmental burdens.

Personnel officer Hilary Simpson stresses that giving employees flexibility about where they work is "an efficiency issue, an environmental issue and an equal opportunities issue", and the council has won a Working Mothers Association Employer of the Year award for its activities. Equipment used includes faxes, mobile phones, answerphones, pagers and laptop computers.

Example 1
Gordon Copping, animal health inspector, can now drive straight from home to markets in North Oxfordshire without reporting to the head office in South Oxfordshire first. The council is making major savings on the cost of journeys back to base, freeing the inspectors to devote more of their time to looking after animal welfare.

Example 2
Pam Block is a management accountant in the department of leisure and arts, and works a 30 hour week contract, of which 10 hours are now home-based. "I tend to work in the office between the hours when my children are at school. Then at home I usually work in the evenings when I can really get my head down."

Example 3
Debbie Dent is head of the trading standards information unit and works 25 hours a week. Normally she spends mornings in the Oxford office, and then does the rest of her work from home.

The risk to data security will depend on the value and sensitivity of the data being handled. The solution is to develop procedures appropriate to these levels of importance. Start by reviewing existing procedures and identify processes which introduce an additional hazard by virtue of being remote. Procedures should cover a series of security layers applied to use of personal computers, access to central computing facilities (using for example dial-back facilities to ensure that an authorised number is linking in, also password control) and data transmission. It may be advisable to retain certain tasks for central processing rather than sending them out to the teleworkers, involving reallocation of some duties. Bear in mind that "hacking" is still a relatively rare phenomenon, and consult specialists in techniques such as "firewalling" where necessary.

Security surveys show that the most likely causes of problems are not viruses or hacking, but more basic issues such as power cuts, hard disk crashes or fire damage, all of which can be minimised as risks by appropriate procedures. An important preventive step is therefore to ensure the integrity of data – having procedures and tools to cover back-up procedures and the introduction of viruses. There are even companies which offer remote backup facilities, allowing automatic dial up and uploading of data to a central repository.

It may be necessary to make specific instructions concerning the storage of important or sensitive papers – both by locking storage to prevent unauthorised access, and by using secure storage such as fire safes for certain crucial papers.

Pay, taxation and national insurance

The introduction of teleworking involves a degree of readjustment in pay and conditions which can have financial implications for both sides. In general, most companies pay allowances to teleworkers to cover their home office costs, and the guiding principle underwriting any new working arrangement, as advocated by sources such as the Equal Opportunities Commission and unions such as MSF and CWU, is that the employee bears none of the additional costs that may be incurred in the new scheme and should be fully compensated by the employer.

This can pose questions about the tax implications of providing equipment, paying expenses for the additional costs incurred, and the issue of costs which would otherwise have been exclusively domestic. Tax rules ensure that all non-cash benefits and expenses provided to employees in the course of their employment are taxed. Once the equipment is available in a home context the employee could be liable to tax on the benefit from personal use of the equipment. The amount involved is not large – e.g. equipment valued at £3,000, annual depreciation at 20%, and used for business for 95% of the time gives tax payable on £30 per annum. In practice the more generous view of assuming that the equipment is used for exclusive business use seems to prevail.

Occasionally an ex-gratia payment has been made to compensate for change in working practices – this has in many cases been deemed as taxable but Touche Ross advise that in certain circumstances this could be exempt from tax. Advice should be sought before making any such payment. People working from home should be made aware of some of the additional potential wrinkles that may face them and provision for this should be considered in the teleworking agreement.

It is difficult to be definitive about types of expenses in isolation so it is wise to verify the detail of compensation arrangements with the Inspector of Taxes and the Contributions Agency before paying the expense. One of our advisers said: "You could line up ten tax inspectors and get ten different answers" – and that suggested agreement should be sought in writing. The problem is not confined to inspectors as different tax advisers also give conflicting advice, reflecting the complexity of interpreting tax law and its changing nature as new types of teleworking develop. Gradually the authorities are beginning to accomodate the new ways of working, however. Last year, the Inland Revenue, in relation to tax relief on mortgage payments (MIRAS) openly acknowledged "it is becoming increasingly common for properties to be used both for residential and business purposes."

Where teleworking schemes involve a degree of part-time work and the use of sub-contractors apparently operating under self-employed working arrangements, it is important to clarify the arrangements with the relevant authorities in order to ensure that the employer does not incur liability for the contractor's tax and national insurance payments. This is also covered in Chapter 7, *Staying Safe and Legal.*

Recompense can be made for proportions of heat, light, cleaning and council tax according to some sources. A fixed amount payable to the

Flexible working at the sign of the Black Horse

Systems developers at Lloyds Bank/TSB Group have jumped at the chance to join a teleworking programme. The stampede has been so great that Nick Benjamin, flexible working programme manager, no longer needs to advertise the scheme to staff.

The pilot scheme started in 1992, involving 24 volunteers from the information systems department of the bank's retail financial services division. Now 180 people out of a total workforce of 560 are teleworking for an average of two to three days a week. Nick Benjamin reports:"The scheme has been promoting itself. It has taken us by surprise – we thought there would be a tailing off but it's going the other way, and we expect to reach 240 teleworkers by the end of 1996".

Once the decision to go ahead with the pilot had been made, the bank drew on internal expertise from other departments on issues such as health and safety, personnel and telecoms. Anyone who wants to take up teleworking is first assessed to gauge their suitability. According to Nick Benjamin: "The person must be an experienced self starter who knows their work well and is able to work unsupervised. They must also be highly motivated, organised and excellent time managers."

The work done from home is varied, ranging from programming, business analysis and design to report writing. "Really, anything to do with systems development can be done from home, with the exceptions of some types of system testing that have to be done in the office," says Benjamin. Staff from all levels of the department have taken up the option, and the decision on how many days a week to telework is a team decision. Performance is measured on results: "It is based on trust. It's down to the individual and their line manager to decide what is going to work for them".

Once an employee is accepted on the teleworking programme, health and safety checks are made to ensure their home environment is safe and conducive to work. Lloyds provides the phone, ISDN links, furniture, fax, filing cabinets, computer hardware and software, and staff sign an agreement to ensure the equipment is only used for bank business. The phone bill is picked up by the company, but there is no allowance for extra heating and lighting. Instead, staff get to keep their daily travel allowance even for days when they work at home. Benjamin comments: "No-one has complained. It is a fair exchange and most people realise that in return for the benefits they get from teleworking, it's a small price to pay."

A recent internal survey showed the advantages of teleworking outweighted the disadvantages, and because the scheme is open to all, there was no resentment. Staff turnover among the teleworkers is lower than for other workers, and Nick Benjamin is now helping other departments of the bank to learn from his experience.

employee revisable on a yearly basis is perhaps the neatest way of proceeding. The sums involved may be based on before and after usage or on an apportionment in relation to space used. These amounts should be declared on the annual P11D form returned by the employer. Alternatively, dispensation for the amounts should be agreed with both the Inspector of Taxes and the Contributions Agency.

A series of guidelines which cover procedures for teleworking needs to be created by any company introducing a teleworking scheme and this should include the procedures for paying expenses and allowances. Other issues which need to be considered when reworking teleworker's employment contracts include:

- sick pay
- use of cars
- holidays
- benefits (replacing central benefits such as canteens)
- low interest loans and advice services
- provision of cheap IT equipment.

Where the teleworker is becoming self-employed, advice to the teleworker on provision of sick pay, health insurance and pensions will be needed (see *Staying Safe and Legal* chapter).

Travel

The good news is that an employee working at home can argue that the home is the real place of work and hence travel to the office is business travel and reimbursable tax free. Maurice Parry-Wingfield of Touche Ross however advises caution in this area : "It is essential that the employee is formally instructed by the employer to work at home rather than at the employer's workplace and to use the equipment at home. If teleworking is purely a matter of personal choice the employee will not be able to claim deductions for domestic or travel expenses provided."

Self-employed contractors

The number of self-employed teleworkers, part-time arrangements, and flexible agreements is continually increasing. Employers need to ensure that they are not, through the nature of their arrangement with the contractor, establishing an employee-employer relationship. Simply creating an agreement which absolves the employer of any responsibility for the contractor's tax and N.I. is unlikely to be valid if the conditions are not agreed by the relevant authorities. Further guidance is given in Chapter 7, *Staying Safe and Legal.*

In the area of computer contracting it has become established practice for the contractor to set up a limited company: the client will engage the company to work and hence is responsible for payment of the company invoices and is not liable for tax or national insurance. This contract model may emerge as a better solution for the regular teleworker and helps remove the uncertainty created by having to assess each new contract on its detailed conditions.

Acknowledgements

Thanks to Croner Publications for allowing us to use text extracted from 'Flexible Working Practices' – a comprehensive guide for employers.
Tel: 0181 547 3333 Fax: 0181 547 2637.

The TCA is also indebted to the following people for their guidance in preparing this section:

Maurice Parry-Wingfield of Touche Ross Tel: 0171 936 3000

Mathew Brown of Independent Accountancy Services Tel: 0171 375 1001
Email: post@iasacc.demon.co.uk

Contributions Agency and Inland Revenue local offices and press office

Stephen Jupp, Home Office Partnership

Bibliography

Changing Places – A Manager's Guide to Working from Home *Date:* 1996
Source: New Ways to Work, 309 Upper Street, London N1 2TY Tel: 0171 226 4026

Flexible Working *Date:* 1996
Author: Steve Simmons
Source: Kogan Page 120 Pentonville Road London N1 9JN Ref: ISBN 0-7494-1713-7
Comment: practical guide to flexible working including tick-box express implementation guide for the project manager in a hurry.

A Manager's Guide to Teleworking *Date:* 1995
Author: Ursula Huws on behalf of Employment Dept
Source: Dept of Employment, Cambertown Ltd., Unit 8 Goldthorpe Ind. Estate, Rotherham, S. Yorks Tel: 0171 273 6969.

Guide to Remote Working - A Practical Manual *Date:* 1995
Authors: Tynedale Network
Source: Tynedale Network, 362 Durham Road, Low Fell, Gateshead, NE9 5AP Tel: 0191 420 028

Teleworking and the Labour Movement *Date:* 1995
Author: Labour Telematics Centre
Source: 3Com Europe Ltd, Eaton Court, Maylands Avenue, Hemel Hempstead, Herts HP2 7DF

Flexiplace Scheme *Date:* 1994
Author: Oxfordshire County Council
Source: Commercial Services Print Unit, Oxfordshire County Council, tel 01865 815672 Ref. C21-17

Homeworking Strategy *Date:* 1993
Authors: Borough of Blackburn Economic Development Department
Source: Shaheen Sameja, City Challenge Access Point, Brook House Business Centre, Whalley Range, Blackburn, Lancashire, BB1 6BB Tel: 01254 676796.

**Self-Employment and Labour Market Restructuring –
The Case of Freelance Teleworkers in Book Publishing** *Date:* 1993
Authors: Celia Stanworth, John Stanworth, David Purdy

Source: Future of Work Research Group, University of Westminster, 35 Marylebone Road, London NW1 5LS Tel: 0171 911 5000

Teleworking Explained *Date:* 1993
Authors: Mike Gray, Noel Hodson, Gil Gordon
Source: John Wiley & Sons, Baffins Lane, Chichester Ref: ISBN 0 471 93975 7
Comments: Extremely comprehensive teleworking guide.

Teleworking in Calderdale & Kirklees *Date:* 1993
Authors: EAP Consultants
Source: EAP Consultants, Enterprise House, 17 Ribblesdale Place, Preston, PR1 3NA

Teleworking in the 1990s – A View from the Home *Date:* 1993
Authors: Leslie Haddon & Roger Silverstone, SPRU - University of Sussex
Source: Mantell Building, University of Sussex, Falmer, Brighton, BN1 9RF Ref: ISBN 0-903622-61-0

Teleworking *Date:* 1992
Source: National Communications Union (NCU), Research Dept, Greystoke House, 150 Brunswick Rd, London, W5 1AW
Comments: Includes section on conditions of service.

Changing to Teleworking and **Teleworking:
A Strategic Guide for Management** *Date:* 1991
Author: Steven Burch
Source: Kogan Page, London.

Changing Work Patterns: A Discussion of Teleworking *Date:* 1991
Author: Fiona French
Source: University of Aberdeen, Department of Sociology, Edward Wright Building, Dunbar Street, Aberdeen AB9 2TY

Homeworking in the Civil Service General Circular 366 *Date:* 1991
Source: Conditions of Service and Industrial Relations Division, HM Treasury, Parliament St, London SW1P 3AL. Tel: 0171 270 4582.
Comment: This document would be a very useful basis for personnel managers seeking to set guidelines for teleworking within their organisations.

Teleworking in Local Authorities *Date:* 1991
Author: Industrial Society
Source: Industrial Society
Comments: Seminar report.

Teleworking (Video) *Date:* 1991
Source: Sunday Times Computers in Business Series, c/o Taylor Made Films. 0171 402 5292
Comment: Includes corporate teleworking implementation guidelines.

Training for Teleworking (2 publications) *Date:* 1990
Authors: The Flexible Work Company
Source: National Council for Educational Technology, NCET, Sir William Lyons Rd, University of Warwick, CV4 7EZ

Contacts and URLs

http://www.collaborate.com is the address for Collaborate Inc., a CSCW consultancy that maintains a useful site with info on Workflow and Groupware/Teleworking systems. They also produce a commercial newsletter.

http://www.dnai.com/~isdw is The Institute for the Study of Distributed Work and has a number of academic resources available.

http://www.eema.org/eemahq is the site for the European electronic message association, a professional group for users of electronic messaging.

http://www11.informatik.tu-muenchen.de/cscw/yp is the address for the Unnofficial Yellow Pages of Computer Suported Co-Operative Working.

http://www.isi.gov.uk is the address for the UK's Dept of Trade and Industry's new "Information Society Initiative", targeted at raising business awareness and use of internet, open electronic networking etc.

UK management consultants MTA have a site with information about their teleworking reports called Mtanet at http://mtanet.co.uk

http://www.ora.com contains information and free 60-day demo CSCW system on WebBoard from O'Reilly. It runs on Windows NT in conjunction with any CGI 1.1 compliant HTTP serve

http://pine.shu.ac.uk/~cmsce/cscwn.html is the address for CSCW (Computer-Supported Cooperative Work) North, which provides an informal forum for sharing and discussing ongoing cscw-related research.

http://www.poptel.org.uk/ltc is the Labour Telematics Centre and its site has guidelines from trades unions for teleworkers.

http://www.RACE.analysys.co.uk is the excellent server operated by British telecoms consultancy Analysys. It contains information on the EU's RACE and ACTS programmes. Do not miss the SONAH section which gives succinct, practical useful summaries of the equipment and software recommendations of several EU projects.

http://www.sisu.se/projects/CoopWWW/coopw~1.htm gives information about the CoopWWW programme which aims to provide a set of interworking tools for group collaboration using WWW.

http://www.softwords.bc.ca contains information on CoSy 4.2 which implements a full email and conferencing system with fully threaded messaging and a full HTML interface. Runs on any VMS or Unix platform. Ports underway to NT

http://www.tagish.co.uk/ethos/ is the website of the EU ETHOS project which gives information on the EU's TAP programme.

http://www.voffice.com is the site for "'virtual' offices for hire in London".

http://www.volksware.com/mobilis is the address for Mobilis: the mobile computing lifestyle magazine.

The following list are groupware sites taken from the Collabra hotlist:

http://www.collabra.com/ Collabra are creators of CollabraShare group conferencing product

http://www.bittco.com/ Bittco Solutions – provides real-time Internet teleconferencing and decision support

http://cu-seeme.cornell.edu/">CU-See Me is a Low cost/low bandwidth Internet videoconferencing tool from Cornell University

http://www.DataFellows.com/ is the site for the makers of Vineyard, a visual information manager for workgroups

http://www.california.com/~meetings/colab.htm is the Institute for Better Meetings and holds info on collaboration, cooperation, technography, and the "fun factor"

http://www.lotus.com/ is Lotus Notes, the best known groupware environment and application development tool http://netwire.novell.com/ServSupp/groupware/nwgindx.htm is the site for Novell Groupware including GroupWise, InForms and SoftSolutions

http://www.prenhall.com/list/wnlist.html is Prentice-Hall giving latest releases from the publishers of many groupware-related books

http://www.teamw.com/ is for TeamWARE Office E-mail, conferencing, scheduling, document management and task routing

http://www.crew.umich.edu/~brinck/cscw.html isTom Brink's Groupware/CSCW page and has various links on Computer Supported Collaborative Work

http://www11.informatik.tu-muenchen.de/cscw/yp is the address for the Unnofficial Yellow Pages of Computer Suported Co-Operative Working.

http://www.collaborate.com is the address for Collaborate Inc. who maintain a useful site with info on Workflow and Groupware/Teleworking systems. They also produce a commercial newsletter.

http://search.yahoo.com/bin/search?p=groupware will give Yahoo search results for the query "Groupware"

http://www.ora.com contains information and free 60-day demo system on WebBoard from O'Reilly. It runs on Windows NT in conjunction with any CGI 1.1 compliant HTTP server.

http://www.softwords.bc.ca contains information on CoSy 4.2 which implements a full email and conferencing system with fully threaded messaging and a full HTML interface. Runs on any VMS or Unix platform. Ports allegedly underway to NT.

Survival guide

This chapter is based on the experiences of members of the TCA, members of the Telework Ireland association, and users of the Telework Europa forum on Compuserve. It represents advice from the horse's mouth on how to take advantage of the flexibility of teleworking and avoid the pitfalls.

Getting the job done

In interviews and media discussions about teleworking, journalists often ask teleworkers: "How do you make yourself sit down at the computer and start work in the morning? Why don't you just stay in bed?" Any self employed teleworker can give them the reason: no work – no pay. You need to pay the rent or mortgage, buy food, buy paper and so on. One contributor said: "I add up how much I owe my creditors or how much I still owe on the mortgage. This does wonders for my motivation." "My main incentive to work is the arrival of the childminder so I know I've got to get stuck in while I've got peace and quiet!"

Another takes things to extremes: "The central heating in my large and drafty house is off until the evening. I keep the room I use as an office heated with a calor gas stove. As well as being more economical, it effectively puts the rest of the house out of bounds during the day unless I put my thermals on, which does wonders for the motivation". The voice of experience shines through this contribution: "Try and plan your work so that the first thing you have to do in the morning is not difficult or unpleasant. Break off in the evening at a point which leaves you an easy start first thing the next day. This means that if you do run into a problem the following day you will already be in full swing."

Behind the simplistic journalist's query is a real dilemma: organising your work when there is no-one physically hammering on your office door to ask where that report/memo/piece of software has got to. To avoid upsetting clients or employers, teleworkers need to get good at managing their time and the projects assigned to them very quickly.

One invaluable aid is to buy a personal organiser package which runs on your computer. Not everyone gets on with these (and it has to be said that a well-maintained handwritten list can do the job equally well), but the best of these packages, such as the inexpensive Time & Chaos, will keep track of your tasks as well as holding information like contact addresses.

Typical teleworker tasks that need to be covered by any personal organiser software you purchase include:

- urgent deadline based tasks
- major projects which may contain a number of sub-tasks
- routine work such as monthly reports

- regular tasks such as backing up computer data or preparing VAT returns
- calls to be made
- appointments and meetings

To carry out this range of tasks you will need:

- a diary function (with meeting alarms and planners)
- a contacts database (addresses, phone, fax and email numbers)
- a "to do" list which is prioritised and which allows automatic prompting of regularly scheduled tasks.

It's also a big help if the time manager has a function that allows you to record what time you spent working on which project for billing or cost centre purposes. Perhaps the most important piece of advice in this chapter is to ensure that you log every hour that you spend working, whether or not you can claim for it. Do it on the same day, or in the morning of the next day, before you forget what you were doing.

Start the day by collecting your email, post, and any messages, and working through your "to do" list in the light of the new messages, prioritising tasks. It is well worth taking the time to eradicate junk mail from the post you have to open by subscribing to the Mailing Preference Service, and its companion the Telephone Preference Service, to have your name removed from mailing lists (for information on preventing junk email see Chapter 8, *Email and Online Services*). Log your incoming post in a book, or better, on a spreadsheet so you have a record of what came in. Stamp it with the date it was received and file it immediately before it clutters up your work surfaces. Your filing system does not have to be complex – it could be just the classic in, out and pending, or action now, action later and information – but if you have one you'll be able to find what you need without having to excavate piles of paper taking over the home office.

Beating deadlines

"If you're working to a serious deadline, put the answerphone on. You can always interrupt it if an important call comes in, otherwise you can call back after the deadline work's completed."

Be realistic about your time estimates. If it's obvious something isn't going to get done by the deadline, inform the customer or client. Often a deadline can be stretched, or the customer or client can rearrange their workload – it is much better to let people know what is happening than to let them down at the last moment.

"Make sure you know all the last posting times and courier pickup times. There's nothing worse than panting into the post office after a day racing a deadline and find that you've missed the van because they changed the pickup routes…"

When agreeing deadlines with clients, don't forget to take account of

> **Voices of experience...**
>
> "I find that it's important to juggle workload according to mood. Some days I am good for nothing but administrative tasks such as catching up on the bills. When I'm working on something involving major writing or creative input, there is always a stage of displacement activities I have to go through before I can start. This is quite stressful at the time because you are ticking yourself off for cleaning out the fridge when you should be in front of the computer racing a looming deadline, but over the years I have realised it is a necessary part of the creative process – whilst I clean the fridge, some sort of composting process takes place in the brain and then the structure, idea or phrase will come that allows me to face the blank screen and get going."
>
> "I used to complete and deliver jobs well ahead of the deadline. Now, I may well finish the job ahead of time but I've learnt not to deliver it until close to the deadline. That way, people think I'm busy and leave me alone! It's not a matter of planning your work but of planning your life, setting yourself targets for both the personal and professional spheres and aim for the proper balance."

regular tasks that have to be fitted in to the working day, such as filing, backing up data, accounts and so on, otherwise you will find that these tasks always get pushed into evenings and weekends to make room for deadline work, and you end up overworking.

It's good to talk...

Teleworkers need to make maximum use of all the tools available to them to keep in touch with the people who pay them. Because you are not physically in the same office, it is vital to respond quickly and effectively so that your client or employer feels secure that you are on top of your work for them and they can rely on you to complete the task. It's good to talk, as the advert goes, but for teleworkers the secret of success is to pick the right communication tool for the job. Telecommuters, or employed teleworkers, may well have a corporate policy laid down about when email should be used, when face to face meetings are needed and so on, but the self-employed usually have to learn by their mistakes. Teleworkers don't have the luxury (or nuisance, depending on your view) of constant face to face meetings, with all the nuances of body language and time for discussion, or of informal "chats in the corridor". It is very easy to pick up the "wrong end of the stick" and make an expensive mistake, or develop a grudge or irritation with a colleague which would never happen in the conventional office environment. Learning to be a teleworker requires good attention to communications tools and skills. On the other hand, face to face meetings for teleworkers often take on new and more interesting roles – they may become about team-building, training, developing relationships and discussing possibilities rather than about imparting routine information.

Telephones

Communicating is about imparting and receiving information, and the most widely used method of communication for teleworkers is the telephone. To make sure there has been no breakdown in telephone communications, always take written notes of telephone calls, and where possible restate any information received before finishing the call to check you have understood correctly. When imparting information, it often helps to write down the points you plan to make before starting the call, ticking them off as each one is discussed. Check the following:

- are you talking to the right person?
- do they understand who you are? Did you introduce yourself and your work context?
- are your communications accurate and complete (have they received the fax you are supposed to be discussing?)
- is your communication timely? (have you missed the deadline for applications already? If so there's no point in going further with the call).

When communicating with your manager or client:

- use current information – have the relevant documents to hand
- ensure your message is clear, unambiguous, understandable and meaningful
- keep it short – the manager's time is precious
- check if people have time to talk and if not, make an appointment for a long call at another time
- don't use excessively costly communication methods such as videoconferencing unless they are necessary
- always try to imagine yourself in the other person's place – empathy.

Often calls made by telephone are discussions or negotiations, or the development of an idea. Be concrete – use examples of what you mean wherever possible to reduce the possibilities for confusion.

A number of other techniques are important in the effective use of the telephone.

"When working alone, it is important to establish trust in your answering machine. Clients must feel confident that leaving a message on the answering machine is as good as a direct contact. This confidence may be established by acknowledging messages quickly, even when it is not necessary to do so and explaining to clients that the presence of the answering machine may only indicate an absence of a few minutes. I, for example, may simply be sitting in the garden with the laptop and will check the machine frequently." Equally, when leaving messages, always state your name, the time and date of your message, your telephone number and leave a clear, brief message.

It is well worthwhile to keep a duplicate message book by the phone,

Telephone communication skills

If you are **imparting information** do **not**:

- assume the receiver sees the conversation the same way you do or hears exactly what you wished to say
- use irritating words and repetitive phrases
- use inappropriate language (swearwords, sexism, jargon) which the other person doesn't understand or feel comfortable with
- mumble, fidget, or use distracting mannerisms
- interrogate the receiver aggressively.

If you are **imparting information** try to:

- speak clearly
- avoid jargon
- ask one question at a time
- listen carefuly to the answer
- be concise.

If you are **receiving information** try to avoid:

- jumping to conclusions and interrupting
- changing the subject
- talking too much
- thinking about what the receiver is going to say next rather than listening to what they are saying now
- switching off or ignoring what is being said
- seeking to score over the other person
- competing rather than cooperating
- pretending to understand when you don't to avoid embarrassment
- being judgmental
- being defensive rather than open to the information you are receiving.

Active listeners, or receivers of information try to:

- signal their interest
- listen between lines
- ask questions for clarification
- avoid criticism
- summarise the message before the end of the call.

for writing brief notes of telephone calls, who from, time and date. This gives you a record of information from the telephone call, and also provides a method for other people in the house to take messages and leave them for you in an agreed format and place. Using message books in conjunction with listening to your answerphone messages can also be useful – otherwise if you get interrupted by another call while listening to the answerphone, you may forget the content of the message.

More and more teleworkers also have mobile phones, and here the difficulty is not receiving the information, but recording the salient details of the message while pulled over at the side of the road, or walking along a railway platform. It can be useful to invest in a pocket memo recorder such as the Philips Voicetrack, or a Walkman with a good recording device to carry with you when you are out of the office. You can record the details of the mobile call straight away, and play back the recording when you return to the office for action. Of course, pen and paper also work well for this task, but small tape machines are also useful for that brilliant idea, or task you've forgotten, which strikes you while sitting in a traffic jam. Another technique is to use your mobile phone to dial your home answerphone and leave details of the message or idea there for collection and action later.

The wide range of telephone features now available to assist teleworkers, including detailed billing and call waiting, are described in the Equipment chapter. It is worth noting here that considerable development work is being put into making CTI technology (computer telephony integration) more widely available. CTI has until recently only been available on mainframe installations in call centres. It uses features such as caller line identification to allow your PC to produce relevant information from your database about a caller, and to record and make calls without having to physically dial. It is particularly useful for people involved in the areas of sales and support. On a smaller scale, the introduction of Microsoft Exchange, part of the Windows 95 software, as a single "send, receive and file" point for your faxes, emails and contacts database is likely to encourage many more teleworkers to make and record their communications on their PC.

One telephone communication method which is often overlooked is the audio or telephone conference. Audioconferences can be arranged through telecoms companies or, if you are working in the voluntary sector, through Community Network (0171 359 4594). Theoretically up to 20 people can join in an audioconference, but from the point of view of running an effective meeting, audioconferences work best with up to 10 people. An effective "chair" who works round the participants collecting views, resolving conflicts and summing up the meeting decisions is vital. Audioconferences are extremely cost effective for a group of people who need to discuss a topic but don't want the time and expense of a face to face meeting

Fax

Faxes are great for urgent written communications, but it's important to use them only as appropriate. For example, if the document is one the recipient will have to work on or edit, it would be better sent by email so they don't have to type it all in again – even if they are receiving their fax on a computer, what they are receiving is an uneditable graphical image, not a piece of editable, computer-readable text. There's also the long-running problem of decomposition of thermal fax paper. If your fax is not plain-paper or computer based, be sure to copy important documents received onto ordinary paper, otherwise when the client tries to sue you a year later and you look in the file, all you may find is a blank piece of paper.

Many people now use fax switches (where the fax shares the voice line) or computer based faxes, but teleworkers disagree on the best practice on these two issues. Fax switches have the disadvantage that some don't work very well, and that you may severely annoy an important client who has to listen to a tinny voice asking him or her to wait, followed by some clunky electronic music, before they can press the button to send you the fax. Also if you only have one line, and are sending or receiving a long fax, then voice calls can't get through. On the other hand, modern fax switches are much more effective and almost transparent in use, and there is the cost saving on the second telephone line to consider.

Computer based faxes allow you to save the cost of a fax machine, but have the disadvantage of often slowing your computer considerably when a fax is being received. As the computer faxmodem is also often used for email, if you handle a lot of messages you may find the fax is occupying the line when you want to send email and vice versa. Also, you will need to leave your computer on all the time so that faxes can be received on a 24 hour basis. If your computer crashes it will affect faxes being received. Most experienced teleworkers have a separate line and machine for faxes because of congestion problems.

When you receive a fax, do check that all the pages have arrived before filing it, especially if it is not something you are going to take action on straight away.

Email

Email is pretty much addictive. Once you have started using it for work communications, the ability to record messages by filing them on computer, plus the fact that the other person doesn't have to be there to receive the message at the time you send it (as with a phone call), makes it the most convenient form of teleworker communication. It is not without its problems, however. Some people are notoriously bad at reading and dealing with their email, whereas they will handle a fax or telephone call with no problem – you need to be sure that the person at the other end of the communication is happy with email. Many people are quite able to send short plain text messages, but aren't clear on the ins and outs of sending files over the Internet (see Chapter 8, *Email and Online Services*), which is crucial for effective teleworking.

It's also frighteningly easy to take the wrong "tone" in an email and end up with an unintended dispute on your hands (hence all the "flame wars" on the Internet). Email requires a high level of facility with written communications, yet it is an informal method – abbreviations and cyberslang abound – and therefore is often used for communications which might better be handled face to face or by telephone. These tensions have led to the development of "emoticons", collections of characters intended to express tone, such as smiley faces. It is interesting to note that these are more widely used in North America than in Europe, and that they tend to be dispensed with by experienced teleworkers. There are three keys to successful use of email:

- use a mail reader which allows filing of messages by project, and which will allow you to sort or search messages by sender, subject and date. This allows easy retrieval of information or instructions relating to a project
- use a mail reader with an easy-to-use address book function, which allows you to quickly "lift" an email address to put into the book from an incoming message
- keep a pad by the computer when you are reading your email to write down information on instructions received which you need to act on, email contact numbers and URLs for web sites. Of course you can print out the whole message, but usually it's only a couple of words that you actually need. Either way, do something to put the information on your action list, or you will just read the email and then forget its contents.

Some online systems also offer computer supported collaborative working tools (CSCW), which are intended to replace face to face meetings by providing electronic "same time same place" communications. Here the participants "meet" online, can simultaneously work on documents and discuss issues. Many of these systems still rely on the participant's ability to type fast, however, which can cause problems.

Other systems, such as the forums on CompuServe, provide a "different time, same place" system where participants look at threads of messages, and add their comments. The discussion develops over a period of hours or days, but the participants are not necessarily online at the same time.

The most commonly used CSCW tools are "different time, different place" tools which allow collaboration or revision of a document between team members, such as Lotus Notes.

Videoconferencing

Videoconferencing is also considered to be a CSCW tool for providing meetings between participants who are "same time, different place" while avoiding travel costs. If you are fortunate enough to have access to videoconferencing, you will find that although the technical standard of affordable systems today is no replacement for face to face meetings, it offers a big improvement over the audioconference, especially for delicate meetings or negotiations where a face to face meeting is not possible. However, most ISDN PC-based systems are still fairly jerky and this means you need to learn to moderate your body language. Also, on many systems only one person can "speak" at one time (rather like a VHF radio system). This means it helps the flow of the conversation if you can indicate clearly by your voice tone or other gesture when you have finished making a point. Otherwise conversations can either degenerate into a staccato cutting from one participant to another as you accidentally interrupt each other, or to a Quaker-like silence at the end of each point while the person at the other end tries to work out if you've finished talking. Videoconferencing facilities are covered in the equipment factsheet. Although they are still beyond the pocket of many teleworkers, a number of telecottages and other bureau services are providing videoconferencing on a local basis.

Post and couriers

In many situations work still needs to be sent by post – even if it's on disk! Unless you have access to ISDN file transfer, the practical limit in cost and time terms for moving files around by email is about 2–3 megabytes. The postal service (or courier where extra speed is required) provides a largely reliable and fast door to door service. It is important to be clear on issues such as the last posting time at your local box or office, the time at which your post arrives (in some rural areas this can be as late as 3 pm, causing problems for teleworkers who need to turn work round fast) and the different services available, such as Swiftair, registered post and Mailsort. Equally, couriers will have last pickup times for your area, and different delivery times for areas of the world. You don't know when you'll need them, so make sure you have up to date pricelists and contact numbers for all your delivery services.

Do log all incoming and outgoing post so that if anything goes missing, you can show when and how it left you. When disks arrive by post, check that they are readable immediately, even if you don't plan to work on that project for a few days. That way if there is a problem, you can request a replacement disk without disturbing your schedule, and the client won't know that you "sat on it" for a few days – it can be difficult to explain phoning up to request a new disk the day before the deadline...

The housekeeping

There are four chores you must find time for regularly if you are to survive as a teleworker:

- **keeping timesheets:** this should be done daily and the hours added up at least monthly. If you don't know what hours you worked on what project, how can you tell whether you are achieving sufficient reward for your work? And why should your employer or client pay you?

- **preparing bills** regularly and chasing payments (at least monthly). Usually regular phone calls will ensure prompt payment (do be sure to bother the accounts department, not your client within the company, who probably has no control whatsoever on when your invoice will be paid). The next step for non-payers is usually a stiff solicitor's letter, which may have to be followed by use of the small claims court (see box below).
- **backing up your computer data** (at least weekly). Backup tools are covered in the Equipment chapter. Most backup programmes can run unattended and automatically, perhaps in the evening after you have finished work for the day. Do not ignore this chore or you will regret it. The average time between failures for computer hard disks is just over two years. Sooner or later it will happen to you – you will lose all your data – so make sure you have backups, that some are kept offsite to avoid fire risk, and that you test and update backups regularly.
- **marketing or researching new opportunities** (if you are self-employed you should be devoting somewhere between a quarter and a third of your time to marketing; for the PAYE teleworker, substantial time should be devoted to keeping in touch with the office, knowing what is going on, and ensuring that people remember you and what you do).

If you are unwell or on holiday, let your most active clients and contacts know in advance or leave a message to this effect, but try not to invite burglars through a detailed answerphone message. However, if you

---

The maximum amount that you can recover through the Small Claims Court is £3,000. The Small Claims Court offers a simpler court procedure which is swifter, less formal and less intimidating. The registrar's decision is binding. Normally the only cost incurred is in issuing a small claims summons which costs 10% of the claim up to a £600 claim, £65 up to a £1000 claim and £70 for up to £3000. If you choose to use a solicitor you should be aware that solicitor's fees are not recoverable by either party, though costs for an expert report of up to £200 can be recovered.

Amanda Walker of home-based publishing company Phoenix 2 has used the service successfully. "The system is cheap and it's efficient – people are usually scared into paying at the point where they get the summons. They don't want to go on record as not paying their bills." The best source of advice on the Small Claims Court is probably the Citizen's Advice Bureau (local offices listed in the telephone directory) or from legal advice centres. Amanda Walker also found that County Courts provide practical assistance: "County courts are not allowed to give you advice but they are very helpful with filling in the form – it's up to you to ask the right questions. The only problem I've had is that sometimes people will send the amount directly to us without the cost of the summons added, in which case it may be best to cut your losses and accept this."

normally use a business name, an answerphone message may be OK, for how is the burglar to know you work from home, as opposed to in a busy office block? While you are away, Royal Mail Keepsafe service can hold your mail at a cost of £5 for a fortnight or £15 for two months. One week's notice is required – ask at your local post office or telephone 01345 740740.

Balancing "home" and "work"

A formal family agreement may be excessive, but prospective teleworkers should discuss and suggest ground rules as to how the family can best help and least hinder the process of working from home. Children's voices in the background of telephone calls create a bad impression to customers and put strain on the teleworker intent on creating a professional image. On the positive side, the teleworker is much more available (by virtue of being there in emergencies and also having freed up commuting time), and there is usually greater appreciation by their family of what they do. Here are some starting points for discussion:

- where is the office?
- is it out of bounds to partners, children or pets? All the time or just at certain times? (Final reports have been decorated by older children with pictures of elephants… two children discovered playing frisbee with backup disks while a third is feeding disks into the CD player "because they fit, Mummy"; pet hair tends to disagree with computer disk drives but cats in particular love to sleep on a nice warm photocopier or laser printer)
- who tidies the office? (Desk is tidied and important paper filed in bin; computer dies during crucial upload of final report as it has been unplugged to make room for the vacuum cleaner)
- is company equipment available to the family? (If not, how can you explain the disappointment to games-mad children whose greatest pleasure in life is saving all those lemmings from certain death?)
- is the teleworker available for domestic chores? Which ones and when? Who does the school/childminder runs? ("What are you doing here? You're supposed to be picking the kids up from swimming?")
- who pays for the extra food needed for the teleworker's lunches and snacks? Who makes sure the food is available? ("But darling, I *always* have Boaster biscuits with my tea…")
- can the teleworker expect help from the family with e.g. mailings? What's the "quid pro quo" for help? A family treat or money?
- how are business calls and visitors to be handled by members of the family? If the teleworker is out, do they let the answerphone go off, or do they answer the phone?

When planning the home office it may be a good idea to draw up a sketch plan, with paper templates representing the various items to be fitted into the room, and get the family to help in designing what should go where. Bear in mind the realities – a loft office may have steep steps that children just love to leave toys all over to trip up the teleworker, whereas a room which is a pathway to others will always cause the teleworker to suffer interruption. And remember: "There is never enough room. The paperless office – the biggest joke of all time!"

It's also worth discussing how you see the teleworking routine working. Some teleworkers report that they need to keep to a strict schedule in order to maintain their work discipline. Others find that it helps their motivation to put on "work" clothes, while for some it is the boundaries that are important. Quite a few report that they go for a walk before and after work time to divide work from home life. Some teleworkers go to the other extreme and may work late into the night. All of these changes and routines can cause strains if they are not talked through, leading to interruption problems such as the "ogre in the spare room" syndrome, with children creeping round the house unnaturally quietly because "Daddy is working".

Most parents find that they need to either arrange for the children to be out of the house at school or a childminder's, or arrange for a childminder to be present in the home if they are to telework successfully. Stresses can arise if the burden of childcare shifts from one parent to the other and everyone is living and working in the same space. "I found I couldn't concentrate because I didn't believe my husband was looking after our daughter properly while I was working. She was at a demanding, toddler stage and he would just watch the telly in the same room instead of attending to her. If I heard her crying it was almost impossible for me to stay in the office. Things did improve when we changed the glass door of the office to a solid one so that she couldn't see me when I was working, but it was still stressful for me". To add to the stress, childcare costs are not tax deductible and must be paid in full.

The support organisation Parents at Work publishes a guide on Balancing Home and Work – contact 0171 700 5771 or fax 0171 700 1105.

On the bright side though, once teething troubles have been resolved, teleworking allows far more opportunity to integrate home and work: "It can be hell when they're small, and friends tell me boys are worse than girls. Always say goodbye and greet them back from school – never be too busy – put the answering machine on instead. Do the taxi runs such as guides, music lessons etc. Make them feel that there are times when they can use the equipment (under supervision when tiny) and that there are things they must not do (format c:); but they must also understand there are times when you are not to be disturbed." It's also a good idea to decide on a review of the situation after an agreed initial period so everyone in the family can have their say about whether teleworking works for them.

"Plan your day around the family. There is no point in getting frustrated with the children coming home from school and interrupting you. Plan breaks at times such as these and enjoy them rather than try to battle on irritably. One of the joys of teleworking is surely that you can have more time for the family when it needs your time."

"I enjoy teleworking because it means I have more time with the family through not having to commute. Also a lovely rural setting and a roomy office make working from home very attractive. The downside is that work is always there, lurking in the corner of your mind and you feel yourself inexorably drawn to it. However, in any conflict with the housework, work wins hands down. I'm often glad of the excuse it gives me to ignore the dust for a bit longer."

"Not everyone may agree but interruptions from family members need not necessarily be unwelcome if you organise your work properly and establish ground rules."

"It is very important when working at home to keep your business and family phones separate. Nothing is as frustrating as continually answering calls for your teenage daughter or discovering that an important caller could not get through because the phone was engaged by family members all afternoon."

Maintaining the worker

A number of physiological complaints can result from long-term use of computers and include eye strain, blurred vision, burning eyes, back pain, sore shoulders and RSI (repetitive strain injury). Teleworker home offices need to be designed with appropriate desks and chairs to minimise these problems, and teleworkers need to be aware of their existence (see Chapter

7, *Staying Safe and Legal*). It usually helps to arrange the work place to face outwards towards stimulating views, and to take sensible breaks at regular intervals.

"The BT directory enquiries experiment in Inverness found that although teleworkers suffer less stress than their office based counterparts, they suffer more snack attacks. I can relate to this totally. The only way I cope is by banning biscuits for the house, and allowing myself a chocolate bar when I take the post to the shop at 4 pm."

Surprisingly, many comments were received about the problem of overworking.

"An important problem I find – and it may seem a curious one – is a tendency to overwork. Your work is always there and it is easy to be tempted to do it rather than something else. I think it important, therefore, to have a clear idea of why you are teleworking in the first place (living in the country, more time for the family, etc.) and carry out periodic audits to see if you are effectively achieving your aims. Resist the temptation to overwork. Make your breaks real breaks away from the computer. Stop and eat; don't nibble and keep going. Plan your social and family life and make your leisure commitments as binding as your professional ones. Comfort yourself with the quantity of work completed rather than worry about the work remaining to be done. Take that walk in the morning if the sun is shining. You can always catch up in the evening when it may well be raining. Set yourself reasonable targets (daily, weekly, monthly) and learn to relax when you have reached them."

"The one thing a teleworker should strive not to be is what I have become. I am addicted to personal computers much as someone could be said to be addicted to crack cocaine. I have two PCs in my home office and they are on from 0700 to 2000 six days a week. The day off is my wife's idea but you should see me get the jitters at 1700 on a Saturday. Holidays away from home and the office can get hairy. Whatever you do, make sure you can walk away from your work without thinking about it."

At least this teleworker has insight into his condition – others becoming tedious workaholics, unable to see that what should be a method of introducing freedom and balance into life, teleworking, has become an excuse for self-imposed slavery. An old hand recommends: "Set yourself a limit on the number of hours a week you will normally work except in exceptional circumstances."

"Make sure that you don't push yourself too hard and that you "leave" work at a regular time. Don't forget how lucky you are to have escaped the commuter lifestyle. But don't forget the bumper sticker that says: "even if you win the rat race, you are still a rat!""

"Take advantage of the flexibility of teleworking by arranging at least one exercise session a week during "normal" working hours – it breaks up the routine and makes you feel privileged to be a teleworker – you get empty pools, cheap horseriding and so on."

"If you're working alone, put the answerhone on or take the phone off the hook when you go for a toilet break."

Another area where "maintenance" is required is the updating of skills through appropriate training. Teleworkers have to adapt to three new areas of skill

- communication
- handling customers and clients
- networking to find work and opportunities.

These areas represent significant challenges to the new teleworker and formal training can ease the transition considerably. However, after a period of years teleworking, it is likely to be core skills such as software packages and professional qualifications which may need updating. For the self-employed, this means planning budget and time to take courses. For those in PAYE employment, training is an issue which needs regular discussion with your manager to ensure you don't end up in a skills backwater.

Loneliness of the long distance teleworker

Teleworkers, particularly those who are disabled or based in rural areas, can suffer from isolation if they work from home for long periods. There are a number of online services which provide "coffee shops" for teleworkers, including Internet listservs and the Telework Europa forum on CompuServe. Professional associations such as TCA and Telework Ireland that provide helplines and conferences can also assist in reducing isolation. Telecottages and telecentres also provide an alternative workspace where contact with peers can be maintained.

Some teleworkers choose to share an office with a neighbour or colleague who is teleworking for companionship and because they find that being "observed" makes them work, even though their companion is not their boss and may well work in a completely different field.

"Based on my experience as a freelance translator, I found that one of the key aspects was the relative lack of praise and positive feedback when working alone. Customers call when there is a panic to sort out, or when they want an urgent piece of work, or when they get a bill and want to whinge. Creative work requires constant positive feedback if it is to maintain its spark. I think most lone workers suffer from a definite lack of professional backslapping. I don't know how to solve this other than by establishing a kind of mutual admiration society for lone workers which sounds dreadful."

"I make a point of getting out to see someone in a business capacity at least once a week face to face. It doesn't really matter who they are – client, suspect, prospect, supplier – but it meets the need for face to face networking and avoids teleworking cabin fever, especially during the early spring. It may even lead to some business!"

"There was one occasion when I was tempted to use the Samaritan's online service. I was owed a lot of money, the work was piling up and my concentration was just shot to pieces. I found I was just reading and re—reading my email messages instead of getting anything done and things were geting out of control. In the end I went to my GP and that solved the problem, but the Samaritan's email address is jo@samaritans.org for anyone else who gets that way."

"Translation is a lonely business at the best of times – you do not really need much contact with your clients and don't want it from anyone else while you are working – so that it is necessary to get the balance right. I find it useful to visit my clients, circumstances permitting, even when it is not really necessary. This puts phone contact onto a human basis afterwards and you get the feeling of belonging to a group of real people."

Other activities which can help to reduce isolation include attending workshops, exhibitions and seminars (these also help to keep your skills and contacts up), joining professional associations, and seeking out discussion groups on the Internet.

On the other side of the isolation equation, city based teleworkers report plagues of neighbours dropping in to borrow envelopes, stamps, use photocopiers, email and so on. A quiet word, or the imposition of a nominal fee for the facility often solves this problem.

Technical support is an area of isolation which directly affects all teleworkers at some time or other. There must be a law about why software problems always develop after office hours. PAYE teleworkers will often have access to company IT specialists to solve their problems, but self-employed teleworkers are usually dependent on their computer supplier: "The main reason for using a reliable small local computer dealer rather than buying mail order". A number of computer manufacturers operate premium phonelines for support which do cover evenings and weekends, but often these give limited help for the first 60 days after a purchase. There is definitely a gap in the market for competent IT support personnel to provide premium line support services to teleworkers. The problem is that teleworkers often have high specification systems with many add-ons which can make it difficult to diagnose the difficulty even where a modem is available for the engineer to use for dialing in.

Perhaps the most fitting piece of advice to novice teleworkers received is this one: "Learn to juggle. It also helps with the invoicing, customer, marketing, and those mountains of backup floppies. I'm still hopeless after 12 years."

Bibliography

Home Run
Author: Sophie Chalmers
Source: Active Information, Cribau Mill, Llanvair Discoed, Chepstow, Gwent, UK NP6 6RD Tel: 01291 641222 Fax: 01291 641777 Email: 100117.27@compuserve.com

Comments: Periodical on running businesses from home available on subscription 10 times per year

Lone Parents & Their Information & Communication Technologies *Date:* 1995
Authors: Leslie Haddon & Roger Silverstone
Source: Science Policy Research Unit, University of Sussex, SPRU, Mantell Building, Falmer, Brighton BN1

Running a One Person Business *Date:* 1989
Authors: Whitmyer, Raspberry, Phillips
Source: Ten Speed Press, Berkeley, California, USA Ref: ISBN 0-89815-237-2

Teleworker Magazine
Editor: Alan Denbigh Tel: 01453 834874 Fax: 01453 836174 Email: 100272.3137@compuserve.com
Source: TCA Tel: 0800 616008 or +44 1203 696986 Fax: +44 123 696538
Comment: Bi-monthly magazine for TCA members

Contacts and URLs

Parents at Work is the new name for the ten year old Working Mothers Association. Contact them at 77 Holloway Rd, London N7 8JZ Tel: 0171 700 5771 Fax: 0171 700 1105

Time & Chaos time management package available from Springfield Publishing Ltd, Springfield House, Llanfynydd, Wrexham, Clwyd LL11 5HW Tel: 01352 770049 Fax: 01352 770816 Email: 100273.2006@compuserve.com

Getting work

Much of this chapter is concerned with a topic of huge interest to self-employed teleworkers: getting work. Some sections are therefore not relevant to telecommuters. For ideas on services which can be offered by teleworkers, see Chapter 6, *Ideas for Teleservices*.

Marketing yourself as a teleworker

Many teleworkers have excellent skills in their areas of expertise, but know nothing about sales and marketing. Think about getting professional help with marketing and assertiveness training if the whole idea of selling makes you nervous. In the UK, your local Business Link, TEC or LEC would be a good place to look for help. In Ireland, talk to FÁS and your local Enterprise Board. But perhaps the first thing to do is adjust your mindset.

From your customers' point of view, they probably aren't that interested in whether you are a teleworker, even though you may see teleworking as a central issue. So begin your marketing review by a simple resolution coined by Horace Mitchell of telework consultants MTA Associates:

"Don't mention the T-word (teleworker...)"

What your customers are probably looking for is higher quality and lower cost than they can get elsewhere. How are you going to convince them that you can achieve this? Here are some quotes from a TCA conference on marketing teleworking:

"If people are sending work out of their office they expect it to be done better than if it was done in their own office. Everything has to be slicker and more efficient. You have to have a control system that makes absolutely sure work doesn't get mixed up, that it's done in the right order, on time and accurately. You have to be more careful than if you were working for one particular business. One of the problems of our company name is that if you pick up the phone and call a potential client, you get the secretary who immediately thinks you are out to take her job away! Big disadvantage!" *Judith Verity, Office Ghosts*

"I looked at what the competition were charging for their reports and tried to get in at that sort of level. People tend not to take you seriously if you are not expensive enough. And when people ring to place an order, we answer the telephone in exactly the same way. To the customer it is a unified response although it may be a different voice. It is like a corporate image over the telephone line." *Anthony Capstick, Instant Search*

The second change in mindset you need to make concerns marketing. Marketing is not selling or public relations. Marketing is the process of adjusting what you are selling (your product) to best fit the demands of your customers. It can cover all kinds of strategies, including the timing and method of delivery of work, the pricing, the technical details of the work (such as the software packages used). Successful marketing is the key to a successful small business.

Establish your objectives

Objectives can be difficult to define for teleworkers. Some teleworkers want a way of working which allows them more time with their families. Others are concerned with improving profits through lowering overheads. Others may be motivated by the desire to avoid commuting to work. This chapter limits itself to looking at business objectives, but it is recommended that anyone considering starting up a teleworking small business should consult the small business guides listed in the bibliography, and spend some time with their family working out a set of objectives – which might cover profits needed to cover living expenses, number of hours to be worked each week, circumstances under which the teleworker can be disturbed in the home office – and which everyone in the family understands and agrees to.

You need a clear business idea and set of objectives before you start thinking about marketing. Equipping yourself with the computer and the telephone is not enough. You need to know:

- what services will be offered? See Chapter 6, *Ideas for Teleservices*
- who is going to use the service? Do some market research – see below
- how do people buy it? By phone and fax? Pay attention to answerphone messages and fax presentation – the "shop window" of a teleworked business
- when do people buy it? Are there peak periods (such as thesis deadlines) that need to be covered in terms of staff levels?
- where do people buy it from? Probably through the Yellow Pages, or through a personal recommendation, or perhaps through a World Wide Web page (see Chapter 8, *Email and Online Services*).
- do others already offer a similar product or service? Is your service an improvement on these competitors? Is there any evidence that customers want an improvement?
- how much is it going to cost? Are you going to be cheaper, on a par with, or more expensive than your competitors? See pricing section below
- what is the business going to be called (e.g. something that relates to your business, your own name, an abstract word, a telecottage, telecentre, telebureau, or teleservice)? The name will depend upon your target market. For example, community resource centres find the term telecottage well understood and reassuring. Commercial organisations may prefer not to use the telecottage name at all, but talk of a business resource centre, or teleservice centre. People offering a teleworked professional service may prefer to use a version of their own name as the business name since the clients are essentially "hiring" that person.

- what happens if a contract goes badly wrong? Do you need professional indemnity insurance in case a customer sues you? (N.B. It is often a condition of professional indemnity policies that you do not tell your customers you are insured because that could make them more likely to sue.) Do you need to take legal advice to draw up a general contract for signature with clients?

Brian O'Kane's guide *Starting a Business in Ireland* suggests two exercises will help in clarifying your business idea.

1. **Write your own CV** for the position of managing director/administrator of your business. What are your skills and experience? Build on these. Look at your technical, personal and business skills.
2. **Write a short description** of the processes which must be completed before you have something for which you can invoice a customer (e.g. receive enquiry, discuss with client, give quotation, use software package on computer and so on). Throughout, keep a list of every item which will be required, from paper to printer right down to the chair you sit on.

Market research

Once you have your business idea clear you need to do some market research. If you are applying for any kind of outside assistance in starting up a small business, the questions which grant-giving bodies or banks will want answered include:

- what is the total market for this service and what are the overall trends in this market area (static, expanding, contracting)? (Look for national surveys undertaken on market share and size – many are available from good reference libraries)
- how much of that total market is practically accessible to your service (e.g. if it is a geographically limited service, check out what percentage of the national market is in your "catchment area")? You would be well advised to research basic figures in your local library such as the population in your area, the percentage of people unemployed, the breakdown of types of employment such as service, manufacturing, agriculture, and so on)
- how much of the accessible market could you reasonably hope to capture? This answer should take into account practical constraints (e.g. maximum number of productive hours in a year which you expect to work) and will look more convincing if you give a minimum and a maximum and then show that you are selecting a fairly conservative figure between the two.
- what competitors do you have? Their strengths and weaknesses? How much do they charge? To provide information on costs, there is little

alternative to ringing round competitor companies to check out prices. This is a horrible job but vital. Make sure you have a "project" for them to quote on or they will quickly realise that you are not a bona fide customer. If you are competing only with other community organizations, you may not need to apply this cloak and dagger approach – just ask! Look through Yellow Pages to see how many companies are working in your area. Don't forget that your competitors may be listed in various different sections of the telephone directory such as secretarial services, computer graphics, desktop publishing, computer training, computer consultancy and so on

- ask existing customers, family, friends. Why do people use your services?

The information from your market research will be used to prepare your business plan.

Business planning

There are many books and guides available which will help you to put together a formal business plan (see bibliography). Many Business Links have advisers who can help with business plans, as do high street banks. The purpose of a business plan is to produce a document, probably only around 10 pages in length for a simple small business, which has four basic functions:

- to help you clarify your thinking – focussing your thoughts and making sure you have done the calculations needed to ensure your plan is realistic
- to establish that your business idea is financially viable
- to provide an accessible, clear document which contains all the relevant

---

Location, location, location

There are plenty of case studies giving examples of people working far from their clients or employers such as programmers working from Australia, or Irish call centres servicing the North American market. Teleworking can allow work to be independent of distance. But all the evidence is that most companies prefer to use teleworkers who are located close enough to be able to pop in and discuss work face to face when needed. The TeleFutures study in Ireland (1996) found that over 80% of companies would prefer their teleworkers to be situated within 25 miles. The exception to this is people with rare skills or combinations of skills, who can usually lay down their own conditions on how they will work. Some people promote teleworking by having two different prices for their work – a lower price if the job can be teleworked without on-site client meetings. Overall, however, the lower your skill set (e.g. secretarial), the more likely it is that your clientele will be local, so build this factor in to your business plan.

information about your business idea for outsiders including advisors such as accountants, and people you want to invest in your business such as bank managers

- to provide a baseline against which the progress of your business can be measured.

There are many different structures for business plans. Here is a simple one which covers the basics provided by Liam Kelly of Forbairt.

1. **Principals:** who are you? Why should anyone believe you can do this? Brief history and objective of your business. Past performance (if available).

2. **Product:** what will you sell and what processes are involved before you have something to sell to the customer? How is it different to other competing services? Is it ready to sell now or do you need to develop it in some way?

3. **Location:** where will you carry out the business? Why have you chosen that location and how does it fit in with how you need to carry out your business? Do you have specific premises in mind? Indicate the purchase cost or rental.

4. **Machinery or equipment:** what is needed for your product or service? Give cost estimates and indicate if you already possess any of the relevant equipment.

5. Are any **raw materials** or parts needed?

6. **Employment:** who will be employed by the business? On what basis? Full-time, part-time, subcontracted? Don't forget all those boring administrative tasks vital to continued successful operation.

7. **Management:** what will the management structure be? Outline the qualifications and experience of the key personnel.

8. **Finance:** where will you get the money from? How much will be invested by the principals? How much will be borrowed and on what terms? How much are you looking for in terms of grants (if any)?

9. **Profitability:** the figures bit. Provide audited accounts for the last two years if you have them. Give projected profit and loss accounts and balance sheets for the first two years of the project.

10. **Marketing:** how will your products be sold? Do you have any firm contracts or orders? Market surveys? Competitors?

Setting prices and quoting

Preparing a business plan can seem to be a bit of a circular process – how can you know how much to charge until you know what the running costs are that you will have to cover? Or how successful your service will be? But in fact, a combination of estimating running costs and researching the prices charged by others for similar services will probably give you a fairly good guide to what you should be charging. This in turn may get you to refine your ideas about your start up costs – what you will really need to get going.

So start by doing the cash flows and other business calculations to find out what you need to earn to cover your running costs. If you aren't sure of how to do this, refer to guidebooks or get professional help from an accountant or business advisor. Your selling price must be higher than this breakeven cost. Selling price affects your choice of target market, means of communication, choice of name and so on.

Many teleworkers find quoting for jobs nervewracking initially. Applying common sense is the best advice. If you aren't sure, ask to prepare a small section of the work as a "free sample". Work out how long it takes you, and multiply up to the size of the whole job. Use the trial section of work to get the exact details of the job agreed with the customer. Novices tend to underquote so think about adding on 20% to the final amount you arrive at. Some customers find it reassuring to know the underlying cost per hour that you are calculating from. Others want you to quote a fixed price for the whole job. If you are on good terms with other teleworkers, ask them for advice on quotes.

Raising finance

The next step once you have a business plan is to raise the necessary finance for starting up. Double check your business plan figures with the checklist of items overleaf which you may need just to get started. Decide which are priority items, and which non-priority or unnecessary. Can you reduce costs by buying secondhand or borrowing? Remember to include VAT in the prices unless you are VAT registered, in which case you will be able to reclaim many VAT amounts.

One important item you will need to decide on with your accountant or financial adviser is whether to register for VAT. You are required to register for VAT if your business turns over more than £46,000 in the UK, or more than £20,000 in Ireland for service-based businesses (the manufacturing threshold is £40,000 but most teleworkers count as services). However, it may be worth your while registering even if you turnover is lower in some circumstances. For most teleworkers, the issues are:

- if you register then you can reclaim VAT on equipment you purchase
- if your customers are VAT registered, it will not inconvenience them that you charge VAT; but if they are mainly *not* registered, then it is actually going to cost them more to use you if you do register
- if you register, you will need to set up, learn and keep VAT accounts and make regular returns. In some ways this is a pain, in others it is a blessing in disguise because it forces you to keep your accounts up to date.

Checklist of items

Item	Priority	Cost new	Cost secondhand
Computer			
Software			
Modem			
Telephone			
Answerphone			
Printer			
Fax			
Photocopier			
Scanner			
Repair contract			
Tape drive for backup			
Surge supressed power sockets			
Consumables (paper etc.)			
Disks			
Disk storage			
Files and shelves			
Online subscriptions for email			
Desks			
Chairs			
Filing cabinets			
Suspension files			
Labels			
Postal scales			
Desk light			
Pinboard			
Reference books			
Stationery - paperclips and pens			
Envelopes			
Postage stamps			
Business cards			
Compliment slips			
Letterheads			
Brochures			
Professional fees (accountant, solicitor)			

You are more likely to be successful if you take a conservative approach to start up costs and "make do" rather than going for expensive items and incurring large financing charges, but beware: a common error is to underestimate start-up costs. Your financing will also need to include working capital – the money you need to start up and keep going until the first cheques come in. Bear in mind that unless you are doing basic secretarial work where people call in to collect their work, and you can extract money as you deliver work, you are unlikely to be paid less than 30 days from the date you invoice a customer. In many cases the delay between completion of the job and invoicing, and payment of the invoice, will be 45 or 60 days. Don't strangle your business at birth by failing to accommodate these delays with adequate finance. The most common cause of business failure is cash flow – so make sure that you invoice at the earliest possible instance, follow up with a statement to remind them, and then chase payment.

The options for raising finance are:

1. Your own equity
2. Other people's equity (shareholders)
3. Debt – fixed or floating, short or long term
4. Grants (almost without exception grant making bodies will require that you raise at least half the cost yourself).

Start by thinking about what finance you yourself can raise, and by taking a careful look at which of your assets you would need to retain if your business went under. You may not want to mortgage your house as collateral for a business bank loan, but other items might include:

- cash
- shares
- luxury items such as jewellery or paintings
- cars
- land/houses.

Now consider the possibility of investment (other people's equity). In general small businesses have difficulty raising equity capital or venture capital except from friends and relatives because the amount of money is too small (normally around £500,000 is the minimum investors want to look at because of the expense of checking and setting up the operation).

Whatever the source of your equity finance, be very clear on the following points outlined in Brian O'Kane's guide:

- are you prepared to allow other people to own (and therefore control) part of your business?
- what reward can they reasonably expect for their investment?
- can your business offer the kind of return that would attract outside investors?

Other sources of finance and advice

Business Links: Originally called 'one stop shops' the intention of Business Links is to provide one source of information and advice for small businesses rather than a huge range of enterprise agencies as had previously been the case. There are now around 250 Business Links covering the UK (called Business Shops in Scotland and Business Connect in Wales) You can contact your local Business Link by ringing the Business Link Signpost line 0345 567765 – in some cases they can put you through directly.

Business Links are partnerships of a number of organisations which include TECs (Training and Enterprise Councils), Chambers of Commerce, local authorities, and enterprise agencies. They are a first point of call and their business advisers should have a good idea of the types of grants, funding, export support, venture capital and other schemes available. Some of the schemes they should be able to advise you about are :

Business Start up Allowance (formerly the Enterprise Allowance): This has recently been changed to a one-off payment of £250 with a requirement to attend 4 days of business training. In certain assisted areas the old style allowance which paid £40 per week for a start up phase may still be available. There are a number of qualifying parameters which include submitting a business plan.

DTI Loan Guarantee Scheme: provides a guarantee for established businesses which have been trading for two years for up to £250,000. There is also a Small Loans scheme for amounts up to £30,000. The DTI guarantees 85 per cent of the outstanding amount to the lender for which you pay a guarantee premium – though the lender should take this into account when making charges. Details of the scheme are available through your business bank.

Enterprise Investment Scheme: the tax incentive scheme to encourage business investment. Here a business creates an investment opportunity and at its own expense arranges for it to be approved by the tax authorities. The investors can then claim tax relief on their investments. You need good legal and financial advice if you are considering this option.

Career Development Loans: this scheme provides subsidised loans for training and retraining purposes.

Local advice: Local Authority Economic Development Departments County, District, City, Metropolitan or Borough Councils' development officers will have information on the grant and funding schemes available within their area. This will include advice on regional funding, European schemes as well as any local schemes such as discretionary rate relief, or business start up assistance. Training and Enterprise Councils (LECs In Scotland) are also a good starting point. Details from your Business Link or the TEC National Council tel 0171 735 0010

Source of advice and finance continued...

Enterprise Agencies: Many of these are being drawn into Business Link partnerships so you may be duplicating information but check your phone directory for local agencies.

You can also consider:

- *Selling unwanted items and equipment*
- *Borrowing against the value of your house*
- *Cashing in shares and stocks*
- *Using credit cards*
- *Borrowing from friends and relatives – when they can afford it and with clear arrangements about when they'll receive their money back, and what interest will be paid.*
- *Buying the book Grants for Business (£39.50) which provides information on many sources of finance (Associated Management Services, 01793 480374).*
- *Contacting the Prince's Youth Business Trust if you are under 25.*

    The amount of debt finance you can raise will almost certainly be defined by what your bank manager is prepared to lend you and will be based on your business plan and available security. An old adage suggests that bank managers are looking for three things: character (your track record), collateral (security against any inability to repay) and cash flow (evidence that your business is financially viable). Arnold S. Goldstein's American book *Starting on a Shoestring* suggests that unless you know the answer to the following points before you go to see your bank manager you may not get very far:

■ why do you need the amount requested?
■ what will you do with it?
■ how do you know that it's enough?
■ how much less can you live with?
■ who else will you borrow from?
■ how do you propose to repay it?
■ how can you prove you can repay it?
■ what collateral can you offer?

    Don't overlook banks as a potential source of finance – most of the high street banks have overhauled their services to small businesses within the last few years and many produce packs of useful information. Lloyds Bank have developed a funder finding service in partnership with the Enterprise Advisory Service (EAS). A computer disk of the grantfinding 'Explorer' database is available, with a price discount for Lloyds customers.

Before you start

PR consultant Lindy Beveridge, who works with hi-tech companies in Cambridge, gives some general principles about what to think about before embarking on any public relations activity. If you have the budget, there is little doubt that using a PR consultant makes sense; sadly few start ups include a sufficient marketing and PR budget in their business plan.

"First, you have to formulate some idea of who you need to address, breaking down the audience into distinct groups, if you can. Then you need to identify the issues for the whole group and sub-issues which may only be of interest to particular groups in your audience. For instance, everyone presumably needs to be convinced that the service your company will produce is reliable, timely, virus-free, affordable and really useful. But only some groups will be interested in certain features.

"The basic aim is to create the best possible climate of opinion in which to do business with anyone whose good opinion will affect the success of your company. That means explaining the whole system clearly and interestingly in the first instance and addressing obvious concerns/issues right from the start openly. So you probably need at the start to formulate a very good and lucid explanation about how it will all work, be charged for, have its quality guaranteed, be delivered etc. After the first package of information has gone out, you need to collect responses – some of these will be fears, some criticisms, some good ideas etc. They need to be analysed and responded to appropriately and promptly.

"You also need to tell everyone how to contact you and what kind of timescale to expect for responses. Don't, for God's sake, undertake the impossible or fail to give yourself time to think things through. You don't know what problems may show up and to maintain integrity and trust that your word is good, you need to make considered and effective responses. These principles would apply to all the sectors of your audience but clearly you will develop a different style to respond to different groups – software developers will need more complexity in their reply than general inquirers and so on.

"You need to establish absolute honesty and integrity over financial and legal issues from the start and make sure that you don't depart from the standards you aim for. You also need to establish a style of communication which is consistent and appropriate and reflects openness – i.e. the intangible but very important qualities that are associated with integrity.

"If all this sounds daunting, I'd like to reassure you. It's not difficult but you do need to think things through before sending out messages to a very diverse and scattered group of contributors/customers. Teleworkers' clients are quite likely to be alone with their screens too, and you don't want preventable misunderstandings or to spend hours disentangling them by email if you can help it."

Antony Capstick of Instant Search gives the following advice:

"With PR and journalism one has to think of a peg to hang the idea on when you are selling it to journalists. When Company House opened up its service to people from the outside, I marketed the idea for my Instant Search business through that 'peg'. I sent faxes off to the newsdesk saying 'Companies House has opened their computer to the outside; however, you can get the service if you don't have a PC because Instant Search are offering it as a mail order instant access services. The best publicity I got from that was the Manchester Evening News. They quoted me and I was flooded with calls from Manchester, lots of orders – it was very good.

"It also helps in background credibility if your name is mentioned for example in the FT or a quality paper; somehow people think you are better. There may be direct sales as a result of editorial coverage, but it also helps when you approach people directly if they have already heard of you."

Your prospective customers may list a number of common anxieties about using teleworkers. Here we look at some organisational suggestions you could implement and use as selling points with your customers.

- computer viruses: can you guarantee that the disks you send to your customers are virus free?
- equipment backup – what would happen if your computer went down? Is alternative equipment available quickly? Do you have ample data backups of work in progress in case of disaster?
- people backup – if you are a small operation, how will you deal with the inevitable peaks and troughs in demand? You can deal with fluctuations in workload through a network of associated teleworkers, perhaps through online systems such as the Telework Europa forum on Compuserve, or the EU's Telemart project. Set the system up before you are in a crisis!
- confidentiality – what happens if another teleworker accesses commercially sensitive information? Could somebody unscrupulous get hold of the client company's stationery?
- make sure your computer system is secure. Use security features such as passwords and file locking to prevent unauthorised access of client's files. Make sure your office is secure. Lock away customers' stationery and files if they are sensitive
- delivery methods: Can you help your customers to get used to teleworking, for example by offering to help them to set up modems and learn to use email? If they aren't on email, do you know everything you need to about collection and delivery services for finished work?

(e.g. what is the cut-off time in your area to get a parcel to DHL for delivery next day in Brussels? How much does it cost to get a motorbike delivery to London? If you needed to deliver a package to an office on a Saturday, which fast postal service does not require a signature on acceptance?)

- presentation: Look at your fax cover sheets, letterheads, business cards. Do they reflect a professional image? How does your office look if a customer drops in unexpectedly? Can customers hear radios in the background when they ring up? Are all staff trained in telephone answering? There are few more effective ways of annoying a prospective customer than putting him or her on hold or asking their name and company several times over before connecting them. Fax cover sheets are often the first impression a teleworker gives to a customer. Give them the attention they deserve.

These issues are related to quality control and are covered in Chapter 9. If your organisation is large enough to bear the time involved, look into achieving formal quality control to ISO9000. Use project management software to track progress on all jobs undertaken. Measure your response time to enquiries.

Handling press and publicity

Properly handled, your relations with the local and business press can be one of the most cost-effective forms of marketing, but they need to be seen as part of your marketing strategy – just as with direct mail or advertising campaigns, identify the target and then look at the most effective means to reach it. Apart from reaching new customers, former *Teleworker* magazine editor Barnaby Page believes press coverage can assist with the following:

- existing customers (reminding them of your existence)
- employees or subcontractors (morale booster)
- suppliers (improved service if they think of you as an important customer)
- bank managers, planning officers (always useful to have them on your side).

To get to these audiences you have to convince an intermediary target – the journalist. The key to success is to treat press relations as a partnership in which both you and the journalist want to reach the same people – the journalist wants to give them an interesting, useful read. You want to make them aware of your product or service. Helping journalists to achieve their objective is the secret of success according to Page, who has provided the following guide to obtaining press coverage.

Step 1: identify the publication. It could be a business to business title, or a specialist trade paper. Be careful not to confuse business and consumer counterparts – mountain bikers don't necessarily read Cycle Trader, and turkey farmers may not have much interest in BBC Good Food magazine. If you're unsure the reference bible is the voluminous and expensive monthly BRAD (British Rates and Data) which gives information on almost every periodical in Great Britain and some in Northern Ireland and the Republic of Ireland. It may be worth using a PR consultant just to identify your market and for access to BRAD – it's rarely to be found in public libraries although the Willings Press Guide is usually available in libraries.

Step 2: draft your press release, always keeping in mind the famous acronym KISS – Keep It Simple, Stupid.

- try not to exceed one page of generously-spaced A4 on your business letterhead
- use a short, clear headline that sums up the story in a few words
- get all the main details into the first paragraph. Further down, include an interesting quote
- avoid journalese – you are writing to attract the journalist's attention, not to do their job for them. Expunge words like "revealed" or "shocked" and keep in mind the news angle – why might your story generate interest?
- avoid jargon and stick to clear, quantifiable facts such as "This is the third government contract Anytown Design has won in two months" not "this places Anytown Design as an industry market leader"
- if you enclose a photo, try to ensure it is a print, not a transparency, label it clearly on the back with the name and job title of each person, and briefly describe what they are doing. Do not use felt pen or biro for this label – in a pile of photographs the ink may come off the back of your photograph and on to the front of the one below, and biros can cause indentations that damage the photograph. Use pencil or a typed label. Don't expect to see the photo again, whether or not it is published
- date it and include your contact details and telephone number at the bottom.

Step 3: make sure you're sending it to the **right person**. A call to the paper to find out, for example, who covers local business may get you a name. If you don't have a name, send it to a relevant sounding job title such as Industrial Correspondent.

Step 4: if a journalist calls you for further details, remember they don't bite.

- be courteous and don't patronise in explaining your story. Today's trainee journalist could be a valuable contact on a national paper in a few year's time
- don't lie or exaggerate – journalists aren't particularly interested in the skeletons in your cupboard until you lie to conceal them
- avoid going "off the record" i.e. giving information which you do not

wish to be published. Although journalists rarely abuse this privilege, mistakes sometimes happen

- understand that you have no veto over what is printed – there is little point in demanding to see an article before it's published

- don't antagonise journalists by complaining. Errors are sometimes made – if they are trivial let it lie rather than be branded as a time-waster. For a major mistake, write a polite letter to the editor.

Step 5: If at first you don't succeed, try again. Keep your name in the eye of the public, and in the eye of other journalists. If there's a subject where you have expertise, you may gradually become established as what's unkindly known as a "rentaquote", so that whenever a feature in your area comes along, you're the first person who comes to mind.

Mailing lists

The mailing list is both a junk-mail curse and a vitally useful tool in the right hands. Today's software tools allow records of contacts to be easily held, and the production of vast quantities of marketing materials which can be personalised to the addressee. However, they can have a negative effect if they are not correctly written and targeted, or waste your resources if they are not well planned.

First, you need to know whom you are going to contact and why. Use your business plan and market research to build up a profile of the likely customer. If you are selling to businesses, your next step will probably be to purchase a mailing list from companies such as Kompass, which hold regularly updated and indexed lists of companies. As you pay "per name" you will need to build up a brief for the mailing list company which may include parameters such as:

- number of employees
- market sector (most have a series of ID codes for different market sectors)
- person to contact within the company (e.g. finance director, human resources/personnel)
- service, manufacturing, export sector
- number of years established
- ownership (e.g. foreign owned or domestic)
- geographical location
- telephone number (vital for qualifying the list – see below).

Mailing list companies have an incentive to get you to buy as many names as possible, whereas you want the smallest number that will give you a good response rate. To avoid this poacher/gamekeeper conflict you may wish to use a mailing list broker. Bill Moss, an experienced broker, explains: "Mailing list brokers get a discount from suppliers such as

Kompass because they buy in bulk. They also know the various mailing lists extremely well. So you can get professional advice from a mailing list broker to produce a well-defined list, get the broker to obtain the list for you, and pay the same amount as you would have done buying direct – the broker pockets the difference between the discount and the standard retail price as the fee for his or her advice".

The broker will also be able to help you ensure that you get the names in a format that you can use. The safest format to ask for is CSV (comma separate variable), which will work with most spreadsheet and word processing programmes. You will probably need to put the list into spreadsheet format whilst you qualify and sort it before using it with your word processing mail merge feature. Other commonly used formats are DBF and ASCII though some suppliers will provide lists in mail merge format for specified word processing packages. Bill also gives a checklist for those buying mailing lists, whether direct or through a broker:

- Does it matter where the client is located?
- What contact name (job function) is needed if any?
- Do you need telephone or fax numbers?
- How/why is the list you are buying compiled, and how old is it?
- Is the list owner registered for data protection?
- Is the list owner a member of the country's Direct Marketing Association. If not, think twice about employing them.

Before you even consider the logistics of sending out your mailing, you must qualify the list. This is a tedious process which consists of telephoning the company and checking that the person on your list is indeed still the managing director/human resources manager or whatever, that you have their correct title, and that they are responsible for the area of activity you are interested in. Be polite, patient and persistent with receptionists – they get many such calls each day and sometimes can be a bit short with the nth enquirer, whom they may well think is either a salesman or yet another jobseeker. If they offer to put you through to the person in question, grasp the opportunity. Briefly explain why you are contacting them and tell them you will be sending a mailing shortly. Don't get depressed if they express no interest – you've just saved yourself a wasted stamp and follow up call.

The next step is to set up a sensible schedule for mailing and follow up. Be realistic – most mail-outs have a very low response rate of less than 5% so build this into your workload projections. For business to business services it is highly unproductive to send out several thousand mailings at once, a large proportion of which will go straight in the bin. Instead, send out small batches in stages, and follow up by telephoning again a few days after the mailing to ask whether the mailing was received, and whether they are interested in your product or service. If they are not interested, ask whether they would mind explaining why so that you can better target your marketing in future (subtext: not bother them with things that don't interest them). This approach may elicit useful information about what's wrong with your service; however some respondents tend to treat it as a hard sell technique and refuse to elucidate.

For consumer/retail services, it may be more effective to use geographical mailings to all houses in a district, usually organised through the Post Office on a cost per copy basis. Such campaigns are almost always more effective if press coverage or advertising is used at the same time.

In either case, before embarking on a mailshot be sure you have costed it properly and that you have put aside resources for the follow-up, and for capturing details of any prospective customers who contact you as a result. Amongst the costs are:

- mailing list purchase
- time and telephone costs for qualifying the mailing list
- design, editing and printing of the mailshot material
- envelopes, laser labels and postage
- responding to enquiries – as a rule of thumb, you should expect around a 10–15% response rate if you also follow up the mailshot by phone.

As well as keeping track of your responses, you will need to have some method of estimating the overall conversion rate between the money you have spent on the mailing and the increased business which directly results from it.

To keep costs and postal rates down, think about printing one-coloured ink onto coloured paper for your mailing, and bear in mind that as long as you have affixed a clear mailing address label and postage, it is quite legal not to use an envelope, but to fold the document neatly and secure with a small adhesive label easily broken open by the recipient. Mailing labels can be printed in sheets on most laser printers. To save licking all those stamps, most post offices can arrange to frank large mailings for you but normally you will have to prepare the mailings with all envelopes the right way round. For mailings of over 2,000 you can use the "Mailsort" service which considerably reduces postal costs, but is only available if the postcode is clearly included in the address labels. Some companies can act as bureau services for Mailsort, including TCA member Global Village Services.

In Ireland franked mailing is available at main sorting offices only and must be paid for in cash or by banker's draft.

Some companies are now using fax shots, although professional marketing people are divided about whether the level of negative reactions from people receiving unsolicited faxes outweighs the value of fax shots. Keep the message short and simple – one A4 page or less. Fax numbers can be found in the fax directory available from BT, and from local business directories. Many specialist business associations will sell their directories to non-members for a price, or have reasonable membership prices.

Advertising

You will probably want to advertise at first so that customers will be aware of your existence. Think carefully about which media (newspapers, local radio) will work best for you, and compare prices. The basic options are:

- newspapers
- trade magazines
- world wide web
- local radio
- TV.

Try to think about how you will measure response to your adverts so that you will know where to spend your money next time. Keep asking new customers where they heard about you.

Directories and networks

An increasing number of businesses are making use of directories to market their services. The best known and most widely accessible publication is the telephone directory (Yellow Pages, or Golden Pages in Ireland). Before advertising in Yellow Pages take a good look at the entries for your area. A problem that many teleworking businesses come across is that there is no obvious place for their services in Yellow Pages at present – or rather too many. Teleworkers would often need to make entries in a number of categories to cover all their services, including office services, desktop publishing, graphic design, bookkeeping, secretarial services and so on. Yellow Pages may be a good option if your business fits into a niche – such as market research – but very expensive if you cover a range of categories. Remember that you are entitled to a basic text entry in Yellow Pages if you pay the business, rather than residential, tariff on your telephone. Make sure you get that and that it is correctly worded – Yellow Pages entries for the

Measuring advertising response

Anthony Capstick of Instant Search comments: "The next area I went into was direct advertising in newspapers. I tried all the national newspapers, the *Sunday Times, Times, Telegraph* and the *Observer*, particularly the small ad section in the back.

We run, for example, a six line ad in the *Sunday Times* advertising our services which costs something like £70 resulting in something like 10 or 15 orders per week, and it's generally busy Monday or Tuesday. You need to run the ad for a specific period of time. I went in and out a couple of times at the beginning because I didn't want to spend too much. But I did notice that when I left it in, I was getting a much better response. People often browse papers, and may see the same ad again and again. The fourth or fifth time they may ring you up. If they have just see the advert once they may think the company is not very reliable. Persistence pays.

But the whole thing is wasted if you do not ask every single person who rings in where they saw your service advertised, where you got that enquiry. Otherwise you are just throwing money away. I constructed a spreadsheet with the cost of the advert, when it appeared, the number of enquiries and the number of conversions from that enquiry. When people call in and their orders are taken, a code is entered about where they saw Instant Search advertised. At the end of the month, when I'm booking the next level of advertising, I can see, for example, that a £200 ad in the *Sunday Times* brough in £500 of business, whereas the Daily Telegraph only cost me £80 but brought in only £60 of business. Stick to the Sunday papers if your business can go overseas – we have agents in Moscow picked up from a three line ad in the *Sunday Times*.

whole country are becoming widely available on CD-ROM so this constitutes a useful form of "free" advertising with wide coverage.

If you decide to pay for a more complex Yellow Pages ad, think through the different options and prices. Often a plain text advert in bold type will be more cost effective and practical than a graphic. In general companies are more concerned about reference clients than they are about the size of your Yellow Pages advert. Think of it in plumbing terms. If you are looking for a plumber, you may indeed use Yellow Pages to find the number of a particular plumber, but you are more likely to choose the plumber based on personal recommendation or reference from friends and neighbours than "cold" through any directory. So it's important to have your contact details accessible but it may not be so important to take a large ad.

Local business directories may also be worth buying entries for – your local Chamber of Commerce or library should be able to give you information on the directories operating in your area. Chambers of commerce and other business networking organisations also often publish

Telemart

The Telemart project is also working to provide work for teleworkers through a job agency with a difference - this time it's the work that travels to the people. The Telemart project will set up a system on the Internet channelling work to teleworkers operating from their homes or from small teleworking centres.

But teleworkers sometimes find it hard to market themselves successfully - it's a costly and time-consuming process for small businesses, and in any case new work often comes via a referral from an existing satisfied customer. Teleworkers also suffer from a "feast and famine" problem of too much or too little work. The Telemart project will connect the teleworkers together into a quality-controlled flexible network of skilled people that businesses can tap into as and when they need work done.

Companies wanting work carried out can either use conventional methods - phone up Telemart and discuss their needs - or they can use Telemart's Internet directory to put in a request and see what kind of skills are available on the network. All the teleworkers involved with Telemart operate quality control systems and use email to send and receive work quickly when needed. Just like a conventional job agency, Telemart performs the introductions and guarantees the quality of the workers. In exchange, it receives a commission on the value of the work performed.

The Telemart project will last for two years, until the end of 1997. During the period to June 1996, the system will be piloted with a pioneer group of teleworkers and companies, before a multinational trial takes place in 1997. The Telemart project is operated by partners in Sweden, Wales, N.E. England, Ireland, Newfoundland, Greece and France and is part funded by the Commission of the European Communities as part of its "Telematics Applications Programme".

For further information on Telemart contact Imogen Bertin
Telephone: +353 21 887300
Fax: +353 21 887402
or send email to imogen@ctc.ie or 100272.1472@compuserve.com.

local directories and encourage their members to use the services of other members.

Individual teleworkers may find it worthwhile to register with employment agencies as some are now taking on board the task of getting in work for teleworkers. A number of agencies advertise on the World Wide Web, although most of the requests are for permanent staff, not for temps or teleworkers.

Get out there and sell!

Many teleworkers have found conventional advertising or mailing too expensive in the long term, and insufficiently rewarding. Other suggestions include:

- prepare a brochure or prospectus of your services for selected mailings. If you want to give names of your existing clients to add weight to your material, don't forget to ask permission. Even better, see if you can get endorsed statements from your clients to use in your marketing material
- work out how much it will cost you to have your own page on the World Wide Web. (See Chapter 8, *Email and Online Services* for further information)
- telecottages can join forces to make joint approaches to larger companies
- teleworkers can form umbrella organizations to market their services co-operatively
- "piggy back" your mailings with those of local computer equipment suppliers by agreement, sharing costs
- speak to local business groups, chambers of commerce, women's institutes (ICA in Ireland), farming groups
- If you have suitable premises, think about organising occasional social get-togethers for your customers and workers so that people can put faces to names, and be aware of all the services you are offering. How about a working lunch involving a presentation?
- personal visits. No-one likes cold calling, but if you can talk to businesses on a one-to-one basis you could get a trial piece of work that will get your foot in the door. Try writing to your prospective customer, then telephone to say you will be in the area, and could you call in? Arm yourself with some facts about the savings to be made by using teleworkers
- if you specialise in a particular area, is there a relevant software user group with a newsletter (e.g. Corel Ventura Users for DTP)? These newsletters are often cheap to advertise in and hit direct to your target market.
- editorial copy is free but you need to do as much of the journalist's work for them as possible in order to get your story into a paper. Talk to all local journalists – press, freelancers, local radio, TV. Keep up the contact. Phone them, write to them, send them press releases and good photographs. Just keep your name in front of them too often for them to ignore. Invite them to visit your premises. Try holding an Open Day. Take photographs of all events – remember you need black and white photos for most newspapers

- follow up professional contacts such as former workmates where appropriate
- the best of all advertising is word-of-mouth. Keep up the quality of your service and you will be repaid by personal recommendations. On the down side, it has been estimated that if a customer has a bad experience of your service, he or she will probably report this to 26 other people.

Acknowledgments

The TCA thanks Brian O'Kane for permission to use material from his guide *Starting Your Own Business in Ireland*, published by Oaktree Press, ISBN 1-872853-17-X.

Barnaby Page, former editor of *The Teleworker* magazine, contributed the sections on handling the press.

Bibliography

101 Ways to Make More Profits
Author: Steve Pipe
Source: Kogan Page, London Ref: ISBN 0–7494–1700–S

101 Ways to Promote Your Business
Authors: Godfrey Harris and Gregrey Harris
Source: Kogan Page, London Ref: ISBN 0–7494–18443

A Marketing Action Plan for the Growing Business   *Date:* 1995
Authors: Shailendra Vyakarnam and John W. Leppard
Source: Kogan Page, London Ref: ISBN 0–7494–1313–1

BBC Complete Small Business Guide   *Date:* 1995
Author: Colin Barrow
Source: BBC, 4th edition Ref: ISBN 0–56337083–1

Business Growth Action Kit   *Date:* 1995
Author: Jim Brown
Source: Kogan Page Ref: ISBN 0–7494–1795

Daily Telegraph How to Set Up and Run Your Own Business   *Date:* 1996
Source: Kogan Page Ref: 12th edn ISBN 0–7494–1969–5

Do Your Own Market Research   *Date:* 1994
Authors: Paul Hague and Peter Jackson
Source: Kogan Page, London Ref: ISBN 0–7494– 1779–X

Enterprise Ireland   *Date:* 1995
Author: Brian O'Kane
Source: Oak Tree Press Ref: ISBN 1–872853–97–8

Lloyds Bank Small Business Guide   *Date:* 1996
Source: Penguin ISBN 0–14–024898–6

Management Pocketbooks: Balance Sheet/Managing Budgets/   *Date:* 1995
Managing Cashflow (three publications)
Authors: Anne HAwkins and Clive Turner
Source: 14 East St, Alresford, Hants SO24 9EE Tel: 01962 735573 Fax: 01962 733637

Running your own Word-Processing Service
Author: Doreen Huntley
Source: Kogan Page, London Ref: ISBN 0-7494-0344-6.

Running Your Own Business *Date:* 1994
Author: David Williams
Source: Allied Dunbar Personal Finance Guides (Nicholas Brealey Publishing) Ref: ISBN 1–85788–092–7

Start and Run a Profitable Consulting Business *Date:* 1989
Source: Kogan Page, London Ref: ISBN 1–850091–927–5

Starting a Successful Small Business/ How to Set up your Own Business/ Successful Marketing for the Small Business (three publications)
Source: Kogan Page, 120 Pentonville Road, London N1 9JN

Survive & Prosper – Rules for Business Success *Date:* 1994
Author: Tony Boffe
Source: Kogan Page Ref: 2nd edn ISBN 0–7494–1276–3

Work for Yourself – A Guide to Self-Employment and Setting up a Small Business/ Earning Money at Home (2 publications)
Source: Consumers' Association, Castlemead, Gascoyne Way, Hertford

The Which? Guide to Earning Money at Home
Author: Lynn Underwood *Date:* 1994
Source: Which? Consumer Guides, 2 Marylebone Road, London, NW1 4DF Ref: ISBN 0 85202 507 6

500 Ideas to Increase Profits
Source: Random House Tel: 0171 973 9000 Fax: 0171 8286681
Comment: Small company strategies put together by financial specialist Tony Grainger intended as a small business manual covering cost reduction, pension schemes, car financing, tax, insurance and shareholder agreements.

Contacts and URLs

Enterprise Advisory Service PC-based database of grants. Details can be obtained by ringing 0345 343434. TCA members should ring 01280 700 102 to contact EAS directly in order to claim a discount on Explorer.

Regional Development Agencies

For information on sources of funds allocated to specific areas of the UK
RDC – Rural Development Commission (areas of rural England) Tel: 01722 336255
DBRW – Development Board for Rural Wales Tel: 01686 627518
LEDU – Local Enterprise Development Unit (Northern Ireland) Tel: 01232 242582
IRTU – Industrial training Research and Technology Unit (Northern Ireland) Tel: 01232 529475
WDA –Welsh Development Agency Tel: 0345 775566
HIE – Highlands and Island Enterprise Tel: 01463 713504
Scottish Enterprise Tel: 01412 482700

CIMTech (Scotland only) is a programme run by the Chartered Institute of Marketing to help companies develop thier businesses through the application of appropriate technology such as the provision of practical advice and support for teleworkers and virtual companies. Contact Mr Donald Malcolm, Chartered Institute of marketing, Burnbrae Lodge, Kellybridge, Dollar FK14 7PG Tel: 01259 743426 Fax: 01259 742631 Email: n.hill@cablinet.co.uk

Local funding

Some funding can be very localised – for example, enquiries to Gloucester Business Link yielded information on:

Gloucestershire Business Angel Scheme (linking potential investors and small businesses Tel: 0800 135235

Royal British Legion small business advisory service (close army contacts) The Cottage, Ordnance Road, Tidworth, Wilts SP9 7QD

Midland Bank Enterprise Fund for the South West has an investment fund of up to £150,000 for application to businesses in the south west. Contact Gloucester TEC 01452 524488.

Funding aimed at Youth :

Prince's Youth Business Trust Age range 18-29 loans up to £5,000 and grants up to £1,500. To qualify must have a viable business idea, be disadvantaged in some way and be unable to otherwise raise finance Tel: 0171 321 6500

LIVEWIRE Grants and support aimed at young people aged 16-25 are available Tel: 0191 261 5584

Teleworker magazine regularly provides information about initiatives relevant to teleworking and telematics projects, small business and rural areas.

General

Management Technology Associates, Clark House, King's Road, Fleet, Hampshire GU13 9AD Tel: 01252 812 252 Fax: 01252 815 702 Email: 100142.31@compuserve.com.

http://www.tjobs.com/" is a telecommuting jobs web page for people to find telecommuting employment. Works two ways, either enter the job-line to check out jobs available, or enter job-seeker area to provide info on type of work sought together with work experience.

Teleworking Associations

National Association of Teleworkers The Island House, Midsomer Norton, Bath, Avon BA3 2HI Tel: 01761 413869 Fax: 01761 419348 Email: 100063.462@compuserve.com

Scottish Teleworking Association, Roy Guthrie, GCS, Tel: 01324 714325 Fax: 01324 714546, Email: 100447.1113@compuserve.com

TCA Tel: 0800 616008 or 01203 696986 Fax: 01203 696538 Email: 100272.3137@compuserve.com

Telecottages Wales, Paddy Moindrot Tel: 01691 648887 Email: 74431.1372@compuserve.com

Telework Ireland (also covers Northern Ireland) Reagrove, Minane Bridge, Co. Cork Tel: +353 21 887300 Fax: +353 21 887402 Email: 100272.1472@compuserve.com or imogen@ctc.ie Web: http://www.cis.ie/tci

Telecottages and Telecentres

A telecottage provides the local community with low cost access to computer and telecommunications equipment, which in turn give access to information services and work. Telecottages also support teleworkers and small businesses. Other terms used in addition to telecottage include telecentre, teleservice centre and electronic village hall.

The first centre claiming the title telecottage in the UK, the Moorlands Telecottage, was set up in 1989, but like many good ideas, it appears that it was being independently "invented" in a number of places. A recent TCA survey turned up examples which predate the first Swedish telecottages in 1985, such as Daily Information in Oxford. Since the early 1990s, numbers of telecottages have grown rapidly to a total of 155 in the UK and Ireland in May 1996. The growth in numbers is set to continue with a number of initiatives planning networks of telecottages, such as the RATIO project for 40 telecentres in Devon and Cornwall, and the inclusion of telecottage facilities in the ACRE village hall improvements project to be carried out with Millennium Fund backing.

Many different forms of telecottage have been set up. Some are community orientated and offer training and use of resources for community groups. Others are highly equipped commercial enterprises. Experience from Sweden, where there are around 20 telecottages, and from the more mature UK telecottages, suggests that centres need to adopt a commercial attitude if they are to survive beyond an initial grant-funded start up. A key to success appears to be creation of a core business, often software training, around which other complementary services are offered. In Newfoundland, the concept has been extended to cover local enterprise support centres where access to a wide range of online resources is also available. The Newfoundland experience has shown the effectiveness of combining a network of online resources which people can access from their homes in conjunction with local centres.

The practice of using telecottages as bases for groups of teleworkers (often referred to in the US as neighbourhood work centres) has been slow to get going. Though a number of centres have housed a variety of individual positions such as rural field officers, there have been few larger scale projects such as the group of 25 county council workers who used the Antur Teifi telematics centre. Recently a number of other county councils have taking up the idea, including Surrey, Notts, Kent and Oxford, as part of their flexible working strategies.

Because rural areas are often short of resources, telecottages can become a focus of community and commercial activity, providing a centre where the isolation of working from home can be broken down. Teleworkers can network through the telecottage, using each other's services to provide backup on larger contracts.

Services

Telecottages usually offer both formal and informal training, computer hire (some offer "take-away" computers too) and access to photocopiers, laser printers and faxes. Other facilities include use of workspace, and meeting rooms. A more complete listing of teleservices which could be provided through telecottages is given in Chapter 6. Trained staff are usually available to provide secretarial assistance, word processing and desktop publishing, which can be invaluable to teleworkers who need additional help. Ideas followed up by some telecottages include:

Product demonstration rooms

Telecottages represent a potential network of centres where product demonstrations can be made to local small businesses. With the level of computer equipment already available in centres, plus ISDN lines in some cases and the office support available, telecottages have been used in this way on a number of occasions.

Sales force support centres

National sales forces often have a far flung group of people who may need to meet up with regional managers, hold small conferences or drop in and use the facilities. Telecottages are being increasingly approached to offer these facilities and would be well advised to network with other telecottages to offer coverage of an entire region.

Product agency agreements

Agency agreements on a number of product lines related to the telecottage business can be arranged such as :computer sales, office supplies and printing.

Mere Telecottage

Our Business is helping small businesses – outstanding range of services at small business prices

- *Photocopying (enlarging/two colour)*
- *Typing/printing (official documents)*
- *Telephone answering service*
- *Foreign language translation*
- *Total accounts package*
- *Computer training RSA/NVQ accreditation*
- *Desktop Publishing*
- *Computer hire by the hour*

No job is too small – our reasonable rates will surprise you!

Homework club
Some telecottages have offered access to computers for children for homework or games useage. By adopting a fixed timetable for this it can be offered in such a way as not to disrupt other telecottage users.

Cybercafe internet access
A number of cybercafes have been set up, usually in town centres, where they have created a lot of interest in the Internet by offering access at £5 per hour. Telecottages could offer an Internet education package - a getting started course followed by a number of sessions at the telecottage.

Local council information centres
A number of County Councils are keen to develop on-line information access points and might welcome a site for an additional terminal which could be rented to them.

CD-ROM library
Some libraries offer a CD-ROM lending service - this can be expensive to set up (eg set of 200 CD-ROMS at £3,750) but shared between a number of organisations it could prove to be an income generator. Contact Ramesis tel 01274 737376

Job club
Telecottages can provide a site for job information , a board, latest job information faxed over or jobs information available on-line contact your local Job Centre for information.

Business adviser outpost
Business Link, your local TEC, council or regional development agency are all potential clients for use of the facilities to meet customers. Using grantfinder database software, the telecottage could also charge an access fee and assist small businesses to use these facilities.

A detailed list of commercial service ideas is given in the Chapter 6, *Ideas for Teleservices*, but a typical example from Mere Telecottage, a community-based enterprise in Wiltshire is given opposite.

Telecottage statistics

At the end of 1994, the TCA supported a survey of telecottage activities by Bill Murray of Small World Connections. The results give a snapshot of the "typical" telecottage which can be useful to those thinking about setting up. All the figures are averages or approximations.

- Centres have 40 regular users and 40 occasional users
- 40% subcontract work to local teleworkers
- One third see themselves as "telecottages"; other titles given include Community Resource Centre, Computer Resource Centre, Office Bureau, Teleworking Centre

- Half are based in towns (the survey did not distinguish between small rural and large urban towns), with a quarter in small villages and another quarter in remote rural settings
- Most telecottages have 1.5 full-time staff, 2 part-timers, 2 volunteers and 1.5 subcontracted workers; in fact patterns are more complex with over half having no volunteer help, and fewer than 25% having subcontracted help. Nearly a quarter have no full-time staff at all and 10% have no employees - just volunteers and subcontractors
- One fifth of telecottages are privately owned. Over a quarter are co-ops or charities or companies limited by guarantee. About half are supported by local councils, colleges or other public authorities
- Half are "breaking even" financially, with one third making a loss (usually the most recently set up telecottages) and about one in seven making a profit. Incomes ranged from £6,000 to £180,000 with an average of £50,000
- Facilities vary widely but almost all have IBM compatible PCs, laser printers and photocopiers. A large number have a flatbed scanner; over two thirds have modems, half have CD-ROM drives. Most have three to four telephone lines, 6.5 PCs, 2.5 portable PCs, two laser printers and an inkjet printer (often colour). Around 20% have at least one Apple Mac.
- Over half see one of their main functions as training, with provision of office facilities a close second. Almost one third see administrative facilities such as word processing as a main key service, but general awareness raising was also seen as an important function.
- Income comes from funded training for over a third of centres, with office services and secretarial services a close second. Niche businesses providing income included: accommodation addresses, message taking, membership subscriptions, online services, bookkeeping and accountancy, newsletter production, conference management, desktop publishing and graphic design.

Case studies

During the 1990s it has become increasingly apparent that successful telecottages fall into one of two models. Under the first model, they develop a core niche business which often creates the infrastructure (equipment and premises) that subsidises the economically priced services of the telecottage. Under the second model, they receive their support from various agencies in exchange for providing training services. Within these two models, there are some interesting variations, such as telecottages which also manage a number of startup business unit premises, telecottages attached to sub-postoffices and/or tourist offices, and integrated telecottages, such as KITE, and WREN, which work to provide training, commercial work and childcare facilities on one site.

Antur Tanat Cain Telebureau

Antur Tanat Cain Telebureau developed out of a community development scheme to revamp Llangedwyn Mill in rural Wales into a number of units. The Antur also trained local people for new technology jobs, but found many were then having to travel long distances to work, or were relocating. The solution was to bring work into the area to follow the training courses, and the first contract was through a locally based consultant who was working with ICL. The telecottage worked to capture historical data using a text scanner. The teleworkers then reformatted the scanned text for an information retrieval system, and this work turned into a number of major contracts providing work for several people. However, a couple of further contracts through Telecottages Wales failed to materialise, and then funding for the Training for Work programme (which the telecottage had been running) was cut further and further until it was not feasible to continue its operation. On top of the funding crisis, the Antur's computers – Amstrad PCWs and 1640s – badly needed upgrading, and local authority support was restricted because the Antur was about to be "moved" across a county border. In the end, the training scheme was discontinued and the staff, a trainer, an administrator and a part-time trainer, were found other jobs. The telecottage manager and two builders stayed on to keep the business units going. Now the new local authority, Powys, through its telecottage support officer Joyce Morgan, is encouraging the telecottage to become a cyber-cafe, reopening the café formally operating from the Mill. An application has been made for European training funding to put 10 people through the teleworking NVQ, and another contract from ICL is in the offing. Maureen Wilde, the telecottage manager, says she has been kept going by the supportive managing body, which includes councillors, local organisations, economic development officers and "anyone interested". She is convinced Antur Tanat Cain is back on its feet, and points to the continuing need for training: "What we need to do now is to retrain many of the people who worked on the original ICL contracts to use the latest software and really, everyone is going to need constant retraining in their working life to keep up."

Barnham Telecottage

Barnham Telecottage near Bognor Regis was set up as a private venture in June 1995 by husband and wife team Jane and Eric Pascal. Jane is a retired teacher, and Eric recently sold off his computer bureau business. The centre is run from a shop at the front of the Pascal's house and follows the pattern of some of the more recent telecottages which run the telecottage on the back of an existing core business. The computer systems and development work which Eric continues to offer provides an income of around £25,000. The telecottage income amounts to a further £6,000, which is expected to grow to £10,000. The telecottage makes use of the equipment amassed through Eric's business.

One of the largest income earners for the centre is training, and the majority of the trainees are women returners. Other services include photocopying, printing, Internet training, dtp and business support. The telecottage is a boon to local home based businesses as Jane Pascal explains: "There are lots of small business converts to the telecottage - people who work from home but probably wouldn't call themselves teleworkers. Also we get students in to type their work or if they've left it too late, to get it typed by us!"

The value of the centre is also backed by an enthusiastic local user: "I think telecottages are an excellent concept - I have been setting up a business venture from the dining room table with no resources. The telecottage has been ideal - I don't think I would have been able to get this far without help from them. I use their email number on my letterhead which has added credibility. I intend to get computer trained in the future - they have put everything they do for me on a space on the computer - and I look forward to the point when I can get going on this myself."

Because they have a core business interleaving with the telecottage, the Pascals have been able to provide economically priced training to the community without any subsidy. Eric is keen to stress that the telecottage would not exist on its own, but it appears to work well with the existing business supplying the basic infrastructure of premises and equipment.

BOON

An example of a hybrid community/commercial enterprise is BOON (Business On Open Network), which is headquartered in the restored Maiden Newton station in Dorset. BOON's manager, Drew Llewellyn, picks out four main activities which have made the company self-financing for over a year. Close links with the original funders, (Dorset County Council and District Council, the local TEC, the Rural Development Commission and Barclays Bank) are maintained through BOON's board of directors.

The Mouse to Mouse Resuscitation™ scheme offers a complete service to local businesses, specifying equipment for them, purchasing, optimising and installing it. "Mouse to Mouse ensures that the system works really well and gives the customer an instant start – a computer that can be used usefully and productively the moment it arrives in the office. We make sure they don't spend money they don't need to on hardware, but that they have the system that they need – and we throw in a free faxmodem. Usually the charge is about 25–30% of the equipment cost, but often we are advising a substantially cheaper computer than the one they originally intended to buy, so that cost can often be "invisible" to the small business."

The Countrywork scheme provides computers to small business to try out for a couple of months. BOON has 8 laptops and 5 desktops for hire, and the costs vary from about £55 per month to over £100 per month depending on the machines. Drew gets round the usual insurance problems in hiring laptops by making customers fully responsible for the value of the laptop, and has had no mishaps or missing machines to date.

Three people, Drew and two others, also work on contracts to install and upgrade software for larger businesses in Dorset and surrounding counties. Recently they completed a project to reconfigure 220 PCs for their local NHS trust, and they take on database publication work as well as supplying IT support to the council's economic development team.

Finally, BOON also acts as a drop-in centre for people to use computers, print out their work and network their skills. One of BOON's associate teleworkers records translations from Japanese to English on tape. BOON transcribes the tapes and emails the results to the teleworker's clients worldwide. Drew's advice to prospective telecentres ("and I speak from bitter experience") is to buy equipment and software on credit card so that you have some comeback if suppliers go bust.

Bronllys and Talgarth Telecentre

Amelia Jones exudes enthusiasm about the progress at Bronllys and Talgarth telecentre despite the prospect of a third move since its startup. "A year ago we began with £21 startup capital. Now our turnover has passed £27,000". Amelia began with a small amount of European Social Fund money to give an eight-week training course, and received support and premises from local enterprise body ATB Landbase. As well as EU funded training courses, Bronllys and Talgarth gives commercial training course and handles secretarial work, picked up largely by word of mouth. Amelia has just heard that the telecentre will receive a further £40,000 of EU funding to deliver training to 20 women returners. She admits that initially they did no marketing, but is full of praise for the recent efforts of her volunteers, who now include a hardware consultant and a marketing specialist, and for their new Community Enterprise magazine which has information on the training courses and local news. Her big problem has been the high rent the telecentre pays: "We are paying about £5.50 per square foot – it was the only place available to rent when we were looking. Since then we've discovered the going rate is about £3.00. Some of the rooms aren't even carpeted, so we're looking forward to moving into new units with access to a custom-built training room provided by the council!"

Cape Clear Telecottage

At the other end of the spectrum, a tiny telecottage on Cape Clear Island off County Cork in Ireland provides office services, photocopying, faxing and word processing from its North Harbour office. The same premises acts as a bookshop and tourist information centre, as well as helping the co-op that runs the island's ferry service. In addition, administrative and billing services for the Electricity Supply Board operate from the telecottage, and the local turbot fish farm has its accounts and records provided by telecottage staff. The island has a population of 150, swelled by tourists and students attending courses in the Irish language to 1,000 during the summer, and the telecottage received a small amount of startup funding from the economic development agency for Irish-speaking areas, Udarás na Gaeltachta.

Daily Information, Oxford City

On the commercial side, Daily Information in central Oxford began as an adjunct to a privately-run broadsheet listing of events which was published daily in the university area of the city. Owner John Rose invested in three giant Philips word processors and a number of IBM electronic typewriters in 1979. "For the first six weeks, the Philips machines didn't work. For the next six months, we had no idea what they were really for. They cost £10,000 each, with annual maintenance costs of £1,000" recalls John. He offered free learning time to customers and soon found that demand was so great the computers had to be available 24 hours a day for thesis and book preparation. The Philips machines were retired in 1985, and Daily Information quickly built up a stock of 30 PCs for hire on site or to take away. Daily Info probably did more than the computer department to introduce PCs to the University. John now turns over £200,000 a year, selling PCs and laser printers, as well as disks, cartridges and paper, and offers access to sophisticated photocopiers and colour printers. "Now that the machines are small enough to take away, we don't have to open overnight. The biggest problem is that technology changes so fast that the business eats up capital just to keep it going", says John. In the past few years, business for printing out theses has fallen as more people have their own printers, but the sophisticated photocopiers and scanners at Daily Info are still proving a draw for customers. Access to the Internet is proving popular, and the broadsheet is now available on the World Wide Web, along with a computer exchange for secondhand equipment. His telecentre, which was operating long before the term was invented, has achieved the status of an Oxford institution.

Eccles House Telebusiness Centre

Eccles House is the brainchild of the Peak Park Trust and arose because a member of the Trust, Godfrey Claff, had visited early telecottages in Scandinavia. A farmhouse with barns had been donated to the Trust by Blue Circle Cement. The Trust spent £400,000 and three years converting the Grade II listed buildings into a number of self-contained workspaces and a telebusiness centre. The centre provides services for the units so far occupied, and trains local people. Some initial funding came from the Rural Development Commission and the European Social Fund. The site has been open since February 1992. Eccles House is managed by a commercial company, Collective Enterprises Limited. Manager Sue Connelly reports that 7 of the 11 units are now occupied, including a software/multimedia training specialist which occupies the two largest units. A percentage of the rents go back to the Peak Park Trust, which has been able to find suitable alternative uses for a traditional building in a National Park, and to improve employment prospects in the area.

Training for women returners is the second major earner for Eccles House, organised through a separate company, Peak Training Enterprises, which receives input from the RDC, local TECs, Collective Enterprises and the Peak Park Trust. In addition to standard training courses, Eccles House also offers enterprise support seminars to help people start their own businesses. The staff offer office support services to the tenants and to local small businesses, ranging from secretarial backup to accommodation addresses. Sue would like to get ISDN installed and add videoconferencing and hotdesking to the facilities available in the next phase of development, but the priority is to fill the remaining units to provide the income stream for technological improvements.

Isles Telecroft, Shetland

At Unst in Shetland, Laura Baisley runs the Isles Telecroft, one of six telecottages set up in 1991 by the Highlands and Islands Enterprise (HIE) with funding from British Telecom under a three year project. Two of the telecottages were schools based, the others were attached to existing community organisations. "One member of our community co-op was keen on IT, which was how we got involved initially", explains Laura. Isles Telecroft began by running two projects. On the first, four women who live on remote islands were trained in telework both through conventional courses, and by carrying out a telework project to put museum records onto a database. The four women had computing equipment provided by the project at home, along with modems for communicating with Unst and elsewhere. Funding for this project came from the local authority, Shetland Islands Council and from Shetland Enterpise. On the second project, seven people with disabilities who live in rural areas of Shetland were trained to achieve an IT qualification. The telecottage derives some income from telework services, but sources of income are limited, especially since the closure of the civilian airport which formerly serviced the oil industry on the island. "We do get pressure to increase the income from telework from the local enterprise company, but we have no budget or resources to do the marketing required at the moment, so it's not easy." The telecottage has recently prepared some World Wide Web pages for Unst, and hopes to expand this area of activity.

At the moment there are four training projects in progress, funded through the European Social Fund (ESF) and the local enterprise company. One caters for disabled people, the second provides training to unemployed and women returners in a socially deprived area, and the third is providing IT skills to members of the Shetland Tenant's Association. The fourth project provides IT training for 10 local women as part of an integrated training scheme for women returners. Re-equipping as equipment becomes obsolete is a problem since ESF funding cannot be used for capital purchases. However, a depreciation charge and maintenance costs are allowed, so Laura does a bit of creative accounting and tries to upgrade the existing machines instead. Separate grants have also provided the telecottage with a colour printer and flat bed scanner. She would like to improve her own IT skills, which have been restricted to the level of the training she delivers, and sees the lack of training and development opportunities for staff as one of the pitfalls of operating on a shoestring.

Her advice to other community telecottages is not to worry about the technological aspects "People are much more important. You can buy technical expertise when you need it. Try to tack the telecottage on to an existing service such as a post office, and make sure there really is local support, and it's not just the brainchild of a couple of boffins. And do a good business plan. That's vital."

A report by the Arkleton Trust in 1993 offered hope and encouragement for telecottages such as the Isles Telecroft which have very small "catchment populations" of users in rural areas. The report studied the six telecottages in the Highlands and Islands, and concluded that three had established a basis for financial self-sustainability, with one already 75% self sufficient. Even in small communities Arkleton found a demand for dtp and office related services, which can often be more cost-effectively provided through a collective facility than through individual purchase of equipment. Arkleton agrees with Laura that the best telecottage managers are generalists, not technology boffins, with community skills and good local networks. The report also noted that 90% of the telecottage users lived within 10 miles of the site, and that 70% of the clients were aged between 25 and 44. Typically they were small-scale, irregular users with no previous computer training.

KITE, Co. Fermanagh, Northern Ireland

Kinawley Integrated Teleworking Enterprise is located in West Fermanagh, close to the border between Northern Ireland and the Republic. It is a highly successful enterprise which sources 60% of its work from North America, and offers childcare facilities as well as training to its employees. The purpose-built telecottage is the brainchild of Sheila and Michael McCaffrey, both of whom have backgrounds in health service administration. Sheila identified four basic requirements to set up the enterprise – childcare facilities, training, computers and telematics to connect them to work from outside the area. The search for funding was long and arduous – in the end, most of the funding came from Europe, including the European Social Fund, the Human Resources Initiative, and the European Regional Development Fund. Other grants came from the Community Business Programme of the Northern Ireland economic development agency LEDU, and the Department of Agriculture.

Because of the low level of infrastructure in the area, KITE had to build its own premises and fight hard to get an ISDN connection put into a rural location. The centre began operations on 25th November 1993, and eight women returners were put through a training programme which included the City & Guilds teleworking VQ, software training, personal development, communications skills and social interaction training as well as marketing skills and European awareness. From the beginning, Sheila and Michael felt that the telecottage needed a commercial input as well as its community aspect, and they worked hard to get contracts such as preparing eye records for Specsavers and handling enquiries for Sandpiper Holidays. But Sheila found that the conversion time for British and European business was too long – the delay between initial contact and the first paying job could be up to a year because teleworking was a new concept. So with assistance from the US State Department as part of the Peace Process funding, she tackled the North American market, travelling to the US for six weeks at a time to meet prospective clients. Now KITE has fourteen staff and prepares work for Boston hospitals and San Francisco recruitment agencies, receiving work by fax or tape and returning it over the ISDN lines. They now want funding to train more teleworkers in anticipation of increased business, but funding is just as hard to come by second time round as it was the first time.

Sheila feels the funding bodies do not appreciate that training has to be carried out in advance of the jobs being available. "If I want to expand the business, I have to start training more people right now so they'll be ready when the new contracts come in." She also feels it is very important to select people through the training process, helping them to work out their own goals and motivations as they develop their skills. "The plan is to get 64 people trained in basic skills on the RSA AOT II course. Of those, perhaps 12 will go on to the one year teleworker vocational training, and in the following year we would hope to employ 10 of those trainees." And if the programme is successful, the McCaffreys plan to double the size of the existing telecottage building – another expense that needs funding.

Mere Telecottage

Mere Telecottage was set up in 1991 by the Community Council for Wiltshire (CCW). The Telecottage's aim was to create a resource centre for local people starting new businesses in a rural area. Its use expanded to include the whole community. An initial investment of £10,000 provided the basic equipment (three computers and printer plus fax and copier on a leased basis), and offset the self-employed manager's salary for the first twelve months on a decreasing basis. The Telecottage is situated in the town library and offers use of the facilities to the library as payment in kind for the workspace. A steering group of local residents has helped to keep the 'sense of ownership' strong. Mere Telecottage has been used to deliver schemes such as Youth Enterprise, Workout (services for unemployed people) and Third Age First. Many telecottages have close links to their local Training and Enterprise Councils (TECs) which enables them to refer people to sources of technical and business advice.

However, in 1995, restructuring of CCW lead to their decision to withdraw support for the four Wiltshire telecottages. A rescue plan was proposed by John O'Dea who ran Goatacre telecottage.

Sue Mitchell of Codford Telecottage takes up the story: " At Codford we decided against John O'Dea's offer because we didn't want the telecottage run by an outsider who specialised in an area unrelated to our activities and we wanted to keep the community aspect. We fought hard to receive our share of the funding and also have received a substantial donation from a local person. Janet Nuth, the former telecottage manager, worked for over a month with no pay during this time and eventually had to leave to find full-time work. Now we are open mornings only, and working to cover our costs. We have appointed a marketing officer and had quite a bit of help from the West Wiltshire Enterprise Business Club, a network whose members use our facilities."

The three other Wiltshire telecottages (Mere, Crudwell and Goatacre) are now run by John O'Dea, a local businessman with interests in healthcare-related businesses. The exact nature of the work at the three telecottages is now confidential for commercial reasons, but involves a call-centre/customer service operation, and the jobs of the telecottage staff have been preserved.

SPEC: Standon Parish Electronic Centre

SPEC, set up in early 1995, is truly owned by its own community - the main financial support comes from an additional £4.50 on the council tax of local residents. The centre was set up with grants from Herts County and East Herts District Councils but running expenses have been covered by the Parish Council grant. Telecottage manager Frank Wallder is on a Community Action programme which pays for 18 hours a week of his time – additional time is provided by volunteers.

Once it had established a local presence, the centre moved to more convenient premises, again funded through the council tax, which include rooms that can be let to the parish council and to other local service providers for field operations.

SPEC is currently launching a Web page authoring and hosting venture run by a local business which will operate within the premises and provide local employment. The telecottage also plans additional training - including establishing links to local colleges with SPEC as a local training outpost. SPEC is working towards a separate company limited by guarantee which

---

21st century village halls bid succeeds

A bid for £10 million pounds of Millennium funding to refurbish English village halls and to include telecottage facilities has been approved. The bid, put together by rural communities charity ACRE and supported by a number of organisations including the TCA, will benefit 180 halls, ranging from extensions and major refurbishments of existing halls to 6 or 7 new flagship halls.

There is much still to be agreed – no specific sum will be allocated for telecottage facilities but all applicants will be required to consider potential for telecottage or telematics facilities. Bids covering Scotland (SCVO) Wales (WCVA) and Northern Ireland (RCN) have been longlisted for the next round of funding.

would enjoy close links with the parish council by having a number of councillors as directors.

WREN Telecottage

Once established, a telecottage can act as a platform for various additional services. The WREN Telecottage was founded as Warwickshire's first telecottage in 1991. WREN "belongs" indirectly to the Royal Agricultural Society of England (RASE), and received startup grants from ARC, BT and Coventry and Warwickshire TEC. Through RASE, WREN has educational charity status and trading status.

WREN combines access to IT, training, open learning, and business services, and has also developed a social and networking function which it considers essential for micro business support, aiding the incubation of new small businesses. WREN works in partnership with a variety of local and European agencies, a role recognised by an EC Local Development Award.

WREN's early development was assisted by contracts to run EC funded training projects, such as Rural Women Back to Business. This provided WREN with a funded core activity and helped train a pool of freelance workers who have become part of WREN's client and supplier network. In recent years, the commercial services side of the telecottage has been developed. Any profits the telecottage makes from such work are used to subsidise local services.

WREN's equipment includes the usual computers and office equipment, but in addition it has videoconferencing equipment, its own email and information service, and offers a nursery where telecottage users can "park" their children while they train or work. WREN has developed a national and international role as a demonstration telecottage, facilitated by its location at the National Agricultural Centre, Stoneleigh and its work in combining community and commercial functions.

Setting up a telecottage

Start by defining your aims. Telecottages can take many different forms and serve a variety of purposes, ranging from community education to economic development, and encompassing purely commercial ventures. Telecottage services include training, equipment hire, services for teleworkers, and jobs agencies. Those who use telecottages include self-employed and employed teleworkers, unemployed people improving their skills and community groups. You need to decide the function of your telecottage and then keep checking that your activities are directed towards that purpose.

Interested parties

The first step is to gather together interested people into a management or steering group. This could be an informal group of like-minded people, or a more formal working group. Try your parish council, chamber of commerce, local politicians and community school. Discuss the services that could be offered, and the premises and equipment that will be needed for the services. Don't forget all the bureaucratic issues – planning, insurance, tax, financial structure. Check that you will have access to a digital telephone exchange, and preferably to ISDN services. Get expert help on the equipment issues.

Visiting a telecottage

Visit an established telecottage. Many hold occasional open days - three of these are:

- WREN Telecottage: based at the National Agricultural Centre, Stoneleigh, Warwickshire. This centre is something of a showcase, and has almost purpose-built accommodation. Open Days are held about once a month, though special visits can be arranged where there is demand. The cost for the half day is £10 per person including VAT, refreshments, online demonstrations and an information pack, and the maximum number is 15. Contact Jane Berry on 01203 696986.

- Moorlands Telecottage: based in school premises in the small village of Warslow, Staffordshire. Users come from a series of villages in the surrounding area, and the telecottage has specialised in developing training materials for teleworkers. Visits are by prior arrangement and cost £30 for up to 10 people. The visit lasts about 90 minutes, and covers what the telecottage does, how it was set up, its training courses and support for the local community and local enterprises. Visits by educational organisations and small community groups are free. Moorlands telecottage is credited as the UK's first telecottage and was responsible for the development of the Teleworking VQ. Contact Simon Brooks on 01298 84336.

- KITE Telecottage near Enniskillen in Northern Ireland provides training, childcare and commercial work for around ten staff. KITE likes to have a detailed advance discussion with prospective visitors on what they want to see, which can cover childcare facilities, obtaining European funding, the teleworking operation (which works for US companies using ISDN links), and initiatives to promote US/Northern Ireland trade sponsored by the US State Department. This allows the visit to be tailored to their needs. The cost is £30 for up to 10 people, and the tour normally takes just over an hour. The price includes an information pack. Contact Michael McCaffrey 01365 348943.

Try contacting a centre in your area using the list and map at the end of this chapter to see whether they would take visitors or offer consultancy on setting up a telecottage. As you are taking up valuable time, remember you may be charged for a visit.

Market survey

Next, assess the need for the centre by performing a market survey of the locality up to a radius of fifteen miles. Try a questionnaire targeted on individuals working from home, small business and community groups. Assess any similar services in the area. You could combine the market survey phase with an open evening to discuss the idea locally. Contact potential sponsors and relevant local authorities as early as you can. Then prepare a business plan (see Chapter 4, *Getting Work*) and examine the available funding sources.

Funding sources and fundraising

Raising money to buy the telecottage equipment is bound to involve a search for innovative funding methods. Sponsorship can be highly productive for both donor and recipient. Many different sponsors, including equipment manufacturers, telecommunications companies and high street banks, have seen the potential of the telecottage idea. Think about linking up with a local bank to provide meeting rooms for their customers who run businesses from home, or charging local agencies for using the telecottage as their base in the local community. Offer to act as a local representative for an office supplies wholesaler such as Office Supplies Online, which offers an online ordering system and recruits local agents.

Try to make sure that your sponsorship idea would create commercial value for the sponsoring company. An equipment dealer may consider a telecottage an excellent place to display equipment so that it can be seen and used by potential customers. A large company which is laying off staff may wish to balance this by helping to create a local service that can train former employees in new skills, and support new businesses. They may also have redundant equipment.

> **European funding will develop Manchester EVHs**
>
> The Manchester network of four electronic village halls (EVHs), which are community-based centres similar to telecottages, is to receive nearly £2 million in funding from the European Regional Development Fund during 1996 for expansion. There will be an additional 8 centres and a 6 person development team based at the Manchester Multi-Media Centre which is due to open in September 1996. There will be a telework agency linked to the EVHs and the network plans to capitalise on the city's reputation as a centre for music and the visual arts.

Because telecottages often use software for training, they may be entitled to educational discounts on software prices. Companies may also be prepared to offload equipment that is obsolete for their uses, and which has low secondhand value. Such equipment is often perfectly functional for telecottage use.

A subscription scheme can be designed to raise money for capital equipment. Once the money has been raised and the equipment bought, the subscription is redeemable against a number of hours of free use of the equipment.

Draws, raffles and lotteries are old stalwarts for the fundraiser. Try to add a twist to the prizes to gain interest – for example, games that children can play on the telecottage computers, business or personal stationery to be designed by the telecottage for the winner and so on.

If you have written a credible business plan and cashflow forecast, don't be frightened to approach your local high street bank. It may be prepared to offer cheaper banking services, or loans, or suggest other sources of funding. Keep in contact with government business support agencies.

Some telecottages think about using professional consultants to find funding for their startups. Before taking any such step, it is worth consulting a checklist produced by the Forum for Private Business which warns against consultancies which claim 100% accuracy or claim special relationships with government. Much of the information offered by consultants may be available free from various sources including economic development agencies. Contact FPB on 01565 634 467. There is a software package which can help in identifying grants available at a discounted price (for Lloyds bank customers and members of the TCA) from Enterprise Advisory Services 01280 700102.

A recent trend has been for telecottages to tie up with a local Internet provider to provide a "cybercafé", or to advertise access to the Internet. However, this can be difficult to bill effectively so think through the charging mechanism.

The National Lottery
Any organisation set up for charitable, philanthropic or benevolent purposes is eligible to apply for national lottery funding but grants cannot be given to individuals. Applications can be made for capital or revenue funding, and the minimum amount is £500. The next round of lottery funding will focus on opportunities for young people to develop their potential, promote information, develop skills and offer disadvantaged young people a realistic chance of becoming economically self-sufficient. Future themes include broadening skills for people of all ages, selfhelp in rural and urban areas, improving the physical and social fabric of communities and so on. To get an application pack, phone 0345 919191. John Lakeman, a director of the TCA and recent assessor for lottery funding, gives the following points to consider for a successful application:

- how well planned and financially sound a proposed project is
- the value for money it offers
- adequate management and staffing
- an appropriate commitment to equal opportunities
- encouragement of community participation
- plans for the project's future survival, or an exit strategy, if the funding is requested for more than one year.

A number of other funding sources are listed at the end of this chapter, and at the end of the *Getting Work* chapter.

State support
Local councils have been very supportive of teleworking in geographically isolated areas. A telecottage can be an ideal support centre for the council's economic development strategies.

In Britain, the Training and Enterprise Councils (TECs or LECs in Scotland) which are responsible for training workers, have used telecottages as a platform to deliver TEC services to rural areas. FÁS and the VECs provide similar services in Ireland. Some telecottages have contracts to provide employment training on behalf of these authorities. The Consortium of Rural TECs (CORT) may be able to advise on TECs involved in telecottage projects.

There are a number of EU schemes which can provide funds to telecottages that deliver specific training services. Women returners are catered for by the NOW scheme. Rurally disadvantaged areas can get funds under the LEADER scheme. Obtaining EC funds requires specialist help – for example from County Council economic development departments. The EU is interested in many areas of teleworking and related technologies (usually grouped together under the term "telematics"), and research into this area is carried out under the ACTS and TAP programmes.

In Britain, Rural Community Councils exist in England, with sister organisations in Wales, Scotland and Northern Ireland. RCCs work at parish council level to assist community development. Some RCCs have become involved in telecottage projects. For details of your local RCC, contact ACRE (the Association of RCCs).

The Rural Development Commission in Britain has supported several telecottages. Highlands and Islands Enterprise, in conjunction with BT, has sponsored six telecottages. The Welsh Development Agency and the Development Board for Rural Wales have also supported telecottages.

Telecottage cash flow: year 1

	Jun	Jul	Aug	Sep	Oct	Nov	Dec	Jan	Feb	Mar	Apr	May	TOT
Income													
Photocopying	200	200	300	400	400	400	300	400	500	600	600	600	4900
Fax	60	60	60	60	60	75	60	80	80	80	80	80	835
Equipment Hire			20	20	30	30	30	40	40	60	60	60	390
Commer. Train				480	480	480		720	720	720	720	720	5040
Commun. Train	250	500	500	500						500	500	500	3250
Teleshopping	50	80	80	120	120	200	200	120	120	120	120	120	1450
Telework			500	500	900	900	900	1600	1600	2000	2000	2000	12900
Publications	50	50	80	80	60	50	50	30	30	30	50	50	610
Room hire				320	320	320		320	320	320			1920
Business Servs	300	400	500	500	500	600	400	400	600	600	600	60	5460
Totals:	910	1290	2040	2980	2870	3055	1940	3710	4010	5030	4730	4190	36755
Expenditure													
Manager	833	833	833	1216	1216	1216	1216	1216	1216	1216	1216	1216	13443
Asst Manager									400	400	400	400	1600
Teleworkers			438	438	788	788	788	1400	1400	1750	1750	1750	11288
Support worker								65	65	65	65	65	325
Rent	112	112	112	112	112	112	112	112	112	112	112	112	1344
Heat/light	55	55	55	55	55	55	55	55	55	55	55	55	660
Insurance	50	50	50	50	50	50	50	50	50	50	50	50	600
Promotion	250	120			250	120			100	100			940
Telephone			255			325			350			350	1280
Stationery	350			350			400			400			1500
Subscriptions	120						200						320
Postage	25	25	25	25	25	25	25	25	25	25	25	25	300
Lease payments	65	65	65	65	65	65	65	65	65	65	65	65	780
Consumables	29	29	43	57	57	57	43	57	71	86	86	86	700
Staff welfare	60	60	60	60	60	60	60	60	60	60	60	60	720
Capital purchases													0
Repairs													0
Service contract													0
Bank charges	25	25	25	25	40	40	40	40	40	50	50	50	450
Equipment lease	260	260	260	260	260	260	260	260	260	260	260	260	3120
Total:	2234	1634	2220	2713	2728	3303	3233	3605	4169	4694	4294	4544	39370
Open. Bal.	0	-1324	-1667	-1848	-1580	-1438	-1685	-2979	-2874	-3033	-2697	-2261	
+/-	-1324	-344	-180	267	142	-248	-1293	105	-159	336	436	-354	
Clos. Bal.	-1324	-1667	-1848	-1580	-1438	-1685	-2979	-2874	-3033	-2697	-2261	-2615	

Notes
The figures for December assume reduced income due to holidays.
Manager is assumed to be self-employed so wage reflects hours worked.
Lease payments are for photocopier and fax on three year leases.
Consumables are supplies for photocopier.
Service contract only applies from year 2 as equipment has one year guarantee.
Equipment leasing costs are based on £8,000 worth of equipment leased over three years.
Once everything is in place in January, the telecottage starts to break even and should show a profit in the following 12 months.

Telecottages and telecentres May 1996

To be included on this list, updated bimonthly in Teleworker magazine, a telecottage must offer public access to computers and other IT equipment, provide training facilities, and supply services to assist other businesses. The location information indicates the nearest post town to the telecottage. However, telecottages come in many different flavours, so to get exact details of services, please telephone the telecottage in question. To add to this listing or make a correction contact Alan Denbigh (Tel: 01453 834 874, Fax: 01453 836 174, Email: 100272.1472@compuserve.com).

1 START (Shetland)
2 Wirral Business Bureau
3 Antur Tanat Cain Llangedwyn
4 Welshpool Telecentre
5 Antur Teifi
6 BOON Ltd.
7 Dereham Digital Centre
8 Hunsbury Telecottage
9 Connemara West
10 Fakenham Technical Services
11 Daily Information
12 Telelink
13 Deer Park Telecentre
14 Durham Dales Centre
15 East Clare Telecottage
16 East Kent Telecottage
17 Eccles House Telebusiness Centre
18 Gittisham Village Press
19 Ileach Teleservices
20 Alford IT
21 Instant Search
22 Sheringham Telecottage
23 Mizen Telecottage
24 CITU Belfast
25 The Resource Centre
26 Llanfyllin Telecottage
27 Wingrave Telecottage
28 Warsop Telecottage
29 Adur Resource Centre
30 Codford Telecottage
31 Colne Valley Trust
32 Comharchumann Chléire Teo.
33 Crickhowell Community Office
34 Telecottage South West
35 Wearhead Community Telecentre
36 Tarbert Community Teleservice Centre
37 Isles Telecroft
38 Kingsley Telecentre
39 Stornoway Telecentre
40 ORBIT Carrefour
41 Mere Telecottage
42 Moorlands Telecottage
43 PATCH, Dublin
44 North Tyne Telecottage
45 Odiham Telecottage (COLCO)
46 Rathcoole Business Centre
47 Cahersiveen Telecottage
48 SIMTRA Aberaeron (see Narberth)
49 SIMTRA Crymych (see Narberth)
50 SIMTRA Fishguard (see Narberth)
51 SIMTRA Llandeilo (see Narberth)
52 SIMTRA Narberth
53 SIMTRA Saundersfoot (see Narberth)
54 SIMTRA St Davids (see Narberth)
55 SIMTRA Tregaron (see Narberth)
56 Stonesfield Telecottage
57 Tele Teach
58 Union Lane Centre Workshops
59 West Cumbria Telecottage
60 Warwickshire Rural Enterprise Network
61 Wolds Enterprise Bureau
62 Ness Telecottage
63 Boston Spa Training
64 Balvenie House Ltd
65 Llanfairfechan Business Centre
66 Chorlton Workshop EVH
67 Launceston Telecentre
68 Midhurst Resource Centre Ltd
69 Global Village Resources
70 Manchester Womens EVH
71 CEB Telecentre
72 Bronllys and Talgarth Telecentre
73 Diss Telecottage
74 Guthrie Creative Services
75 The Business Base
76 Goireas Business & Computing Centre
77 Kington Connected Community Co.
78 Daventry Tertiary College
79 Colwyn Telecottage
80 Menter Bro Ddyfi
81 Network Personnel Ltd
82 Rural Business Centre
83 Naver Teleservice Centre
84 Porthmadog Telecentre
85 Hindon Telecottage
86 Aberdeen Teleworking Centre
87 CATS 2000
88 Menter Bro Preseli
89 U-Compute
90 Reydon Infobase
91 Kinawley Integrated Teleworking Enterprise (K.I.T.E.)
92 Moira Telecottage
93 Goatacre Telecottage
94 Mevagissey Telecottage
95 Strathyre IT Centre
96 Hackney Resource Centre Telecentre
97 York Telecottage
98 W.C.E.I.R.D.
99 Brackley Telecottage
100 Declare Business Centre
101 Barra Telecottage
102 Worth Telecentre
103 Rhondda Enterprise
104 Honeybun Secretarial Services
105 RNIB Teleworkers
106 Impakt Assistance
107 Honeytree Services
108 York Word Processing Bureau
109 Varitech Telecentre
110 Castell-y-Dail Telecottage
111 Romney Resource Centre
112 Crudwell Telecottage
113 Rutland Business Communications Centre
114 Gwynedd Telecentre
115 Llanwrtyd Wells Telecottage
116 Miracle Graphics
117 The Business Base
118 Support Shop
119 Premier Services Telecottage
120 Presteigne Community Resource Centre
121 Rivermark Centre
122 Beara Community School
123 ITS Marlborough Telecottage
124 Commpact
125 SPEC
126 Lambourn Bake House
127 IT Drop in Centre
128 Stuart House IVNU
129 Downham Telecottage
130 Elbowroom
131 Barnham Telecottage
132 Slamannan IT Centre
133 Wirral Telecottage
134 Basford Hall CFE
135 Soho Computing
136 Burford Telecottage
137 business Focus
138 A M Computer Services
139 Leek Telecentre
140 Highland Teleworking Centre
141 Sledmere BARN
142 Skills Station
143 Longton Telecottage
144 Hendon Telecentre
145 Yeovil College Telecentre
146 CTF Training
147 Newport Advanced Teleservices
148 Clydesdale Telecentre
149 Phoenix Telecentre
150 Skye International Teleservice Centre

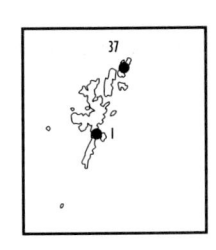

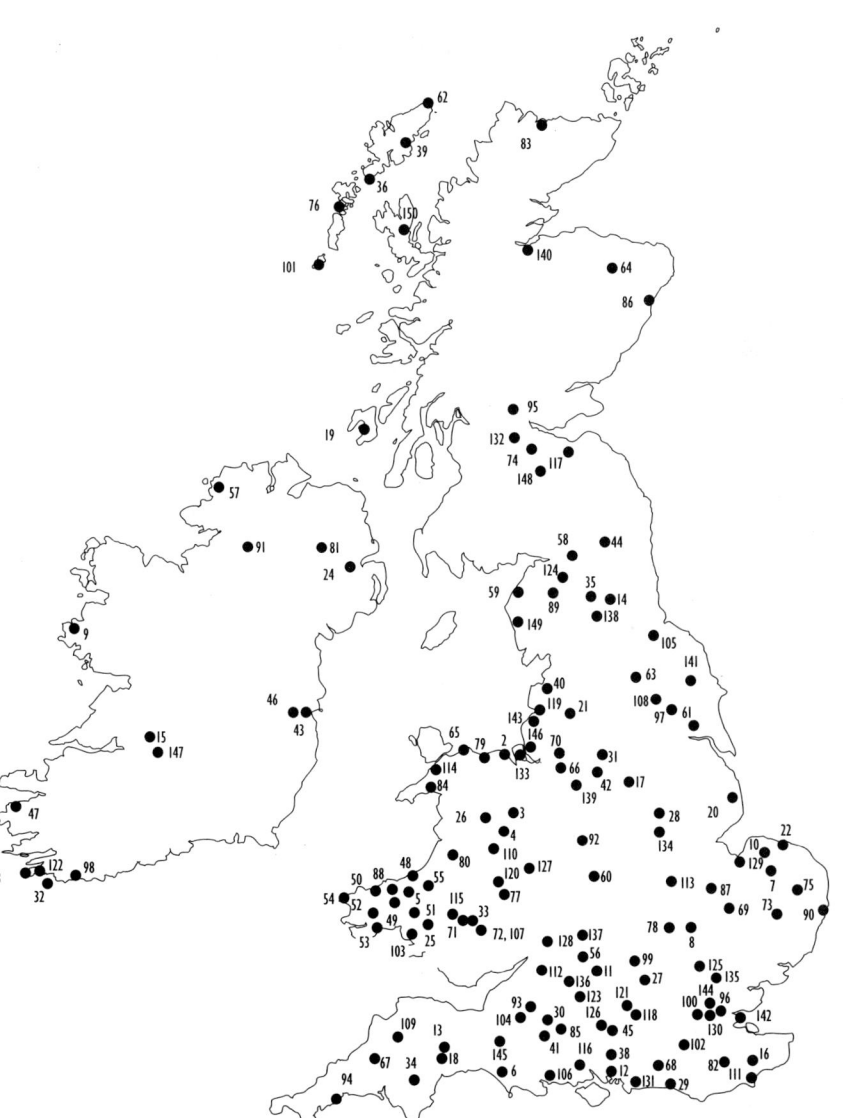

TELECOTTAGES AND TELECENTRES

Bibliography

Why Teleworking? *Date:* 1996
Authors: Stoney Stanton Telecottage
Source: Stoney Stanton Telecottage, P.O. Box 7, Stoney Stanton, Leicester LE9 4ZW

British and Irish Telecottages *Date:* 1995
Author: Laura Burt, University of Edinburgh
Source: Laura Burt, 27/3 Blair Street, Edinburgh, EH1 1QR, email 9157561@lewis.sms.ed.ac.uk
Comment: Dissertation following 1994 large-scale survey of telecottages. Available in paper or disk format.

Community Economics *Date:* 1995
Source: The New Economics Foundation, Tel: 0171 377 5696

Survey of Telecottage Activity and Finance *Date:* 1995
Authors: Small World Connections with support from the Telecottage Association
Source: Bill Murray, Small World Connections, Tel: 0161 4456 0630.

Sussex Telecentre Network *Date:* 1995
Authors: Sussex Rural Community Council
Source: Sussex Rural Community Council, 212 High Street, Lewes, East Sussex BN7 2NH, Tel: 01273 47342 Ref: ISBN 1 873850 13 1

Telecottages: How the Usage of Information Technology can counter Rural Disadvantages *Date:* 1995
Author: Tatjana Gosau, MA in European Business Administration
Source: University of Northumbria

A Survey of the Users of Selected Telecottages in Britain *Date:* 1994
Author: Colin Cummings, University of Plymouth
Source: Seale-Hayne Faculty of Agriculture and Food, University of Plymouth

Golden Valley Information Project - Initial Report *Date:* 1993
Author: K A Webb
Source: County Libraries Service & BLCMP Ltd, Libraries Division, Shire Hall, Hereford, HR1 2HY

Telecommuting Centers and Related Concepts: A Review of Practice *Date:* 1994
Authors: Michael Bagley, Jill Mannering, Patricia Mokhtarian
Source: Institute of Transportation Studies, University of California, Davis, California 95616 Ref: ISBN UCD-ITS-RR-94-4

Telecottages, Teleworking and Telelearning *Date:* 1994
Author: Lilian Holloway
Source: Teldok, Sweden, Tel: +46-8-23 00 00 or Fax +46-8-10 13 27

Final Report on the Evaluation of Community Teleservice Centres in the Highlands and Islands *Date:* 1993
Authors: John Bryden, Stuart Black, Frank Rennie
Source: The Arkleton Trust, Coulnakyle, Nethy Bridge, Inverness Tel: 01479 821 393, Fax: 01479 821 441.Ref: 0 90 6724 41 4

Marketing Telecottages and Teleworking Date: 1993
Author: ACRE/Telecottage Association
Source: ACRE, Somerford Court, Somerford Rd, Cirencester, GL7 1TW Ref: ISBN 1 871157 33 1

Best Practice in Developing Community Teleservice Centres *Date:* 1992
Author: Steve Graham

The Ratio programme

Ratio (Rural Area Training and Information Opportunities) is a programme to set up 40 local telecentres in parts of Cornwall, the Isles of Scilly, Devon and Somerset which fall into the European Union's Objective 5b areas. Each centre will provide computers, email, digital satellite reception and videoconferencing, which can be used by people seeking information, work and training.

Ratio is a collaborative venture bringing together education providers, local authorities, government departments and regional bodies, as well as businesses and the voluntary sector. Its main function is the provision of access to training and information (such as information on grants, local authority services, the EU, employment, education and welfare). The centres will begin to come onstream during 1996, and each will have a facilitator. The facilitators are volunteers, chosen for their commitment to the aims of the project and trained by the project. Each centre will also be sponsored by a local company.

The total cost of the project is around £5 million, including £2.3 million from the government's Regional Challenge prize, local authority funding and EU funding.

Source: CASR, Faculty of Economic and Social Studies, University of Manchester, M13 9PL

So You Want to Start a Telecottage *Date:* 1992
Author: Beverley Shelley
Source: Gloucestershire Community Council, 15 College Green, Gloucester, GL1 2LZ

Telecentres - Australian Experiences
Authors: Graham MacKay and Ian Reeve, University Of New England *Date:* 1992
Source: Dept. of Learning, Devt & Comm, RDC, University of New England, Armidale, Australia

Telecottages – The UK Experience *Date:* 1992
Author: ACRE
Source: ACRE, Somerford Court, Somerford Rd, Cirencester, GL7 1TW Ref: ISBN 1 871157 31 5

**Community Technology Audit: East Manchester
Electronic Village Hall** *Date:* 1991
Source: Centre for Appied Social Research, Faculty of Economic & Social Studies, University of Manchester, M13

Telecottages – Dossier *Date:* 1991
Revi. 1993
Author: Various
Source: National Rural Enterprise Centre, NAC, Stoneleigh Park, Warwicks, CV8 2LZ

Telecottages: The Potential for Rural Australia *Date:* 1991
Authors: David Horner, Ian Reeve, University of New England, Armidale
Source: Australian Government Publishing Service, Canberra Ref: ISBN 0 644 14585 4

Telecottages Today Date: 1991
Editor: Alan Denbigh
Source: ACRE, Somerford Court, Somerford Rd, Cirencester Ref: Seminar Report, ISBN 1 871157 22 6

Contacts

Partners in the Countryside is a non-profit making organisation established to promote a business approach to rural regeneration. The organisation provides information about rural intiatives and uses its sponsor's funds to support a range of rural projects. Contact Anne Harris 01273 695776.

The Community Investment Fund created by English Partnerships is for projects from priority areas such as rural development blackspots, former coalfield areas, city challenge areas and so on. Grants of between £10,000 and £100,000 in value are possible and can be for capital works to buildings or for revenue projects that are expected to produce social and economic benefits. Contact Sukhvinder Stubbs on 0171 976 7070.

Calor Gas and **Country Living** make annual prize awards to innovative and successful country based businesses in the UK which offer original services or products and demonstrate support for local businesses. Contact Richard Butler, AIMM Ltd, 01462 675600.

The Rural Development Commission publishes a guidebook to financial and other forms of assistance available to entrepreneurs in rural areas. Copies are available free of charge from the Information Section, RDC, FREEPOST, SA122 141 Castle Street, Salisbury SP1 3BR.

Community Development Organisations
There are a number of regional rural community organisations which may be potential sources of information and advice for organisations starting telecottages and telecentres.
ACRE – Action With Communities in Rural England. Acre can put you in touch with your local rural community council who may know of other schemes or funding awards in the area. Tel: 01285 653477
WCVA – Wales Council for Voluntary Action Tel: 01222 869224
SCVO – Scottish Council for Voluntary Organisations Tel: 0131 556 3882
RCN – Rural Community Network - Northern Ireland Tel: 01232 242582
NCVO – National Council for Voluntary Organisations (UK wide) Tel: 0171 387 9898
British Coal Enterprise – a number of locations in the UK principally in ex coalfield areas.
NIAA – Northern Informatics Application Agency – aims to improve communications and information access in the Northern area including Northumberland, Tyne & Wear, Cumbria, County Durham and Cleveland. Tel: 0191 549 6577 Fax: 0191 549 6578 Email: chris.drew@niaa.org.uk Web: http://www.nia.org.uk

Ratio programme Contact Steve Simmons, Tel: 01736 332736 Fax: 01736 69477 Email: 100021.2563@compuserve.com

http://www.ronneby.se/ronneby/infoc/projekt/attach.html is the home page for the Telematics Applications project ATTACH (Advanced Transeuropean Telematics Applications for Community Help)

http://ctr.cstp.umkc.edu/nevadatelecommunity/ is the Website for the Nevada Telecommunities project.

For details of other regional funding bodies, also see the Bibliography to Chapter 4, *Getting Work*.

Ideas for teleservices

This chapter lists ideas for services, some of which are already offered by other teleworkers. Some of the ideas are only suited to telecottages. For teleworkers, many forms of consultancy not listed here, ranging from quality management to market research can be teleworked, but you need to already have the relevant skills and industry contacts to make them work. General issues of how to sell your teleworking services are covered in Chapter 4, *Getting Work*. You should also find Chapter 11, *Teleworking Equipment* relevant, although it does not cover software in detail. When considering what services to offer, be careful to evaluate the cost of software that will be required, and avoid substantial investments in this area without thorough market research on the demand for the proposed service.

Abstracting, editing, proofreading and indexing

Many teleworkers have skills in the publishing area such as copy editing, proofreading and indexing. There is strong demand for these skills if they are combined with the ability to handle scientific subjects. A much-publicised example of a teleworking business based on these is skills is Crossaig in Scotland. Crossaig arranges abstracting and indexing of biomedical articles for Elsevier's EMBASE database. The printed journals are

Proto-type

Ann Collins runs Proto-type, a remote word processing business based in Essex which services business in the City of London. Their main client is a quantity-surveying group. Work is received as audio tapes or handwritten faxes, typed in and returned by faxmodem. At the beginning of each week, the customer gets a list of all the teleworkers and their availability, with the possibility of extending the service beyond normal office hours if needed. "We are effectively providing the organisation and quality control behind the teleworked service," says Ann. "The people we use need to be technically very good at the word processing package so that there are no problems if the client later needs to correct or alter the document. I interview all the teleworkers before they are registered with the client and confidentiality declarations are signed. Some of our teleworkers also offer translation services. The going rate for temping in central London is £12-£15 an hour, so we are undercutting this rate at the moment, but we really sell on quality and the fact that clients only pay us for productive time. We have regular customers whose ways of working we know, and unlike temps, we don't need half a day's training to get into the swing of things." But Ann is realistic about the future as more and more managers do their own typing, and voice activated dictation systems become widespread. "I believe this solution only has an eight to ten year lifespan, but teleworking has tremendous potential and we will need to develop new services."

OCR-scanned into computer text files at the company's offices and then sent by ISDN file transfer to the teleworkers around Scotland. The teleworkers work on a piece rate, but many have specialist skills and PhDs in areas such as marine biology or pharmacology and can earn up to £17.50 per hour for their work. This arrangement gives Crossaig access to the skills it needs, and the teleworkers access to work from remote rural areas.

Audio typing, remote typing, document formatting

Work arrives by fax, or on audio cassettes, is transcribed onto computer and returned as disk, printout, email or all three. For audio typing you will need a transcribing machine. This is a tape recorder with a foot pedal for playing the tape, stopping it and rewinding where necessary while leaving the hands free. There are three main sizes of tape: standard audio (C-size), Philips mini cassette and Dictaphone mini cassette, so talk to your prospective customers about the sizes they use before buying. The work can range from correspondence to whole books or conference proceedings. Perhaps you could link up with conference organisers in your area? However, be aware that this market is under threat from advances in systems which allow direct dictation to computer. If you plan to go into this area you will need to specialise or add value to your transcription services, and consider areas such as proofreading, indexing, editing, and translation.

Bookkeeping and accountancy services

Accountants may be prepared to send out the more tedious areas of their work such as putting purchase receipts and invoices onto computer. You will need specialist accountancy skills to succeed in this area. Alternatively, self-employed accountants and bookkeepers might want to hire your computers and software to work on themselves. There is a multitude of software packages in this area, and every company has its personal favourite. Be careful to check this out before investing in expensive software. Accountants who plan to telework from home themselves need to take account of the likelihood of client visits, and provide suitable parking and insurance cover.

Computer programming/software support

Several telecottages have been started up by small computer dealers who offer tailor-made programming services to customers as well as software training and support. If you have specialist skills in this area it could be for you. Offering technical support over the telephone to new computer users could also be a winner. But beware: you should think about getting professional indemnity insurance to cover yourself in case your advice leads to a financial loss for one of your customers – what would happen if you recommended a backup procedure that led to the loss of vital data? This kind of insurance can be very expensive. Specialist areas for computer programming and software include CAD/CAM (Computer aided design and manufacturing), computer design of PCBs (printed circuit boards), mathematical and financial modelling, stress calculations for engineers,

The Dyer Partnership

Mark and Bill Dyer have been profiled in publications about Britain's Information Society Initiative for the way in which they have used the World Wide Web to expand their accountancy partnership. Mark Dyer explains: "Our website has generated interest from all over the UK and the world. For example, we've had contacts from the British Consul in Messina, Italy, and quite a number from the US, Canada and even Australia. We're doing business with people through email, acting as their accountants."

The Internet also helps with client credibility closer to home: "Where clients use the technology themselves, the minute you say you have email it establishes a lot of credibility and provides a good way of conducting business – we can send data files attached to email." Setting up the website took around 150 hours of work, and a further 100 hours has been spent marketing and maintaining the site. "Of course we are not the only accountants on the Internet, but we have interpreted the information, giving people a taster of what we can do on items such as why companies should pay dividends rather than bonuses – rather than putting up a page of detailed corporate tax law on the web."

quantity surveying and project management. The BOON telecottage in Dorset offers a tachograph analysis service.

Conferencing

Conferencing services help with "telemeetings". Telecottages can offer videoconferencing and audioconferencing facilities. For videoconferencing, you must have an ISDN telephone line and a videophone. Audio conferencing for up to three people is available using standard digital telephone services. For larger numbers, you will need to use either BT's audioconferencing service, or if you are a charity or resource centre, Community Network. Organisations using conferencing regularly may want to invest in a high quality telephone loudspeaker unit.

Data conversion

Converting data from one disk format to another, or from one software package to another, is a commonly requested service in telecottages. Software format conversion does need some knowledge of the package involved, and it's important to quiz the customer on exactly what they want to do with the resulting file in order to provide an appropriate format.

Data input

Many of the first generation of telecottages financed themselves with contracts from companies and government institutions to put large volumes of data onto computers. The more basic end of this kind of work is less available now because most historical data needed by companies has already been entered. However, some companies need to continue to process data on a regular basis and, if you can offer low cost and high quality, might be interested in a teleworking arrangement. The KITE telecottage in Northern Ireland recently won a contract to put customer records held by the SpecSavers chain of opticians onto computer. Data input work is not generally well paid, and is usually quoted as piece-work. However, specialist areas such as the construction of mailing lists can be more remunerative and could be tied in with preparing mailshots or faxshots (mailings by fax). An experienced person can design the database while the less skilled enter data.

Call centres

Call centres, where staff handle large volumes of telephone traffic, have been highly successful in the commercial sector and are used to deliver a wide range of services which fall into two major categories – telemarketing and data processing.

Telemarketing

- central reservations services for hotels, airlines and car hire
- technical support centres for computer hardware and software
- outbound and inbound telesales
- order processing
- consumer information centres
- market research.

Data processing

- abstracting and indexing
- health claims processing

- banking administration
- financial analysis
- magazine subscription administration
- medical transcription
- VAT reclamation
- central order processing.

The development of computer-telephony integration (CTI) is now making it possible for call centres to become smaller and more specialised – previously the equipment required meant that large operations, usually with mainframe computers, were important for paybacks. CTI distributes calls to operatives, brings appropriate customer records up on screen, helps staff to fill in information correctly according to a pre-prepared script, and to enter appropriate data. CTI systems also provide statistical monitoring of call handling.

Call centres are a highly specialist area, both in terms of technology and marketing, and in the appropriate training of staff. Call centre projects are best approached through the services of a consultant.

A typical telesales operation could involve ringing retailers and getting their orders for a manufacturing company. You need a telephone headset to allow hands free for computer data entry. Some companies with high pressure selling techniques like to ring round prospective companies and question them by phone. This work can easily be done on contract by teleworkers. See if your can tie in telesales to mailing list and mailshot work. It is vital to recruit people with a good telephone manner for this kind of work and to give training where necessary. Several London agencies use "resting" actors because of their persuasive skills and good voices.

Equipment rental

This is a major source of income for most telecottages. It can take several forms:

- hire of computers and software on site (e.g. for people who want to use word processing, either for private use or to offer a service)
- hire of computers for private study for those who want to start using computers on an informal basis, perhaps before attending a formal training course, or who want to use software based tutorials
- hire of equipment to teleworkers such as high quality laser printers and colour printers
- hire of equipment to "take away" such as portable PCs, small inkjet printers, for occasional teleworkers or overload work. The BOON telecottage offers a "try before you buy" hire service.

Farm skills

Farmers need secretaries, bookkeepers and people who know how to fill in complex EU forms and maps. A teleworker with specialist knowledge in

> **The Virtual Office**
>
> Richard Nissen has been running the Virtual Office for nearly fifteen years in Piccadilly, London. His business provides serviced offices, meeting rooms, telephone answering, fax forwarding, a mailing address and secretarial backup. Charges are £150/month for call answering, and £50/month for use of the prestigious London mailing address. Office manager Rebecca Benbow explains: "We have a lot of customers who have left large corporations and are used to having a hundred people running after them. They are there to make money, and we do the menial things."

these areas could prove invaluable to a rural community, though many farmers are uncomfortable about using someone who also works for their neighbours and may know details of their cultivation plans. The WREN telecottage initiated a scheme whereby four farmers clubbed together to buy some crop management software and used it on a collaborative basis rather than each having to buy their own computer and software. It may be worth contacting suppliers of specialist products such as Farmplan and Optimix to discuss possibilities.

Faxing/photocopying services

Copying charges average about 10p/sheet for low volume. Fax varies at £1–£2.50 per sheet. Colour photocopying or high quality laser photocopying comes in at about £1/sheet. Think about your location before buying equipment for bureau services. If you are based half way up a remote valley, are people really going to drop in for a few photocopies? On the other hand, if you have the only decent photocopier on an island, you could be in business.

Home shopping

Some telecottages offer access to Kay's mail order catalogues. Shoppers can consult catalogues in the telecottage and then order goods not available locally such as clothes and electrical goods. The telecottage staff use a terminal linked to the retailer to place the order, and the telecottage receives 10–15% of the price of the goods as commission. This service works particularly well in telecottages which are attached to post offices or similar community services.

Information broking

Almost every business sector needs facts of some description. Information brokers are experts at accessing paper and online information sources and distilling the results into a product they can sell to clients. Examples include Watchdog, a business based in Kinsale, Co. Cork, which surveys EU legislation relating to the food and pharmaceutical industries, providing its clients with briefings on new laws that could affect their businesses. Stepping Stones, based in London, provides information on European tenders through its TED and BC-Net agencies. Alert Publications, also based in London, searches online sources for telecoms news, which it summarises and provides to clients via daily fax bulletins. Most brokers are specialists who know the resources in a particular subject area intimately. Good personal contacts are also important. Charges are usually via an hourly or daily rate, or by subscription to a briefing document. (see information about Instant Search in chapter 4, *Getting Work*).

Information services/booking agency/tourist information

Teleworkers can provide box office services for professional and amateur theatres. They can arrange bookings for coach services, village halls and sports facilities. Other related ideas include registers of business services and local organisations. These could be computerised if there is sufficient volume of information. Tourist information such as B&B lists, sites of interest and events diaries are provided by several telecottages in holiday areas. This seems to be a service that fits in well with other telecottage activities, and can attract funding or sponsorship from government agencies.

LETS

The Local Enterprise Trading System (LETS) scheme can provide telecottages and teleworkers with additional resources. Under LETS, local services are exchanged in cashless trading, with different services attracting different rates of LETS. Each subscriber gets a cheque book for their LETS tokens, and abuse is discouraged by monthly statements showing the indebtedness (or otherwise) of each subscriber. The system is promoted as encouraging local trading, and re-enfranchisng people on low incomes by allowing them to exchange services and goods without money. Telecottages in particular can operate as administrative centres for local LETS systems.

Office services

A number of virtual office services have grown up over the past five years providing an official "front" for businesses including telephone answering, accommodation addresses and meeting space. These services aim to fulfil all the functions of a traditional receptionist/secretary, without of course the expense.

Telecottages can also be used as accommodation addresses by very small businesses. As well as correspondence services, think about message taking – the advantage to the businessperson is that their customers do not have to leave a message on a machine, they can speak to a real person. The telecottage can help the small businessperson to present a more professional image. Local enterprise agencies can often help telecottages by handing out cards to those enquiring about starting their own businesses.

Publishing, design and multimedia

There are a number of areas where teleworkers can be involved in publishing, including preparing diagrams on computer, editing text, layout

> **Neighbourhood work centre facilities at Antur Teifi**
>
> Antur Teifi, a combined business park and telematics centre in Wales, participated in the OFFNET EU project to provide services to workers that would reduce their commuting burden. The social services and trading standards departments of Dyfed County Council began using the centre in March 1993 for field workers who spend over 50% of their time out of the office, travelling at last ten miles to return to the office between visits. The council workers can deal with their workload more effectively, and use their normal database and word processing facilities on the council mainframe over an X.25 link. Initial uptake was low, but after 5 months over 30 individuals were regularly booking in to the four reserved workspaces. Contact: Lynne Davies 01239 710238 or email 100141.2166@compuserve.com

work, proofreading and graphic design. However, they all require specialist skills. It is not just a case of buying the DTP software! Related areas include preparing overhead projections and 35 mm slides for presentations, as well as the growing market for computerised presentations incorporating sound, graphics and animation (multimedia).

Remote office services

A few corporations have created telecentres remote from their main offices where much routine correspondence and administration is done. Examples are Glaxo in Teesdale, and Rank Xerox. The advantages for the companies are that, rather than relying on disparate teleworkers with varied equipment, they can specify the equipment to be used and the procedures to be carried out, as well as controlling the teleworkers more closely. By locating these centres in rural areas, they can reduce labour and premises costs.

Scanning

Scanners are used for three purposes: to scan text, to scan line graphics and to scan photographs. For text scanning, you will need a flat bed scanner with an automatic feeder, and specialist OCR (optical character reading) software. Text scanning works well on clean, typed manuscripts. It does not cope well with heavily edited typescripts, or with handwriting (yet). For scanning line graphics such as simple company logos, a cheap hand-held scanner will be sufficient. To scan photographs at high quality, you need a high quality flat bed scanner, and specialist knowledge of printing processes such as halftoning to get best results. For colour reproduction, expensive colour separation drum scanners are used. These are normally provided on a bureau basis by reprographics or typesetting companies. Standard desktop colour scanners do not provide sufficiently good quality for high volume colour printing, although they are excellent for adding interest to short print run documents such as internal report covers.

Skills register

Many telecottages now maintain a local skills register of individual teleworkers and can refer work to them. Sometimes the telecottage takes a percentage of the value of the work if a contract is arranged through the telecottage. In others, because the teleworkers are using telecottage equipment, no commission is taken. Some telecottages simply maintain a skills noticeboard that teleworkers can advertise on, whilst others hold social events such as lunches where teleworkers can exchange ideas and form business relationships. But beware: if you are acting as an employment agency you need a licence from the Department of Employment (see *Staying Safe and Legal* chapter).

Training

Most telecottages offer a variety of training courses introducing people to information technology. Other areas you can consider include training in specific software packages (particularly word processing, spreadsheets and databases), training in business skills and special vocational qualifications for teleworkers. Much software training is now done by means of interactive tutorials or videos. These are usually based on CD-ROMs.

Funding is often available for these courses from Training and Enterprise Councils (TECs). Larger telecottages could think about becoming examination centres for qualifications such as the RSA word processing examinations, the City and Guilds diplomas and the Cambridge syllabus information technology modules, including teleworker training qualifications such as the VQ in teleworking.

Telecottages should also consider linking up with their local Further Education college as TCA member Su Pointer did, following up an article in *Teleworker* magazine "I immediately contacted a senior member of one of the colleges in the area, some 30 miles away. He was more than willing to meet and discuss possible developments. Three months further on, and we have already run, and been paid for, three successful subsidised computer courses."

A number of colleges are starting to look at providing courses supported by remote means such as modem and videophone (eg Open University, Stroud College of Further Education). A telecottage can provide a learning base for students without these facilities.

A related area of opportunity is the production of training courses and materials. Such documents can run to hundreds of pages, and command high prices, especially where they are prepared for professional bodies or large corporate clients. The preparation of distance learning materials is a major growth area, but requires skills in editing, teaching, high level word processing and/or desktop publishing.

Translation services

Translation services are increasingly in demand, and translation work is often received and delivered via email these days. Translations can be tied in with word processing and desktop publishing services. By connecting together a number of language teleworkers, telecottages can provide a complete European service. Try contacting local chambers of commerce, enterprise agencies and so on to sell this idea.

Word processing and desktop publishing

Word processing (typing) services can be offered to home workers, businesses, political parties and pressure groups, community newsletters and societies. If you are in a university area, see if you can get involved in typing theses and academic papers. Another area which is more within the skill range of most telecottages than full-blown publishing services is using desktop publishing or sophisticated word processing to prepare brochures, newsletters, pricelists and instruction leaflets for local companies. One telecottage combines producing the local community newsletter with training exercises for word processing trainees. Another, Daily Information, arguably the first telecottage in the UK, began by combining word processing training and services with the production of the Daily Information free broadsheet covering activities in central Oxford. Think about making commission arrangements with a local printer to provide printing of documents as well as typing and layout. You may also want to invest in cheap forms of binding such as a comb binding machine, or a colour transfer machine for beautiful report covers.

WWW pages

The production of World Wide Web pages is something that many teleworkes have tried their hands at. It is "flavour of the month", with many businesses requiring help to advertise their services on the Web. To produce Web pages, you need appropriate authoring software and a working knowledge of HTML, the programming language used. It is a big help if you have graphic design or information editing skills, as many client companies are not good at putting together clear information, or understanding how to structure it for use with hypertext. Some Web sites include forms and other areas for users to enter information. The forms have to have corresponding processing software which handles the responses, normally provided through a "cgi script". Programming skills in cgi scripting, and in HotJava, the programming language used to send small, self running programmes over the Internet, are in high demand. Some telecottages already have their own Web sites and are letting space within their sites to local businesses.

Bibliography

Online Business Information and Business Information Basics (2 publications)
Source: Headland Press Tel: 01429 231 902.
Comment: Useful publications for those interested in information broking.

Online Notes
Source: ASLIB Tel: 0171 253 4488
Comment: Useful publication for those interested in information broking.

Contacts and URLs

The Institute of Information Scientists, 44-45 Museum Street, London WC1A 1LY, tel 0171 831 8003, is a useful organisation for those interested in information broking.

The Dyer Partnership, contact Mark Dyer Tel: 01420 473 473 Fax: 01420 487 695 Email: info@netaccountants.com, http://www.netaccountants.com

Staying safe and legal

This section is intended for employers, employed teleworkers and self-employed teleworkers. If all the laws which could be applied to teleworking were enforced absolutely rigorously there would be very little telework. There is a great deal of anachronism around because legal reform has not kept pace with the speed of change of work practices. In general, the advice has to be to inform yourself, use your common sense and not to worry unduly – few authorities want the headache of regulating home offices. Get yourself a good accountant and solicitor, and ask for advice about anything you're not sure of, either from your advisors or from the relevant authorities. If you encounter a problem that is not easily solved, let the TCA know about it so we can try to resolve the issue and warn others who may be affected.

Health and safety

Health and safety authorities have draconian powers of inspection and enforcement, and all HSE legislation includes workplaces in the home. However, in reality the HSE does not have any register of teleworkers, or the resources for a large number of inspections. There is nothing in health and safety law that prevents working alone at home providing it does not affect the worker's health and safety, although strictly speaking all workplaces should have an approved safety statement.

Some may feel the 1974 Health and Safety at Work Act means that teleworker's employers have less onerous duties as they cannot be deemed responsible for the safety of an employee's home. However, any equipment used by the employee in the course of their employment should be deemed safe by the employer. In general it is advisable that the employer should provide the teleworker with all equipment and ensure that the equipment is inspected and checked on a regular basis, and in accordance with the company's on-site practice.

In order to reduce risk of RSI or other injuries due to poor work furniture, the employer is also advised to supply all working furniture. The main relevant law to teleworkers is the Display Screen Directive 90/270/EEC which requires:

- clear and stable screen, bright and free from glare, which should swivel and tilt easily
- adequate arrangement of keyboard characters, adjustable keyboard with sufficient space to support the hands and arms of the user
- sufficient user space to change positions and vary movements. Work desk sufficiently large, document holder adjustable and stable
- satisfactory lighting conditions

- minimised glare and reflection at the workstation, and minimisation of radiation levels
- work chair adjustable in height including the back rest
- a foot rest available if required
- environmental factors should be minimised including effects of reflection/glare, noise, heat and humidity.

Employers should put in place a system for their teleworkers to report accidents or hazards, as there would be in a conventional workplace. Practical experience within the TCA suggests the following are also often problems:

- insufficient power sockets leading to over-use of extension leads, trailing cables and adaptors
- shelves situated inconveniently so that heavy files have to often be placed and replaced, causing stress on the spine and overbalancing
- inadequate office chairs and tables which are not the appropriate height or adjustability for long periods of work
- reading glasses not correct prescription for close work. Anyone working with computers should have their eyes tested, and the optician informed of the computer work.
- lighting – spotlights and anglepoises are generally less tiring than fluorescents in small spaces. Light levels should be about 350 lux. Screens should be positioned at right angles to windows. Blinds to prevent sunlight making screens hard to read should be installed where needed.
- temperatures should be as near as possible to 18.5 degrees centigrade. Where a small home office is intended for use it is important to remember that IT equipment generates heat, and temperatures may become uncomfortably hot in summer unless adequate ventilation can be provided
- the use of IT equipment usually requires an additional 2 power outlets, and 1 or 2 telecoms sockets. Safely stowing cabling is important.
- psychologically, most teleworkers prefer to be situated so that they can see out of a window if possible, although it is important to avoid problems with glare and reflection on computer screens.

Prolonged computer work can also cause discomfort and fatigue to the back, shoulders, neck, head, eyes, buttocks, legs and wrists. Maintaining posture in a static position also causes blood flow to the muscles to be restricted. Ergonomics expert Eilis Duggan of Workright Consultants advises the following guidelines to maintaining a comfortable and efficient work posture:

- feet should be flat on the floor with knees bent at 90° or 100° angle
- the front edge of the chair seat should not be touching the back of the knee or press into the underside of the thigh as increased pressure on the back of the leg may lead to numbness, fatigue or knee swelling
- knees should be level with or slightly above hips
- the chair seat to chair back angle should be slightly backwards (10–20°)
- document being typed should be placed by the screen at the same distance and height, and as close as possible
- change body position frequently, moving feet up and down, adjusting chair and/or keyboard height
- organise work so that you can take "mini-breaks" to stretch muscles
- exercise regularly and eat well.

Planning

There is no question that setting up a home office does constitute a "change of use" in strict planning terms; however, as far as planning departments are concerned, the average teleworker is unlikely to require planning permission, particularly if they are not creating a nuisance to neighbours. There is considerable argument and variation between different councils on whether home offices constitute a "material" or "ancillary" change of use (i.e. turning an outhouse into a garage and car repair workshop is rather more material than putting a computer into a spare bedroom). Material changes of use require permission; ancillary changes or temporary changes probably don't.

Decisions on whether the change of use is "material" are based on whether it will cause increased traffic, changes to the visible appearance of the property, nuisance such as noise or smells, or unsocial working hours. Unfortunately few local authorities have taken into account that teleworking is a form of homeworking which reduces traffic and generally involves no alterations other than provision of electrical sockets and telephone lines. Oldham Borough Council is an exception, recognising teleworking formally in its planning guidelines, and regarding home offices as ancillary changes of use. The Oldham document is available to other planning authorities, who can use it as a blueprint for their own guidelines.

The Department of Transport issued guidelines in 1994 which request local authorities to encourage teleworking. The document, *Planning Policy Guidance 13* (PPG13), contains recommendations for local authorities to "facilitate home working and the provision of facilities for small groups of employees to work together locally". In Ireland there is no overall guidance on teleworking, and policies vary between councils and corporations.

MIRAS mortgage tax relief

Most taxpayers who have a mortgage in Britain can claim tax relief on their interest payments, known as MIRAS (Mortgage Interest Relief at Source). MIRAS is normally available for 15% of the payments on the first £30,000 of the loan. In 1995, the Inland Revenue made changes to its rules to acknowledge that many houses are now used partly for residential purposes and partly for business purposes. Under these rules, the house is notionally "split in two". The interest component on the work or office part of the building is fully deductible from your tax liability as a business expense. For the residential part, MIRAS can still be claimed.

At first sight this looks like a breakthrough for teleworkers – however, if you classify part of your house for business purposes, there are wider implications. The "work" part of the house is potentially liable for Capital Gains Tax, although as house prices are still fairly static, and the first £6,000 of any capital gain is exempt, it is unlikely to be a major concern for most teleworkers. Perhaps more worrying is the possibility that your local authority may try to levy business rates on the "work" part of the house on top of normal Council Tax charges (see below). Other problems could include business rates being charged for gas and electricity, and the possibility of higher insurance charges. However, the Inland Revenue says it treats tax information as confidential and does not pass on information to other public bodies, so these risks may appear more worrying than they actually are.

One home based salesman, Andrew Wood, found that his building society removed him from MIRAS after he informed them of his homeworking. The society told him he would have to reapply for inclusion through his tax office. Because the tax relief is automatically accounted in mortgage payments, building societies in effect administrate MIRAS. Fortunately the tax office disagreed and Mr Wood was allowed to stay in – otherwise he would have had to wait until the following April for reinclusion, followed by a further delay before receiving his missing MIRAS via an adjustment to his tax return and standard tax bill. In response to TCA enquiries, the Inland Revenue has said that building societies do not have the right to remove people from MIRAS simply because they work from home. If you find yourself in this situation, refer your building society to your local tax office, and if that doesn't work contact the TCA so we can try to help.

Restrictive covenants

Some properties, particularly estate houses and flats, may be subject to covenants which could in theory restrict working from home. The origin of these covenants is usually a condition put in place by a vendor selling land to prevent business rather than residential developments. A TCA member discovered his flat was affected by a covenant imposed by a local authority when selling land to a builder, and intended to prevent business use other than by a dentist or doctor. Another TCA member, Peter Fowler, a solicitor working on business related legal matters and commercial property, fills in some background information on the two types of covenant, freehold and leasehold:

Freehold covenants

A typical restriction on a housing estate would be that no trade or business could be carried out on at the property, and no use is permitted other than as a private dwelling house. The power of enforcement lies with the original estate owner or his successors, and in some cases owners of other properties on the estate who could be affected by physical damage or a fall in value of property. Most teleworkers are unlikely to cause damage as they are working entirely inside their home, although some problems could be envisaged (excessive parking obstruction from multiple visitors to a business). In general, it will be a case of common sense and keeping disturbance to neighbours to a minimum.

Sometimes old estates may flex their muscles and request payment for a licence to vary the original covenant, but often they have no direct right of enforcement and may no longer own any nearby property which could be affected. The threat of action is likely to be a bluff as the cost of enforcement could be prohibitive. They could also face a substantial claim from the teleworker if their claim failed, but in the interim the teleworker had been prevented from working by their injunction.

Leasehold covenants

Houses on very long leases such as 999 year leases will fall into the same category as freehold and the comments above apply. However, some small developments of houses or blocks of flats on long leases with ground rents pose a different problem. There will probably be an existing landlord or management company (possibly owned by the residents) who could enforce the covenants although, as before, they will have to prove that damage is being caused. Such proof is easier where covenants have been established for the common good. All that is needed to cause a problem is one resident who has been inconvenienced and an active resident's committee.

In general, if you are prudent and do not cause any nuisance from your business, even if you are in technical breach of an estate covenant, you will probably be safe enough to carry on teleworking. In many ways, the planning authorities are a bigger source of worry to potential and existing teleworkers.

Business rates

If you do go through the process of receiving official planning permission for your home office, then you are liable for commercial rates or council tax on the portion of your house that you are using for work.

A big bill from the meter man

Roderick Prescott, a retired Edinburgh civil servant, was shocked to discover that he had to pay an extra £300 a year on his electricity bill because he runs a business from home. Roderick has a property business which he spends only an hour a day on. His problems started when he chased up a problem with Scottish Power on behalf of one of his tenants, but wrote the letter from his home address. "A man came from the electricity board saying he had come to read the meter. Afterwards he was having a chat with my wife who said we were retired but that I run a business in the spare room. The next thing I knew, a letter arrived which said we should be charged on an industrial tariff, which is intended for factory owners." This was later reduced to the "farm and combined premises tariff" which is intended for people with B&Bs, aimed at people who use a lot of electricity for washing machines, baths, and so on.

In the UK, as far as liability for business rates is concerned, a large grey area exists. The accepted advice is typified by internal Treasury guidelines issued for the management of its own homeworkers: "Generally when part of a home is used as a workplace where the non-domestic activity precludes the use at any time of that part of the property for living accommodation, the part will be non-domestic and therefore subject to the business rate. In practice where domestic use can take place after work has finished, it is unlikely that liability for the business rate will arise."

This view was confirmed by a local rating officer: "We apply what we call a six o'clock rule – if after six, the room reverts back to domestic use, then it would not be subject to business rates. Generally as most home businesses wouldn't need planning permission we would only get to hear about this if a neighbour complained. It is highly unlikely that a home office business would require business rating." However, the same officer described an example of a publisher operating from home and using two rooms – one entirely for stock and the other as a computer room which resulted in an (amicably agreed) annual rate of around £300.

More recent experiences suggest that "home businesses" are more of a target than employed teleworkers and if moving a business from a rated office based premises to home, you may well be visited by a rating valuation officer as a matter of course.

Dublin chartered surveyors HPSG Hanson International give the following hypothetical case in Ireland: for a house in a rural area with a room of 15ft x 15ft in use as a home office, the General Valuation Office rateable value would be of the order of £5. Most councils levy a rate of around £45 so your annual rate bill would be around £225 per annum. Paul Kennedy of HPSG Hanson points out that the process involves a surveyor being sent out from the General Valuation office in Dublin, and that because of the expense of this in relation to the rates collected, some county managers may take a view that teleworking is a temporary arrangement not liable to commercial rating. Tongue-in-cheek, Paul suggests that perhaps in the future we may see the Belgian approach – in Brussels, instead of taxing property, they tax each computer in use.

"Business" charges by public utilities

Unfortunately for teleworkers, many power utility companies have a policy that to qualify for the minimum tariff, premises must be used wholly for domestic purposes. The practical situation is that they would have to know you are working from home before any change could be made, and that the exact conditions vary from company to company. Check with the regulatory body such as OFFER or OFGAS, and contact the TCA if you have a problem.

For telephone service, BT does not compel people to use the business rate, but points out that business service has the advantage of a Yellow Pages entry, and a Business Pages entry. BT also puts business users on a higher priority for fault correction than residential users. In both cases compensation is paid if the fault is not repaired within 24 hours.

VAT (4th schedule)

Another area of confusion concerns "4th-schedule" VAT. Where a teleworker is registered for VAT and performs data processing tasks for a VAT registered business located in another EU member state, no VAT is chargeable despite the transaction being for a service rather than goods. The existence of this rule is particularly important for Irish teleworkers because if they were forced to charge their export clients the high Irish VAT rate of 21% and oblige the clients to go through the cumbersome process of reclaiming the difference between this rate and that pertaining in their own country, they would be at a competitive disadvantage compared to teleworkers in other EU member states with lower VAT rates. Unfortunately, the existence of this VAT category is not widely known in regional revenue and excise offices.

Employed or self-employed?

Many teleworkers and telecottages have reported confusions and difficulties when they wish to get help from other teleworkers to complete work. The difficulty comes over whether the other teleworkers are employed (PAYE) or self-employed. The definition used to distinguish between self-employment and PAYE employment is that of a contract **for** service against a contract **of** service.

- contracts for services are agreements for a specified piece of work to be completed. In teleworking terms these normally consist of the completion of a specified project by the teleworker for his or her client as a self-employed activity on which no PAYE (or PRSI in Ireland) is levied

- contracts of service are standard employments – a teleworker operating on a payment by the hour for one single client is likely to be considered to have a contract of service, on which PAYE and national insurance (PRSI in Ireland) are payable, regardless of the location of the teleworker in relation to the client/employer.

On occasion the tax authorities have taken a retrospective view that regular telework contracts which both teleworker and client thought were contracts for services were in fact employments (contracts of service), and have levied back tax and penalties. This confusion damages the willingness of businesses to use teleworkers, particularly as the "employer" can then be liable for both sets of taxes.

Are you employed or self-employed?

The main criteria to be taken into account are listed in a free Inland Revenue bookled *Employed or Self-Employed?* which states that if you can answer yes to the following questions, it will "usually" mean you are self-employed.

- *Do you have the final say in how the business is run?*
- *Do you risk your own money in the business?*
- *Are you responsible for meeting the losses as well as taking profits?*
- *Do you provide the major items of equipment you need to do your job, not just the small tools which many employees provide for themselves?*
- *Are you free to hire other people on terms of your own choice, to do the work that you have taken on? Do you pay them out of your own pocket?*
- *Do you have to correct unsatisfactory work in your own time and at your own expense?*

If you answer "yes" to the following questions, then you are "probably" an employee:

- *Do you yourself have to do the work rather than hire someone else to do it for you?*
- *Can someone tell you at any time what to do or when and how to do it?*
- *Are you paid by the hour, week or month? Can you get overtime pay? (even if you are paid by commission or on a piecework basis you may still be an employee)*
- *Do you work set hours, or a given number of hours a week or month?*
- *Do you work at the premises of the person you are working for, or at a place or places that they decide?*

Proto-type's points for self-employment:

- *The teleworkers provide their own equipment*
- *The client deals with the teleworker direct*
- *There is no guarantee about the level of work the teleworker might expect*
- *It is the responsibility of the teleworker to correct poor work at their own cost*
- *The teleworker's ability to take on other work is not restricted*
- *Separate invoices are issued from the teleworker to the main "work getter" (such as Proto-type) and from the work getter to the client*

The erratic nature of telework contracts can also cause difficulties; two teleworkers may collaborate closely on a project for a third party for three months and then not work together for a further six months after that – are both self-employed, or is one employing the other during the three months, but not afterwards? The answer will depend on the extent to which one controlled the other's working patterns, how many other clients each had, whether one required the presence of the other at specific premises and times and other factors.

Richard Nissen of the Virtual Office took this issue up with his local tax inspector: "The fact is that you can employ people and have them working on a self-employed basis as long as they are not directed by you. The easiest way to do this is to send the terms and conditions for the worker you want to employ on a self-employed basis to your local PAYE office for confirmation that you can employ them in this way before you start paying them. However, even if you cross this hurdle, then there is another problem. If you ask a teleworker to do some typing for you that is then charged out and sold on to a third party, you fall slap bang into the scope of employment agency law (section 134 ICTA 1988), so you would have to act like an agency and pay John or Jane PAYE and national insurance. Yet if the person you employ is from another EU country then no PAYE is payable – it's actually easier to use a cross-border teleworker."

Whatever the exact situation, where it is important to either the employer or employee that self-employed status is assured, get advice on formulating a contract and working conditions from your financial advisor and verify it with your local tax assessor.

The corresponding situation in Ireland is controlled by the Employment Agency section of the Department of Enterprise and Employment and is based on the 1971 Employment Agency Act. At first sight this act appears to cover someone obtaining work and distributing it among other teleworkers; however, in the case of the Telemart online work agency, the department has ruled that as long as the other teleworkers are demonstrably self-employed, that they are not being charged in any way by Telemart for its service in obtaining the work, and that the client company pays Telemart, not the teleworkers themselves, then no agency licence is required. Due to the complex and confused status of Irish employment agency law at present, it is recommended that expert legal advice be taken for similar enterprises.

Ann Collins of Proto-type, a TCA member, has successfully established a situation where the four teleworkers she works with are classified as self-employed. Proto-type is a remote word processing service based in Essex and operating for city-based firms. The company's main client is a quantity surveying group. Handwritten documents and audio tapes are received by fax, typed and returned by modem. Ann explains: "We started off with just myself and we are still small, using four teleworkers, with very tight margins. The additional cost and the time in administering PAYE and National Insurance for employed status would have been sufficient deterrent to stop us from continuing the business. From the teleworkers' point of view, self-employment gives them greater flexibility. We had to argue the point with the local tax office, but a number of points eventually convinced them."

So what expenses can you claim for your home office? The best advice is to talk through the issues with your tax advisor, but you can claim part of your mortgage or rent, expenses for heating, lighting, and telephone, depreciation of the fixtures and fittings, installation of extra power points, cleaning costs, business insurance, refurbishment, office equipment, postage and stationery.

Tax changes – self-assessment

The tax system in Britain is being changed to "self-assessment". There are two main elements to the reform. From the tax year 1996-97, taxpayers will be asked to do their own calculations on how much income tax they are due to pay, and new forms will be issued from spring 1997 onwards. At the same time, existing self-employed businesses will move to a "current year" rather than "previous year" basis for paying tax (this is already the case for businesses started after April 1994), bringing the self-employed in line with PAYE employees. For most existing self-employed teleworkers, this means that two year's profits (1995–1996 and 1996–1997) will be taxed together for the year 1996–97, with the tax payable in January and July 1997. In most cases, taxes will be levied on half the profits of the two years and tax-allowable business expenses currently being run up will only benefit from half the normal rate of tax relief. There is a cumbersome overlap accounting system for businesses whose trading year does not coincide with the tax year, involving tax credits being carried forward through the lifetime of the business. A self-assessment enquiry line is available on 0345 161514.

In the Republic of Ireland, self-employed people have been taxed on the current year basis for some years so no equivalent change will take place.

Trade union guidelines

The isolation from co-workers inherent in teleworking can restrict negotiations for appropriate rates of pay, as shown in the University of Westminster's 1993 Work Research Group survey of self-employed teleworkers in the UK publishing industry. Over 100 respondents indicated that loneliness, isolation and lack of contact with clients and colleagues was a problem. Over half of the interviewees did not receive a "living income" due to insufficient workload and low rates of pay. The report noted that "Neither the National Union of Journalists or the Society of Freelance Editors and Proofreaders has been able to foster sufficient solidarity amongst freelancers to maintain any generally observed rates of pay."

To date, the only union which has published guidelines to address the problem of representation of teleworkers, including self-employed teleworkers, has been MSF:

1. Home based working should always be voluntary.

2. Home based workers should be employees (enjoying full employment rights) and not self-employed subcontractors.

3. Ideally, home based teleworking should operate from a separate room in the home properly examined by qualified health and safety experts to ensure a safe working environment.

4. There should be regular opportunities for teleworkers in the same organisation to meet each other, as well as non-teleworking colleagues and managers, so that people do not feel isolated or excluded.

5. Teleworkers should have access to electronic mail and telephone links with each other - using the scope of the technology to expand contact between people and avoid further isolation.

6. Each teleworker should be assigned a particular manager whose responsibility it should be to keep in regular contact and who would also meet the teleworker on a regular basis.

7. Teleworkers should enjoy the same rates of pay and other employment benefits as non-teleworking employees in an organisation.

8. Teleworkers should be included in the career development programme of the organisation in which they work.

9. All equipment used should be supplied and maintained by the employer.

10. Financial arrangements should be agreed to cover the extra costs of teleworking, such as heating, lighting etc., and it may also be appropriate for a rental to be agreed for the use the employer makes of the employee's home.

11. Employers should be responsible for the health and safety of teleworkers and have specialist health and safety advisers to give advice and to regularly visit and monitor health and safety.
12. Teleworkers should be represented, through their own employee representatives, on health and safety committees of the organisations that employ them.
13. Teleworkers should enjoy the same rights as other workers to join trade unions and should have access to representatives, including the right to elect their own. In this regard, trade unions will need to think about the services they may need to offer teleworkers, including access to electronic mail, notice boards etc.
14. Employees who transfer from conventional based working to home based teleworking should be entitled to a trial period and should have the right to return to the previous arrangements. All teleworkers should be entitled to an annual review of the arrangements and have the right to revert to the previous employment arrangements if they wish.

Source: Bill Walsh, National Officer, MSF (UK branch), September 1993 – 'The Best of Both Worlds', MSF

MSF has also set up a Teleworking Interest Group to examine how it can meet the needs of teleworker members running their own businesses, covering ideas such as help and advice on cashflow, health and safety, taxation, legal issues and other small business problems, as well as partnerships with suppliers to supply discounted business equipment, travel and insurance.

Pensions

Those who begin teleworking are often entering self-employment for the first time and consequently losing the security of a former occupational pension. This area of financial services has been in turmoil for a number of years after the Maxwell scandal and investigations into sales advice about personal pensions given in the late 1980s. It can still be hard to get clear, unbiased advice because most pension advisors receive commissions on the pensions they sell. The best option is to look for an independent financial advisor (who should be a member of the regulatory authority FIMBRA) whom you can pay on an hourly rate (around £30–£100) to look at your situation and advise you – that way the advisor is paid by you to look after your interests, and not by the pension company to sell their policies.

The two types of pension – occupational and personal – differ widely in their tax breaks and regulatory regimes. In general, a well funded occupational pension scheme is likely to be preferable to a personal pension, but fewer and fewer people are eligible for occupational pensions, which were designed in the days of "jobs for life". Both types of pensions are paid on top of the state old age pension, which is a flat rate payment available to those who have paid into the state scheme for a sufficient number of years through their National Insurance contributions. Because of the increased number of older people in the population, and long term underfunding of the state scheme, it is likely that the value of the state pension will fall far below the present basic level as we move into the 21st century, and contributions to an occupational or personal pension scheme are to be strongly recommended where affordable.

An occupational pension scheme is normally run by an employer and provides a pension based on a percentage of your final salary rate at retirement, as well as on the number of years of membership of the scheme you have. Occupational pensions cannot exceed two thirds of final salary, and to achieve this maximum you will need at least 40 years membership of a pension scheme. Normally both the employee and the employer contribute to an occupational pension. Added benefits can include death in service grants and payments to widows or widowers.

When someone changes jobs they have two main options available for their pension – deferred pension or transfer value. If they become a deferred pensioner, they leave their contributions in the scheme untouched and quietly growing until they reach retirement, beginning a new occupational scheme with the new employer. If they opt for a transfer value, the pension scheme calculates the value of your pension based on existing contributions and arranges for its transfer into a new scheme. TCA officer Alan Denbigh found that when he became a teleworker, by taking out his new personal pension with the company that had operated his previous company pension, he was able to avoid the normal penalties of withdrawal – his pension was "converted" from an occupational to a personal pension with minimal pain.

Personal pension plans by contrast are based on how much pension you have "purchased" by your payments throughout your working life. What you receive depends on your contributions, and how successful the pension fund managers have been in selecting good investments. The big difference is that employers usually will not contribute to a personal fund, so the whole pension burden is borne by the teleworker.

However, contributors to personal pension schemes are entitled to tax breaks. As you get older, the amount of money you can put into a pension scheme tax free increases:

Up to 35	17.5%
36-45	20%
46-50	25%
51-55	30%
56-60	35%
61 plus	40% up to the earnings cap of £75,000

In the Republic of Ireland the tax free amount is 15% regardless of age until you reach 55 years, when it rises to 20%.

If you are starting a personal pension plan it pays to begin early – the rule of thumb used in calculating how much you should contribute is to halve your age and convert it to a percentage (so a 30-year old should begin contributing 15% of their income).

Many self-employed people wait until towards the end of the tax year, when they know what their total income is likely to be, and then buy single premium pension plans to allow them to use up all the available tax relief on the grounds that it is better to spend money on a pension than to give it to the government. The alternative is monthly regular premium policies, but these can be inflexible if your income varies – if you fail to make payments there are penalties. It is very inadvisable to stop payments in the first two years of a regular payments scheme. One company, Equitable Life, offers a regular scheme where there is no penalty if you cease contributing or vary your contributions. Equitable Life is also the only company which does not pay commission on its policies to salespeople.

To avoid a cashflow crunch at the end of the tax year when pension payments have to be made to qualify for tax relief, it can be worth looking at having two policies: one for small regular payments, and the other a single premium whose value depends on the maximum tax relief you can obtain. Single premium policies allow you to spread your investment over a number of different companies, reducing the risk that you might "pick" an underperformer, but regular premium policies are a lot less painful to the bank account.

In Ireland, proposed pension payments can be taken into account when calculating your preliminary tax liability in October. The payment must then be made by 31st January of the following year.

When selecting a personal pension plan, you are likely to be faced with a plethora of graphs and figures indicating how different companies have performed and many different options, such as with profits schemes and index linked bonds. The main points to watch for are:

- underlying trends of performance – the final value will depend partly on inflation and partly on the growth of the funds invested. Look at how your proposed pension company has fared compared to others over a period of years
- administration charge percentages (these can vary from 8% to 32% for regular premium policies, and from 13% to 39% for single premium over a 25 year period)
- commission charges, which can be more than half the first year's payments.

Within each company there are options on funds which carry risk and growth tags, such as investment in shares of companies trading in the Pacific Rim, or in property, or in index-linked bonds. A with profits policy is a calculation based on the bonuses of the company that reflects its overall level of profitability. Ethical funds are a recent development which invest only in companies conforming to certain standards, and avoiding areas such as arms production.

At retirement, you can take up to a quarter of your pension as a lump sum. The remainder has to be used to buy an annuity, which provides a regular income for the rest of your life. You can choose which company to buy the annuity from, and it is a crucial decision for a comfortable old age.

Health insurance

In Britain everyone has access to the National Health Service for free medical care but you may need to think about extra health insurance if you are opting for self-employment. Typical needs are:

- access to fast, private healthcare to reduce time out of work
- insurance against critical illness preventing you from working and earning
- access to welfare benefits or insurance payouts to replace your income should you become unable to work.

Private healthcare policies are available from a range of suppliers in the UK such as BUPA and PPP. These regular payment policies are not the same as the critical illness insurance policies currently being marketed which need very careful assessment, as many cover the basic unhappy events such as heart attack, stroke or cancer, but not chronic conditions such as arthritis or endometriosis which can prevent you from working just as effectively. The small print is well worth reading!

Self-employed people do pay national insurance, but it only entitles them to the health service, disability benefits and the old age pension – not to unemployment benefit if their business goes under, although depending on circumstances other means-tested benefits may be available. The benefits system has become increasingly complex in the past few years, and it is worth consulting your local library or Citizen's Advice Bureau on your entitlements.

Any teleworker becoming self-employed should think seriously about taking out personal health insurance (PHI) to secure their income level should they become unable to work through ill-health. PHI does not pay your medical bills – instead, it replaces your lost income. Normally the policy provides around 75% of your usual salary (to give you an incentive to go back to work…). Premium levels depend on your medical history when you take out the policy, your deferral period, and any exemptions you select. The deferral period is normally around 13 weeks, and is a time delay between the onset of illness and the date when the policy begins to pay out. The longer the deferral, the lower the premium. Exemptions are usually created where you have a pre-existing problem (such as back trouble) which makes your premiums very high. If you agree not to claim with regard to back problems, you can get insurance for other conditions at more reasonable premiums. It is extremely important that you ensure your medical conditions are fully disclosed when taking out a permanent health insurance policy (check your doctor's report and make sure you let the insurer know if you think anything's been omitted). Otherwise, if you need to claim and have to undergo an independent examination, your claim may be denied. Permanent health insurance isn't a particularly remunerative sector for insurance companies, and many will only offer these policies if they are taken out in tandem with personal pensions. Friend's Provident does offer stand alone permanent insurance policies, however.

In Ireland membership of VHI is to be recommended to ensure swift treatment of health problems for the self employed. VHI premiums can be partially claimed against tax.

Small businesses can also buy "key person" insurance for owner managers so that the business receives a payout if the key person dies or becomes incapacitated.

Data Protection Act

The British Data Protection Act is over ten years old, but as many as 150,000 firms have still to register, risking fines of up to £5,000 plus costs. Many small companies complain that the data protection forms are overly complex and that registration is too expensive. Yet if you hold any personal data, including mailing lists, on your computer then you should be registered.

The Data Protection registrar will want details of the data you hold and control, the purposes for which it is used, where the data is obtained and to whom it is disclosed, both here and overseas. If your information handling practices are found to be negligent, you can be liable for civil action due to damage caused by inaccurate data, unauthorised data, loss of data or

Data protection principles and definitions

- *Obtain and process information fairly and lawfully*
- *Keep it only for one or more specified and lawful purposes*
- *Use and disclose it only in ways compatible with these purposes*
- *Keep it safe and secure from unauthorised or accidental disclosure or loss*
- *Keep it accurate and up to date*
- *Ensure that it is adequate, relevant and not excessive*
- *Retain it no longer than is necessary for the purpose or purposes*
- *Give a copy of his/her personal data to any individual on request.*

Personal data is any information relating to living, identifiable individuals processed by computer

Data users are any company or individual who controls the content and use of a collection of personal data

Data subjects are those to whom personal data relates

---

destruction of personal records, including liability for related distress caused.

Data subjects can request access to their personal data, and where appropriate, demand correction or deletion of a record. In return, data users can charge up to £10 for a copy of the data.

In general, if you are processing information on behalf of an employer, it is the employer's duty to register, not the employee's. The cost of registration is £75 and the forms are long and complex; however, you can have your forms "prefilled" as templates by expert staff before they are sent out to you if you ring 01625 545740. The general enquiries number is 01625 535777.

The data protection laws in the Republic of Ireland by contrast are clear and unrestrictive. Only those directly involved as the main part of their business in processing or holding financial or personal data need to register. Teleworkers who keep their client's mailing lists on their computers do not normally fall into this category. For telecommuters, it is the responsibility of their employer to register. The forms are clear and easy to fill in, and the fee is £50. However, regardless of whether or not you are registered, you still have a duty to safeguard personal computer data that you hold and you must abide by the data protection principles.

Intellectual property and copyright

Although prosecutions for infringements of copyright and intellectual property rights (IPR) are rare, it is important to have a basic grasp of your rights and responsibilities, especially with regard to online material. In practical terms, most people don't necessarily want to be paid if you re-use something of theirs in your work. However, they almost certainly do want to be asked, and to have their IPR acknowledged in your document. Barry Mahon of information management association EUSIDIC comments: "Publishers would like you to believe that quotation is a cardinal sin, but that is because they make authors sign away their rights to allow quotation without payment. Equally, if you are an author, take advice before signing away all your rights to a publisher – it is possible only to grant limited rights". Many authors and agents distinguish rights for paper publication from those for online distribution these days.

Most countries in the world operate to the Berne convention, which means that even if a document does not have a copyright notice or use the © symbol, the work is copyright, even if it's merely a shopping list. Pictures are covered as well as text, and it is irrelevant whether or not you charge for your publication – even if you give it away free, if you include someone else's copyrighted material without permission it's an infringement of their IPR.

If you want to assert your own copyright on a document, add:
Copyright © [date] by [author].

With regard to information on the Internet, including newsgroups and listservs, nothing is "in the public domain" and therefore free to use unless it has an explicit statement granting it to the public domain attached. This particularly applies to material from online news services; you may be able to extract information, rephrase it and sell it on in some circumstances, where it could be regarded as "fair use", but in general beware of all but the most minimal quotation.

An excellent guide to copyright and IPR by Brad Templeton is available at http://www.clari.net, and includes this summary of "fair use":

"The "fair use" exemption to copyright law was created to allow things such as commentary, parody, news reporting, research and education about copyrighted works without the permission of the author. Intent, and damage to the commercial value of the work are important considerations. Are you reproducing an article from the New York Times because you needed to in order to criticise the quality of the New York Times, or because you couldn't find time to write your own story, or didn't want your readers to have to pay to log onto the online services with the story or buy a copy of the paper? The first is probably fair use, the others probably aren't. Fair use is almost always a short excerpt and almost always attributed. (Do not use more of the work than is necessary to make the commentary.) It should not harm the commercial value of the work – in the sense of people

> The security survey of telecentres carried out by the Telecottage Association in 1995 showed particular problems with user supervision
>
> - One third felt people could get into their offices undetected during office hours
> - Once inside the building, visitors were generally supervised by centre staff or clients, but less than half reported supervision "all the time"
> - Over three quarters had no signing in or visitor's badge procedure
> - Almost half allowed access to the office outside office hours by clients
> - Only a quarter had an alarm system
> - Almost half described their environment as "loosely controlled"
> - Only 30% had any kind of disaster recovery plan
> - Only 40% had plans for provision of alternative telephone lines
> - Only 20% had plans to cope with power supply loss
> - Less than half required users to employ passwords when accessing PCs
>
> 53% of telecottages reported at least one security incident, at an average cost of £1300, although half of the cases were described as very low impact (one incident costing £10,000 substantially skewed the average cost). No incidents of hacking or computer fraud were reported, and the level of deliberate computer misuse was low compared to national surveys, although misuse incidents including loading of illegal (copyrighted) software, introduction of viruses and running up large unauthorised online charges were reported.
>
> A series of security guidelines and policy suggestions entitled *Keep It Safe and Secure* for telecottage managers is available from the association. Send an SAE with 47p stamp to KISS booklets, WREN Telecottage, Stoneleigh Park, Warwickshire CV8 2LZ.

no longer needing to buy it (which is another reason why reproduction of the entire work is generally forbidden.)"

Training materials do not normally fall into the fair use category, a point of particular relevance to telecottages who may be copying training modules.

Another important area to consider is that of defamation, particularly when "flame wars" break out on the Internet. In general you should resist putting anything which could be considered defamatory in an email message, even one that is sent on a one-to-one basis. In ordinary written correspondence, a letter from one person to another in a closed envelope is considered to be "privileged" correspondence and it is unlikely that a defamation lawsuit could be made to stick in such circumstances. Email is not the same at all – it is not assumed to be private unless previously agreed between the parties. It's also very easy for a slip of the finger to send an email to entirely the wrong person. If in doubt, leave it out, particularly on public forums or newsgroups.

Security

Teleworkers need to address issues of data security as well as those of physical security (preventing theft and damage). Telecottages, which allow public access to premises, also need to look at the problems of supervision of visitors and casual users.

Issues of fire and theft head the likely list of incidents. Many home offices do not have fire extinguishers, smoke alarms, first aid kits or clear evacuation routes. Given the high proportion of electrical equipment, it is to be recommended that home offices should have a CO_2 extinguisher to deal with small electrical fires with minimum damage to equipment. For those in remote areas far from fire stations, the purchase of a substantial powder extinguisher for general fires is also recommended. Fire extinguishers should be located close to the exits from the building. Upstairs home offices should be assessed for evacuation routes in case a fire were to break out downstairs and prevent escape by means of the usual staircase. If you are worried that an official fire inspection by the fire brigade might lead to your office being "banned", ask advice from a supplier of firefighting equipment on suitable measures.

No one is immune from crime, and in many ways a burglary has a much more drastic effect on a home office than on a conventional office. In an office, the employer takes responsibility for equipment, and can afford security measures such as closed circuit TV (CCTV). At home, you will be dealing with the consequences of any burglary.

Computers have a high resale value and are likely to be the main target for a break-in. However, the advantage of most home offices is that they do not advertise "expensive kit in here". To all intents and purposes the risks of burglary are actually lower than for an ordinary house because working from home means there is someone on the premises for most of the day and night, but you might look at installing blinds if your office is on the ground floor so that the computers are not visible to passers-by. In general it is wise not to allow visitors into your home office unless necessary – the fewer people who know about your equipment the better. Check the credentials of utility company or other officials who call at the house.

Physical security advice will be available from your Crime Prevention Unit, contactable via your local police station, or from your insurers. Common sense measures include:

- five lever mortice locks on outside doors
- key operated window locks
- key operated bolts on back doors and patio doors

- ensure ladders or other tools that could be used to gain access are locked away
- a separate lock which allows the home office door to be secured against the rest of the house.
- arrange for e.g. lights to be switched on and off by timer if away on holiday and notify police
- leave a radio or light on in the house if popping out during the day.
- lock all doors and windows before going out or retiring for the night.
- photograph and keep a description of your IT equipment including serial numbers in case you have to report a crime or make an insurance claim.

Specific deterrence device for computers include:

- Trojan, an anti-tamper alarm that fits inside a computer
- Wobbler, an extremely loud alarm which goes off if the computer is moved
- PANDA Protected, a system of hard-to remove labels which contain a code held on a national register
- Retainaguard, a system of etching an ID number onto a piece of equipment such as a fax or mobile phone
- workstation cabinets that allow computers to be locked away out of sight when not in use.
- cable security devices that lock computers to tables or other fixed items which cannot be removed from the room such as the Secure-it lock from Tomco.

Telephone and electricity supplies are often not considered when analyses of security risks are being made, but problems in these areas can effectively stop a business from trading. For most people the cost of providing an uninterruptable power supply, or generator backup for a whole office will be prohibitive, but systems are available which at least give you sufficient breathing space to close down the computer after a power cut without losing work in progress – check the Radio Spares (RS) catalogue which lists devices that will keep one computer powered for about 15 minutes costing around £130. It may be worthwhile to pre-arrange for the use of workspace elsewhere in the area should you suffer a loss of power for more than a day. The arrangement could be with a neighbouring teleworker or office services company, or with a telecottage.

Faster repair times are probably the main reason for paying business rather than residential rates for your telephone lines. However, if you have a residential line, and no need for the directory entries provided as part of business services, but still want fast repairs, you can pay BT £8.25 a quarter to get Total Care, which aims at a 4-hour repair time every day except Sunday.

Association member Stephen Thomas found that it is also possible to arrange with BT for an alternative number while your own is out of service, so that clients hear a message and can leave voicemail or speak to you, rather than getting a frustrating engaged tone or, more commonly, the phone appearing to ring out as though you were out. Dial 154 to ask for this service – but as it operates through call diversion, you need to have another, functioning number for the calls to be diverted to.

The most effective form of data security is to ensure that you take regular backups and that one set of your backups are held "offsite" in case of fire or other extensive damage to your computers and onsite backups. As well as physically swapping backup tapes or disks with a co-worker or local business, you could look into backing up your data remotely via modem or ISDN line – a number of specialist companies offer safe archiving services in this way. Remember that on average a computer hard disk will fail once every two to three years – and that the inconvenience hard disk crashes cause can be hugely reduced by even once-weekly backups.

Insurance

The insurance market is moving rapidly to catch up with the shift to home working. It is still the case that a standard home contents policy is unlikely to cover your home office equipment, so now specific policies targetted at home offices are being produced to replace the plethora of computer, office and home policies previously designed to confuse the teleworker. These new policies also cover important business issues such as public liability, employee liability and loss of earnings which can affect teleworkers.

Standard domestic policies, even if you have remembered to inform your insurer that you are working from home, usually don't cover more than £5,000 worth of goods and may exclude single items worth more than £1,000 (which means many PCs won't be covered). Commercial office and computer policies will cover the computer equipment – but at a high price caused by the dramatic rise in computer theft. Home office policies generally cover equipment valued in the £5,000–£20,000 range and cost about 60% of the cost of an equivalent office policy. The higher the value of the equipment, the higher the premium. Whether your office is part of the house or a separate outbuilding may also affect the premium (in the house is considered more secure because it is constantly occupied). When adding up the cost of your equipment, don't forget add-ons and small items such as mice and tape drives which can easily turn a £1,000 basic PC into a £2,000 replacement cost. Do be sure to make your calculations on a replacement, value not current value, particularly since computers depreciate in value so quickly. Also remember to inform your insurers about any changes, such as purchase of new computers, or a change in the number of visitors or employees, which affects the risk insured. Failure to inform can cause problems if you have to claim.

If you employ a broker who, on your behalf, moves your policy around different insurers to get the best deal, check that the material details (such as serial numbers of equipment) are properly recorded every time the policy is renewed.

Other items which affect the premium vary from insurer to insurer and include:

- client visits to your premises
- employees
- window locks
- mortice locks on doors
- presence of burglar alarm
- membership of neighbourhood watch (Community Alert in Ireland)
- age of policy holder.

Mobile phones, eminently portable and stealable, are often excluded from home office policies. Another area often omitted is stock held for resale such as paper, disks, publications. Other areas to consider (which are usually available at the cost of extra premium) are:

- loss of data (e.g. through virus or malicious attack)
- public liability or employer's liability insurance if people visit or work at your home office (this is a must for anyone operating in the Republic of Ireland).
- business interruption insurance, which compensates you for your time spent putting your business back together and other costs incurred after an incident
- computer breakdown insurance – in some situations this can be cheaper than holding a maintenance contract and ensures that expensive part replacements are covered
- cover off the premises e.g. portable computers on business trips.

Because teleworker situations vary so much, it is well worth shopping around. Here are two example quotes from early 1996:

1. Professional teleworker

35 year old graphic designer working in a converted outbuilding in the garden of her house in postcode LE15 (small market town in Leicestershire) looking for insurance for £5,000 worth of PC equipment against fire, flood, theft, accidental damage and business interruption:

Insurer/broker	Policy	Cost per year	Excess	Notes
Burnett and Associates	Computer From Home	£184	£100	
Direct Line	Home Insurance	£62	£50	
Guardian Insurance	Blue Plan Home	£33	£50	no business interruption cover
Independent Insurance	HomeWorkers	£38.75	£50	as part of overall home policy
Mathews Comfort	Computer/ Office insurance	£76.87	£50	
S-Tech	Homebase	£125	£100	
Tolson Messenger	Home Business Insurance	£95	£100	

The variation is mainly due to some insurers not taking into account the location or business details which works against people in low risk areas of the country who do not see clients on their premises.

2. Office services

28-year old providing secretarial services from the spare bedroom of a semi-detached house in postcode SE26 (Sydenham, a medium-income outer London suburb) Clients frequently visit the premises. Wants to insure £2,000 of office equipment against fire, flood, theft and accidental damage:

Insurer/broker	Policy	Cost per year	Excess	Notes
Burnett and Associates	Working From Home	£274	£100	
Direct Line	Would not quote due to frequent client viists			
Guardian Insurance	Blue Plan Home	£45	£50	depends on frequency of client visits
Independent Insurance	HomeWorkers	£42	£50	as part of overall home policy
Mathews Comfort	Computer/ Office insurance	£76.87	£50	recommend additional cover at £25.62
S-Tech	Homebase	£125	£100	
Tolson Messenger	Home Business Insurance	£120	£100	

Several expressed concern about client visits – resolving doubts before taking out a policy would be vital in case a claim has to be made. Contact details for insurers dealing with home offices are listed at the back of this book. Tolson Messenger also produce a free guide to insurance for people working from home; (Ian Jones, Freephone 0800 374 246), and have recently added professional liability and mobile equipment modules to their specialist policy.

In Ireland, Hibernian Insurance operates a home office policy designed in conjunction with the Telework Ireland association.

Bibliography

Keep IT Safe and Secure (Security and Telecentres) *Date:* 1995
Author: Bill Murray, Small World Connections
Source: Send SAE with 47p stamp to KISS Booklets, WREN Telecottage, Stonleigh Park, Warwickshire CV8 2LZ
Comment: Part of 1994 security survey analysis, available free of charge to TCA members, subject to availability.

IT Security Breaches Survey Date: 1994
Source: National Computing Centre (NCC) Tel: 0161 228 6333 Fax: 0161 237 1558.

Employed or Self-Employed?
Source: Inland Revenue Ref: Booklet no. IR56, free of charge

Contacts and URLs

Inland Revenue self-assessment enquiry line Tel: 01345 161 514.

UK **Health and Safety Executive,** HSE, tel. 01422 892 345.

Data Protection Registrar Tel: 01625 535777.

Law Centres Federation Tel: 0171 387 8570.

Oldham Borough Council have revised their **planning guidelines** to take account of teleworkers. Their guidelines are available to other planning authorities. Contact Dave Hashdi, Oldham Borough Council Tel: 01619 114 154.

Peter Fowler is a solicitor with a niche practice in businesss-related legal matters and commercial property. Tel 01202 849 242, email p-fowler@lds.co.uk, website http://www.lds.co.uk/pw.html.

The following **insurance companies and brokers** offer home-office insurance:

IBM PC User Group Tel: 0181 863 1191 (runs computer insurance plan)
Tolson Messenger Tel: 0800 374 246

Health and Safety issues: Eilis Duggan, Ergonomics consultant Tel: +353 45 861148

Information on trade unions guidelines for teleworkers is available from the http://www.poptel.org.uk/ltc Labour Telematics Centre in Manchester

http://www.state.mn.us/ebranch/admin/ipo/giac/ is the site for a report on Minnesota Government Use of Copyright and Intellectual Property.

http://www.imprimatur.alcs.co.uk contains information on the Imprimatur project on copyright issues and you can register your interest in being involved in the Special Interest Groups currently being organised.

Email and online services

Exploring electronic mail and online services is probably the most difficult but also the most rewarding task there is for teleworkers. Using email and online services, teleworkers can receive and send work to their employers or clients, get technical support or product information, and "network" socially with other teleworkers. They can also create "virtual companies" – teams of people who can be located anywhere, and who come together to work on a project, but may never meet physically. Instead, they pass around the elements of the project by sending messages and computer files by email. Online services – information sources accessed by computer and modem – also offer many opportunities for teleworkers to create service businesses by obtaining information, reprocessing it and adding value, and then selling it to customers. There's a world of work, friends and fascinating information awaiting the determined explorer – all that's needed to get started is common sense and a little help.

What you need to get online?

The elements needed to get started are:

- computer
- modem
- software to control the modem
- telephone line
- access to the online service – often paid for via credit card subscription.

Computer and modem purchases are covered briefly in the *Teleworking Equipment* chapter. You need to check what ports (connections) your computer has free for attaching the modem. Modems usually attach to the serial ports on PCs, and to the port marked with a telephone icon on a Mac. The standard entry-level modem is now the 28.8 kbs or V.34 model. "Vfast" modems are also available which use software compression to achieve even higher transfer rates. However, local conditions such as the speed of the connection at the other end often restricts the practical speed at which Vfast modems can be used. Speed is measured in kilobits per second (kbs) or baud rates, which are not quite the same thing, but usually treated as identical and interchangeable units.

Modems are notoriously difficult to set up for beginners, and because of their low cost, computer sales operations are not keen on devoting time to modem technical support as the support costs erode profit margins. Some providers of online services also sell modems, and it is worth considering buying from this source because they have a vested interest in making sure your modem works properly so that you can spend money on their service. Do check that the modem has the correct connector for your telephone socket (British sockets differ from American, Irish and other European equipment). It is also illegal to connect a modem that is not BABT approved (green circular sticker) to British telephone networks.

Basic communications software to control the modem should be supplied with it. Alternatively it can often be obtained as shareware, such as Procomm for the PC, or RedRyder for the Macintosh. More sophisticated commercial software contains preset definitions for most modem models that ease setup problems, and may also have helpful scripting modules that allow users to automate their connection procedures. Increasingly, online service providers, like your local Internet service provider or systems such as CompuServe, provide their own Windows or Mac based "client" software to control the modem and navigate the service, which you receive as part of your membership of their service. These software packages normally allow you to select from a list of modem types as part of the installation process, and may not cater for some more esoteric models; it's worth sticking to the well known names when buying, or to ask your online service provider to recommend a modem. A separate class of software programmes are the "offline readers", packages that download your mail in bulk, minimising the time you spend connected to the online service, and so helping to keep your bills down.

If you encounter problems in getting connected and need to ask for technical support, make sure you have details of your modem make and model before you phone. You will also probably need to know five bits of jargon about the settings in your comms software if you can find them: the speed; whether it accepts 7 or 8 bit "data words"; how many "stop bits" are in use; whether the parity is set to none, even or odd, and whether error correction is in use. The middle three are often expressed as, for example, N-8-1 (no parity, eight bits, 1 stop bit). The fifth piece of information is more complex. Most error correction tools (where the modems at either end keep checking on the data) confirms to the MNP standard, which has several levels such as "MNP5". A good rule of thumb if in trouble is to try turning error correction off, at least temporarily. Fortunately you do not usually have to worry about any of this if you are using dedicated "client" software, such as the CompuServe Information Manager, which handles these minor details for you. If you have difficulties with your client software, it's probably because you've misunderstood some of the information the package is asking for, such as "domain name server" or have mistyped your password (the upper and lower case characters are important). Check these thoroughly before calling technical support.

You do not need a dedicated telephone line for your modem unless you plan heavy usage. Many people switch over their fax line for the short time they spend online. Most telephone connections should allow you to connect at 9600 baud minimum, and in many cases up to 28,800 baud. If you are only achieving low speeds, and your modem is functioning correctly, get your line quality checked.

When you succeed in contacting the service you want, you will often be asked to identify yourself (your user-id) and to give a password – a process known as "logging in", although increasingly these details are held in the comms software you use so that the logging in process is automated. In some circumstances you are allotted these passwords by the service; in others you choose them. It is strongly recommended that whenever you have control over the choice of password, you choose a random mixture of letters and numbers, upper and lower case. Do not use standard classics such as Fred, God, your middle name, your partner's name or a pet's name. Never reveal your password, but do give people your email address so that they can contact you.

What's out there in cyberspace?

Cyberspace is an overused term intended to express the "virtual" world to which computer communications give you access. The services that you can connect to once your modem and software are installed fall into four categories:

- bulletin boards
- specialist online information services such as newswires or databases
- proprietary online services that provide email, opportunities to "conference" with other users on topics of special interest, electronic shopping and often access to technical support for particular software packages such as America Online or CompuServe. Most proprietary services now also offer connection to the Internet and World Wide Web through their services.
- the Internet and the World Wide Webare both open-access to anyone who has a subscription with an Internet service provider.

Specialist bulletin boards (BBSs) are not covered in this book because they are being superseded by Internet functions such as Web pages and listservs. Computer magazines regularly give listings of BBSs, with details of their specialities, telephone numbers and the modem settings needed to access them.

To access a specialist online service such as the Dow Jones Newswires, or Dun & Bradstreet's credit ratings, you will usually need to contact the supplier and arrange contract details and payment methods. Then the service provider supplies you with an access telephone number or an Internet address, a user-id and a password. Some of these premium services offer free training on the basis that the more you know about the system, the more you will use it, and the more money you will spend.

Both standard Internet service providers, and proprietary services like America Online offer access to Internet email and the World Wide Web. Standard Internet service providers are usually cheaper than proprietary services, which provide a number of "bells and whistles" of use to teleworkers. Many experienced teleworkers have two or more email accounts to guard against one service being unavailable due to technical problems and preventing the teleworker from getting online, or else to take advantage of particular facilities such as conferencing.

Email: cheaper, faster, better?

Why send a message by email rather than by fax or post?

- it's cheaper. If you are using the email system efficiently, the cost should be in the region of 10p per message
- it's more flexible. As well as text messages, you can also send complete computer files such as spreadsheets or dtp layouts. If you are working collaboratively on a project it can be much more efficient to send a computer file that the person at the other end can use and edit themself, than to send a fax which can only be read and annotated
- it's faster. Email is much faster than traditional post, and many teleworkers deliver their finished projects by this method
- It's convenient. Email can be sent at any time. The recipient does not have to be there to receive the message – it is stored until they are ready to receive it. It is also easy to send group communications, and many systems offer facilities for creating customer emailing lists

Email has its disadvantages, but most are easily overcome. Peter Flynn of University College Cork explains: "Most email is restricted to the 96 printable characters of the ASCII character set (A-Z, a-z, 0-9 and punctuation). That means you cannot send binary files in their raw state. Binary files are those containing programs, accented characters, non-Latin alphabets, pictures or sounds. However, you can wrap, or encode the binary files, either using facilities provided in your email software, or by pre-processing the files with widely available programmes such as uuencode or binhex or MIME. The encoded file is converted to 7-bit ASCII, sent by email, and decoded back to binary format by the recipient. Many services can do this automatically. It is also important to remember that many email systems are not secure while in transit, so email is best regarded as an equivalent to a postcard, not a letter."

Many companies already use email for internal messaging over their local area networks (LANs). The most popular LAN based packages are Lotus cc:Mail (and Lotus Notes), Microsoft Mail and QuickMail. Internal email packages often flash up a message on the screen to announce newly-arrived mail so that the recipient can decide whether to read the message immediately or continue with their work and read their mail later. It is usually possible to create "gateways" from LAN based internal messaging systems to access external sites and recipients over the Internet. But however you are using e-mail within in an organization, it will need managing. Peter Flynn comments: "Someone has to be responsible for setting up and maintaining the software, for keeping an eye on queue lengths and disk space, and for handling wrongly addressed messages." Security is also a major issue for larger companies, usually handled through a number of access restriction techniques.

To use email well, it is important to take advantage of productivity tools such as computerised address books that avoid the need to keep retyping the recipient's email address, and computer based filing systems so that you read and reply to your mail in a structured fashion. Like traditional mail, email has its downsides. You will, in all probability, get some unsolicited messages from rather odd people, and you will also have a depressingly high stack of messages on your first day back from holiday. Email is only one aspect of online services, so it usually best to pick a service that includes email, rather than to go for an email only service, unless budgets are tight.

If you are planning to use email to send large files, you will need to obtain a compacting utility such as PKZIP for the PC or Stuffit for the Mac. These programmes squash your files, commonly to about half their original size. You can then email the "stuffed" or "zipped" file in half the time, and with any luck save half the phone call costs. The recipient usually needs to have the appropriate programme in order to unpack the file to its original size, such as PKUNZIP. Some compacting programmes, such as Compactor on the Mac, allow you to create "self-exploding" files – the recipient double clicks on the compacted file and it expands itself back to normal size. Just for added confusion, remember that zipped files are binary files, and therefore still need to be "uuencoded" or "MIMEd" before they can be sent over the Internet.

There are a number of different messaging formats, and it may be worthwhile talking to your customers and suppliers about the systems they use to ensure that your email system can connect to theirs. The most widely used standard is Internet email with any binary files sent as "uuencoded" attachments. But many large corporates and government departments use systems based on the secure X.400 messaging standard. X.400 systems can exchange messages with the Internet, or CompuServe, but when X.400 messages are routed via North American gateway computers there can be problems as these gateways may not recognise European X.400 country codes reliably.

There are also some applications where a direct modem-to-modem link or an ISDN link is cheaper than using an email system. For example, dtp files for a four-colour magazine can easily exceed 10Mb in size. Many typesetting bureaux offer their own high-speed direct links to keep the cost of transferring such large amounts of data down, often using the widespread 4-sight ISDN file transfer software. There are also a number of PC packages to assist with direct dial-up access to office LANs, some of which use the technique of "spoofing" to disconnect the computer from the ISDN line when it is not active (see Chapter 11, *Equipment*). Increased availability of ISDN telephone lines, which allow extremely fast connections from remote computers (typically 1–2 seconds to log on), are likely to increase the use of links using what is called "client-server" architecture. If you are involved in large scale file transfer, it is worth comparing prices between different modem speeds and ISDN lines to work out the cheapest methods for different file sizes. This will allow you to work out whether the additional installation and rental costs of ISDN are justified in your situation. The graph below prepared by John Kissane of Cork Internet Services can be used in conjunction with information on the costs for the services you are being charged in your location to aid your decision making.

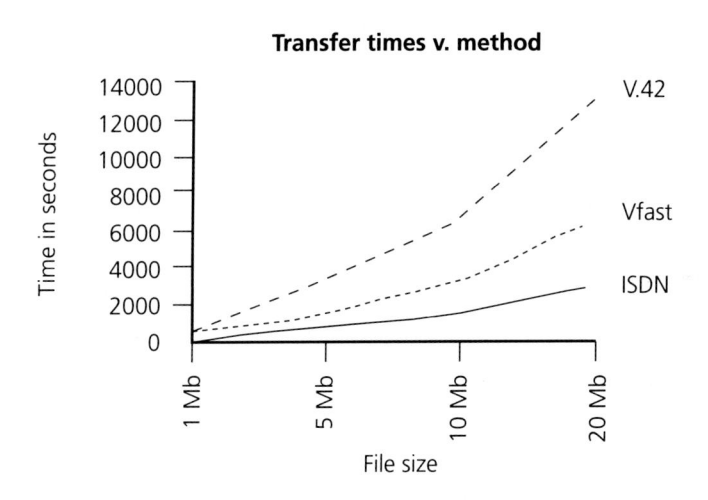

Transfer times v. method

(Time in seconds vs File size: V.42, Vfast, ISDN curves at 1 Mb, 5 Mb, 10 Mb, 20 Mb; y-axis 0 to 14000)

Online Services

This chapter covers the two most widely used services, CompuServe and the Internet, in some detail. Internet service is available from a wide variety of suppliers, some locally based, while others such as Pipex, Demon and BT operate nationally. Other services include CIX, an inexpensive system much favoured by journalists in Britain, and the Manchester Host, an imaginative service that links education, community and commercial groups in the greater Manchester region. New entrants to the proprietary online services market include America Online, Microsoft Network and Europe Online, as outlined in the summaries below, kindly provided by Freddie Dawkins of Media Training.

CompuServe

CompuServe is the second largest proprietary information service in the world, with approximately 4.2 million subscribers. CompuServe provides a worldwide network of access nodes for widespread local call access. The node network is of particular use to those who travel regularly (such as project managers) as it provides easy access from almost all parts of Europe.

CompuServe email can reach a wide variety of architectures including Internet and MHS. Internet access is also provided including the ability to subscribe to Internet mailing systems and to browse the World Wide Web, as well as facilities to build simple personal Web pages. However, Internet users cannot browse CompuServe unless they have a CompuServe account.

CompuServe forums cover areas of special interest from telework to vintage cars. Each forum has messaging sections where users can communicate and receive help from "sysops" (system operators), normally volunteers with expertise in the topic of the forum. There are also file libraries related to each message section. The forums can also host online conferencing where several users type onscreen and view each other's comments. Average telework use (say around 10 messages per day plus some Internet browsing or forum usage) would incur bills of about £7 a month.

Europe Online

Originally planned as a true European system (minimum three languages) in contrast to the perceived American bias of CompuServe, EOL has had a very disrupted history. Just prior to the planned launch date of July 1995, EOL abandoned its original bought-in technology from AT&T and decided to offer open Internet service. EOL is beginning to attract subscribers in the UK, Germany and Luxembourg (where it is headquartered). To date there are very few "content" areas and the operating software available to subscribers has not met the targetted service levels. The monthly cost to subscribers has been reduced to £3.95 and this includes 3 hours of online time each month. Additional hours are charged at £1.85.

Bertelsmann/America Online

The German publishing conglomerate Bertelsmann has joined forces with the world's biggest electronic information service AOL to provide online services in Europe, with a customer service centre located in Dublin. AOL has extensive experience in running subscriber driven services and has tried and proven operating software. Bertelsmann intends to make much of its content material from its magazines available electronically. The monthly cost will be in the region of £10 for basic subscription and full Internet access. The worldwide membership of AOL is now in excess of 5 million, but in tone it has previously been fairly American oriented. One strong application is homebanking, already implemented by many German banks.

Microsoft Network (MSN)

The initial launch of MSN, which took place through bundled Internet access supplied with copies of Windows 95, has so far not been the huge success predicted. MSN had virtually no information content or services available at its launch and was not available to non-US users. The company is now preparing a relaunch for summer 1996, with costs expected to be low at around £5/month for full Internet/WWW access. Potentially MSN could be the world's largest Internet service provider with up to one million subscribers within a year of relaunch. Estimated membership world-wide is some 500,000 at present.

First Class

First Class is an email and workgroup software system combined, which operates on a number of different platforms including Mac, Windows and Unix. In many ways it is a hybrid between old fashioned bulletin boards, with racks of modems for direct dial in, and a fully fledged online system. As well as simple point to point messaging, First Class integrates group conferencing with cross-platform person to person messaging. Workgroup features include graphical "office memo" message forms, simple name-based addressing and file attachments, and online cross-platform graphic viewing. Other First Class features are drag-and-drop mail filing in custom folders, auto expiry of old mail and comprehensive built-in message tracking (showing who read your mail, when, whether they forwarded or replied or downloaded any attached files). First Class servers can be attached to the Internet via gateways. The First Class client software is available for different languages such as French Canadian, German, Portugese, Spanish, Japanese, Swedish and others.

First Class is a fast spreading technology, but does not offer the breadth of access that CompuServe or the Internet provide, due to the implementation of the Internet gateways. The alternative is direct dial-ins, but for cross-border teams this can be prohibitively expensive. However, the rapidly growing popularity of First Class means it is a platform to be watched.

There are a number of issues that are common to all of these services, of which the most important is probably netiquette.

Netiquette

The general etiquette of online services (network etiquette or netiquette for short) is one of consideration for other users. Most breaches of netiquette are due to ignorance, rather than any desire to offend. A simple example would be that typing in capital letters is the online equivalent of SHOUTING. Instead _underscore_ words or *asterisk* phrases. Because online communications do not allow body language such as ironic grins and shoulder shrugs, some people use symbols such as <bg> for big grin and "emoticons" such as the smiley face :-) (look at it sideways) or {%—)) (crosseyed smiling man with hat and double chin) to embellish their messages . There are also a number of acronyms such as IMHO (in my humble opinion), AFAIK (as far as I know) and BTW (by the way) in common usage. Probably the most important piece of netiquette to understand is that blatant commercialism and marketing is disapproved of, especially on the Internet. Sales messages are likely to result in your being "flamed" – sent a hailstorm of rude replies. If you post sales material on CompuServe forums, you may be barred from that forum. Internet netiquette, particularly as the Internet was originally an academic and non-commercial network, is even stronger.

Help and how to ask for it

Help comes in various shapes and sizes on different systems. When you get stuck online in a proprietary system, typing ? or help will often provide you with a page of context-sensitive help. On the Internet, most World Wide Web pages will contain an email address to which you can send messages with queries or problems. Almost all proprietary online services have sysops or system operators, who look after the technical and administrative issues. Sysops also come in a range of colours. On some BBSs, the sysop will also be the person who operates the host computer, and sorts out connection problems. To contact the sysop, you usually send a message to the user-id "support". For internal email systems, the sysop will probably also be the network administrator, and in all likelihood also issues user-ids and passwords, as well as ensuring that old messages are deleted to free up storage space. On CompuServe each forum has several voluntary sysops, lead by a wizop (wizard sysop). CompuServe sysops check files that are uploaded, contribute to message threads and try to provide advice and support to forum users, so if you are not sure, ask a sysop. There is also a centralised CompuServe support staff. Another source of help are FAQ lists, or files of Frequently Asked Questions (and answers). On the Internet, an archive of FAQ files is held at rtfm.mit.edu. Internet sites have postmasters who deal with message failures and wrong addresses, and moderators who check the contents of some news groups. Each Internet site will usually have a technical bod who can help with problems but there are no standard sysop arrangements. The Internet has two useful newsgroups – news.newusers.questions and news.announce.newusers which may also have the answer to your problem.

Offline readers

Once you have done some initial exploring to orientate yourself to your on-line service, think about using an OLR or offline reader. Manually checking through forums or newsgroups for new messages or sendng and receiving your mail can be time-consuming and therefore expensive. An OLR is a programme that creates a customised, automatic script for all the actions you would take yourself, and performs them as quickly as possible. A typical script would check for waiting email, check for new forum/newsgroup messages in those areas you are interested in, and summarise any new library files. When you log on, the OLR zips through all the actions you have requested and logs off automatically – typically taking around two minutes for a simple script. You can then, at your leisure and without incurring further telephone charges, peruse the messages that have been downloaded onto your computer by the OLR. Once you have composed your replies and new messages, you send them as a batch using a second OLR script, again minimising connect time and keeping costs down.

Be properly addressed

Email addresses vary in format depending on the email system used by the person you are trying to send a message to. If the recipient is on the same system as you, normally you just address the message with their user-id. If you don't know their user-id, there is probably a command to help you find it. On CompuServe and many other proprietary systems, all you need to know is the person's name, and their location to find their user-id using the membership commands. On the Internet there is a "whois" command, but it can only find people who have chosen to register their identity on that particular server. An Internet X.500 "white pages" directory is under development by InterNIC (at ds.internic.net). Fortunately, any message you receive by email will contain the sender's address, and normally you just "reply" to the message – your software will pick up the address from the original message automatically without you having to worry about formats.

When it comes to sending messages to someone on another, linked system, you often have to give an Internet address format as the Internet frequently routes the message. This is why, if you are putting an email address on business communications, it is wise to use the Internet format. X.400 address formats are not dealt with in detail here for reasons of space. However, if you are in difficulties you can "convert" Internet to X.400 addresses and vice versa using the WEP (well-known entry programme) available via telnet at wep.ucd.ie and other Internet hosts if needed.

To message Internet user fbloggs on the Greennet Internet host (gn.apc.org) from elsewhere on the Internet:
fbloggs@gn.apc.org

To message Internet user fbloggs on the Greennet Internet host from CompuServe:
INTERNET:fbloggs@gn.apc.org

To message Fred Bloggs, CompuServe user-id 100001,1001 from the Internet:
100001.1001@compuserve.com

To message CIX user flbloggs from the Internet:
fbloggs@cix.compulink.com

To message CIX user fbloggs from CompuServe:
INTERNET:fbloggs@cix.compulink.com

To message Fred Bloggs on an IBM X.400 mail system in Ireland from the Internet:
C=IE;A=IBMX400;P=IBMMAIL;S=BLOGGS;G=FRED

Handling junk email

The following information was kindly provided by Gerald Abrahamson on the Telework Europa forum. The obvious method of stopping junk email is to politely ask the sender to stop. Unfortunately, because junk email arouses such hatred on the Internet, usually the junk emailer will have given an invalid return address to prevent furious recipients "bombing" them back with a hailstorm of email insults. Another sneaky trick of the junk emailer is to force you to read their message in order to find out how to turn it off. If this happens to you, check the domain of the junk emailer (the bit of the address after the @ sign) and send a message to the postmaster (e.g. to postmaster@xxx.yyy to the effect that you cannot get hold of the the junk emailer and you would like their assistance in getting your name removed from their mailing list. Almost all Internet sites have a postmaster. However, this may also bounce, by which time steam will be coming out of your ears.

The next step is to use the WHOIS command to find out who really is the emailer. Log in using a standard text interface to your Internet service provider (not a web browser), and give the command:

WHOIS xxx.yyy

If the junk emailer has registered themself on the Internet X.500 directory, you will then get the name, address, telephone number and so on of the company or person owning the domain name. Most junk emailers are based in the US, in which case you can now get your revenge. Send a notice based on the following:

NOTICE REGARDING UNSOLICITED EMAIL

Please remove my personal email address from your mailing list. If your message was intended as advertising, it may be in violation of federal law (Telephone Consumer Protection Act of 1991), and collateral Code of Federal Regulations (47 CFR 64.1200).

Legal notice:

The Telephone Consumer Protection Act of 1991 (TCPA) and collateral Code of Federal Regulations (47 CFR 64.1200) define an unsolicited advertisement sent via fax as the equivalent same sent by email. To wit, if your computer has:

– a modem connected to a regular telephone line and

– a printer connected to that computer

unsolicited advertising sent via email to that equipment is considered (by definition of law) as sent to a fax. The TCPA allows a private right of action against the sender of such unsolicitied advertisinig. The recipient can sue for $500, or actual damages, whichever is the greater.

CompuServe – on balance, the tops

The CompuServe Information Service is known as CIS in short and is the easiest online service to understand and use effectively for telework, though not necessarily the cheapest. Increased competition sees CIS regularly winding prices down and functionality up. CIS is an American system based in Ohio. It is strongly represented in Britain and Germany, but less so in the rest of Europe.

When you join CIS, the first thing to do is to find out whether there is a node (connection point) in your local call charge area so that you can keep your telephone charges to the minimum. In Britain many users log on via BT's Dialplus nodes to keep connection charges low. It is also possible to log in via your local Internet service provider, using the Compuserve Internet Dialler software, but this means you will have two online subscriptions – one for CompuServe and one for Internet – which seems like overkill but can provide a cheaper alternative if you have no node within your local call charge area. CIS only accepts payment by credit, or debit card from individual members, but business accounts can pay using a standard invoicing system. Online charges are around £6 per hour but may decrease again. Charges levied by CIS depend on the hour of the day (NB their cheap rate does not begin until 7 pm), and on whether you are using "basic" services such as email, or "extended" services, for example some of the technical support forums or scientific research paper services. CIS also provides shopping services and information on stocks and shares and weather forecasts. It is recommended that you use these sparingly to begin with until you have received your first bill.

As well as email, CIS offers forums. These are special interest areas on topics ranging from rock music to the Apple PowerPC. Each forum has a messaging area divided into a number of sections. Each section covers a topic of interest to the forum members, and contains a number of message "threads". Any forum member can start a thread by leaving a message in the appropriate section. Other forum members read the threads, and chip in with their comments or advice.

Threads can seem a little disjointed when you first start reading them, because they consist of a group of interconnected messages, and if you missed the beginning of the thread they can be confusing. Also, someone can read a thread that is a week old, and decide to reply to one of the first messages in the thread – threads are not time sequenced like a spoken conversation. Once you get used to them, they are a fascinating source of information and comment on many different subjects. To add your comment to the thread, just reply to a forum message – the CIS software will notice that it is a forum message, not private email, and route it accordingly.

Each forum section has an associated library, where members of the forum leave files that can be retrieved by anyone who is interested. The files are checked by the forum sysops before they are made publicly available, to ensure that they are virus-free, that they do not contain illegal or defamatory matter, and to check that the file matches its description (e.g. if it is described as a Microsoft Word file, that it can be read in Microsoft Word). Library files are usually zipped ASCII format, but can be in proprietary graphics formats – the library description will tell you the size of the file and its format before you choose to download it.

The forum that is likely to be of most interest to teleworkers is the Telework Europa Forum (GO TWEURO). This forum was started as part of an EU initiative to promote teleworking, but it now largely run by and for individual teleworkers and members of the various European teleworking associations. It also contains a lot of information about the EU's ACTS and TAP programmes (see Chapter 1, *Overview*).

You can "conference" or chat interactively with anyone else who is logged into the same forum at the same time. Telework Europa sysop Kevin Tea explains: "If you think of a forum as a town, the message section is where the townsfolk meet and greet each other daily. The library is like – well, a library, and the conference section is like the town hall where people meet formally to discuss a specific topic, although informal, non-agenda led conferences can be held. Conferences have not taken off much in Europe because of the high cost of access compared to the US, where local calls are often free."

CompuServe subscribers can create their own World Wide Web pages (see below) using Home Page Wizard software which can be downloaded from CompuServe. However, to date CompuServe has not adopted the worldwide HTML standard for browsing its system, opting instead to update its servers using proprietary "NISA" software. There have been problems in the implementation of this software, and speculation is rife that eventually CompuServe will move to HTML structures. In particular, although CompuServe forums offer limited search commends for files in forum libraries, there is no equivalent to the powerful search engines such as WAIS available on most Internet sites which help users to find what they want by searching every file and listing those relating to the user enquiry by their level of relevance.

The Internet is where it's at...

The Internet is a global network of computer networks. There are estimated to be 2.2m computer "hosts" on the Internet, with about 25 million users in 137 countries. The Internet was originally a US government funded academic network, and still has a mild academic flavour, but is rapidly becoming commercially minded with much research targeted at providing secure methods of payment for services and goods bought online.

Most teleworkers link to the Internet via dial-up links such as those provided by Demon and Pipex in Britain, or Ireland Online and Indigo in Ireland. Telephone companies have also started to move into the market – BT offers an Internet service with local charge dial nodes throughout the country. For these services you pay a joining fee and a monthly sum and are given a user-id and password on a computer connected to the Internet. This allows you to log in and send and receive email, and to browse the World Wide Web. Some service providers offer discounted email only accounts which do not provide graphical access to the Web. If you want to have your own Web pages to market your services, you will normally pay a separate fee to "rent" space on a Web server for your pages, usually at a rate dependent on how much space your pages take up.

Mailing lists and listservs

The Internet has a vast number of mailing lists on subjects of special interest. As with most Internet functions, the difficulty is finding what you want in the first place. A giant "list of lists" is maintained which you are unlikely to need to download yourself – your Internet host will probably have a copy that you can peruse. Once you have the name of the list, and the address of the computer that administrates the list, you can subscribe automatically using the ingenious listserv command. You send an email to listserv@address.of.host containing one line:

subscribe name-of-list yourname

The listserv programme will add you to that mailing list and send you information about the different address where you can send your contributions to the mailing. From then on, you receive all messages that are sent to that mailing list – so check you also know how to "unsubscribe" and how to "nomail" while you are on holiday. Do remember that the address for subscription commands is different to that for contributions to the mailing list.

Usenet News – world's largest BBS

Mailing lists and newsgroups are easy to confuse at first. Internet newsgroups are a subset of Usenet News – a set of machines that exchange articles tagged with universally recognised newsgroup labels. There are over 3000 groups and Usenet receives tens of megabytes of postings each day. Each machine collects all the newsgroups each day and allows you to download only those groups that interest you. To get news, you must first subscribe to newsgroups using a newsreader utility, which is usually supplied by your Internet service provider. The same utility should allow you to browse through the groups to find the ones you want to subscribe to. Any subscriber can contribute to a newsgroup, either by replying with mail to the author, or by "following up" to continue the newsgroup messages. As well as the publicly available newsgroups, there are others, such as Clarinet, which are commercial services; your host must have a contract with Clarinet before they will be available. The main newsgroup categories are:

comp computer science, hardware, software
news news networks and software
rec recreational activities, arts, hobbies
sci scientific research and applications, including some social sciences.
soc social issues
talk discussion on controversial topics
misc all the rest – including the useful misc.jobs and misc.forsale
alt alternative ways of looking at things. Includes many bizarre topics. Unregulated
biz discussions related to business. Allows advertising, unlike many other sections of the Internet
k12 teachers, students, topics related to the "kindergarten through twelve" age group.

How to get and put files – worldwide

"Anonymous ftp" allows Internet hosts to devote part of their disk space to public files in a way that doesn't require everyone who wants a file to have a user-id and password. You will need a piece of "ftp client software" to do this – many are available on the Internet, such as the public domain package winftp.exe. Normally you log in to the host computer by issuing the command

ftp somewhere.domain

eg ftp gn.apc.org. When you are connected, an information line will appear, and then you can log in with the user-id anonymous. Netiquette requires that you give your email address as the password. Once connected, you use the dir and cd commands to move around the host computer. When you find the file you want, first be sure whether it is an.ascii or a binary file. Tell the ftp software the file type by giving the command binary, or ascii as appropriate. Then:

get filename

Alternatively, if you are contributing a file to the host computer you "put filename".

The speed of file transfer depends on the speed of the links between the user and host, and on the number of people simultaneously ftp-ing. Netiquette suggests that you try to ftp outside normal business hours, to avoid slow speeds for other users.

The World Wide Web

The World Wide Web (commonly abbreviated to WWW) is a distributed information source accessible from anywhere on the Internet via "HTML browsers" such as the ubiquitous Netscape Navigator. It is much harder to describe than it is to use... It consists of files located on Internet hosts around the world. Each file looks like a page of text with certain words highlighted. These highlights are hypertext links – points which, if you click on them, jump you to another page of information. The links are often to pages located somewhere else entirely on another computer. The beauty of WWW is that it hides the confusing fundamentals of the Internet, providing a standard look so that all you need to worry about is where you want to go and what you want to find. You don't need to worry about where in the world the information is or about logging in and out from different Internet host computers – you just ask your Web browser to save the interesting file you've found on your computer, or to print it, and the software does all the rest. A good way to understand how the hypertext system works is to start your WWW browser and give the help command, which is usually held as hypertext.

For the technically minded, WWW files are written in HTML, a hypertext application of the ISO standard SGML text description language. Web browser software on the user's computer interprets the HTML commands to create a graphical display of the pages. Web pages can contain graphics in GIF or JPEG formats as well as text, and even (though these are not widespread) audio and video clips. The hypertext links are made by using URLs, or Uniform Resource Locators, which are a unique form of address for every page of WWW information on the Internet. You can recognise URLs, often seen at the end of press articles, by the initial characters http://www.

Creating Web pages

Most people create Web pages either for personal "hobby" interest, or to market a service or product. The Web has been the focus of a great deal of marketing activity because it is cheaper than conventional print advertising or direct mail, and the content of the "advert" can be altered at any time, although it is still extremely hard to measure the response to Web advertising, or "cost per hit". Many Web sites are really PR activities rather than conventional marketing tools. However, Web users are likely to be young, affluent and educated, as well as being keen on "teletrading" over online systems, so they represent an excellent audience for certain products. But it is important not to get carried away by the hype: only a small proportion of the world's business customers are on the Internet at all, and of the 40-odd million Internet subscribers worldwide, only about 10–15% currently have access to the Web – most use email only. Also many people using 14,400 baud modems find the Web so slow as to be almost unusable unless they choose not to see the complex graphics provided on many sites by turning off graphic viewing in their Web browser. Congestion is a problem at many popular sites.

Web pages are normally "hosted" by an Internet service provider – they have to be available 24 hours a day, so renting space on existing servers is usually cheaper than setting up your own. Many providers will also design pages for you if you don't want to learn to use HTML authoring tools or don't have graphic design and editing skills. HTML itself can look intimidating, but is actually a clear and well structured language. It does have strict rules, however, so most people use an authoring package which allows you to specify the structure of the document (heading levels, graphics and so on), and then inserts the correct codes to produce the desired effect, checking for adherence to the rules as it goes along. Web authoring tools include:

HTML Writer, available at ftp://lal.cs.byu.edu/pub/www/tools/hw9b4all.zip
HoTMetaL Pro, available at http://gatekeeper.dec.com:/pub/net/infosys/NCSA/Web/html/hotmetal
HTML Assistant, available from http://cs.dal.ca/ftp/htm/asst/htmlafaq.html
Microsoft Word has an add-on called Internet Assistant, available from http://www.microsoft.com for converting Word files to HTML.
Hot Dog Pro is available at http://www.sausage.com.
WebEdit by Ken Nesbitt is available at http://www.nesbitt.com

---

WWW browser software

The latest version of Netscape is available at:

http://home.netscape.com/comprod/products/navigator/version_3.0/index.html

or ftp.mcom.com/netscape, with the Mac version at ftp.mcom.com or ftp.demon.co.uk/pub/mac/,,,/macweb

The original NCSA Mosaic software can be found at ftp.ncsa.uiuc.edu

Cello is available from ftp.law.cornell.edu/pub/LII/Cello.cello.zip

Websurfer can be found at ftp.netmanage.com

InternetWorks Lite is at ftp.booklink.com/lite

IBM OS/2 Warp users can get Web Explorer from ftpq1.ny.us.ibm.net

CompuServe users can download the Home Page Wizard from CompuServe to create their own pages, an approach now being taken up by a number of local Internet service providers in order to provide customers with very basic pages. This kind of software is not appropriate for creating complex sites with sophisticated graphic design.

For Mac users, Adobe has produced a set of commercially available packages including PageMill for Web authoring and ScreenSaver for converting existing Postscript graphics and photo scans to the correct formats for the Web.

When designing Web pages, it is important to keep information short and well structured, and not to go overboard with complex graphics which slow down browsing for the user. Graphics should be interlaced - a version of the GIF and JPEG formats which allows a browser to quickly sketch out the graphic on the page while it is waiting for the rest of the information from the host. This is less frustrating for the user than watching a slow counter ticking off the bytes as a graphic is downloaded. Use the facility of hypertext – instead of creating very long pages, make small pages with logical links that users can select to get more information on a particular topic.

The Web also provides facilities to create online forms for collecting feedback from users. The information in these forms has to be processed on the computer where the Web pages are hosted, so if you want to use forms you will need to create what is known as a "cgi script" to process the form information. If you do not have experience with graphics, information provision, cgi scripting and HTML, but need to create a complex site, then you should consider paying a consultant to prepare the pages for you.

Once you have created your pages, you need to signpost them so that people can find you. The cheap but time consuming way to do this involves visiting each catalogue site and filling in a request form. Alternatively, use Postmaster, a commercial service which will post your details to a variety of sites (http://www.netcreations.com/postmaster/postmaster2.html). Postmaster offers one free trial posting to 24 sites, but further postings cost around $500.

Finding what you want on the Web

How do you find the information you want? A common criticism of the Internet used to be that it was like being dumped in the computer equivalent of the British Library, but without a catalogue. To find what you want on the vast, global network of Internet servers, you will need to use an online catalogue by browsing to a catalogue site and entering a query. The most widely used catalogue is Digital's Altavista at http://www.altavista.digital.com, because it offers both simple and complex searching tools. An Altavista search will give a summary of pages and their URLs, plus sophisticated search functions including Boolean, proximity, wildcards and include/exclude tools. You can use Altavista to find the other major catalogues such as Excite (http://www.excite.com), Infoseek Guide (http://www.infoseek.com), Inktomi, Internet Search, Lycos (http://lycos.cs.cmu.edu), Open Text, WebCrawler, World Wide Web Worm and Yahoo (http://www.yahoo.com) – most people develop a "favourite" amongst these.

IRC – wild chatter on the Internet

Chatting on the Internet (similar to conferencing on CompuServe) is carried out using Internet Relay Chat. Once you are in IRC, commands begin with a / but everything else you type is broadcast. To join a chat, type /join channel name. Internet chats are unmoderated, and can be chaotic, but they are very useful for emergency technical support on a Sunday afternoon. The Finger command on the Internet tells you who else is logged in for chatting

Acknowledgements

Peter Flynn, Academic Computing Manager, University College Cork. Internet: pflynn@curia.ucc.ie

Kevin Tea, sysop on the Telework Europa forum. CompuServe 100136,1426.

Freddie Dawkins, Media Training, Premier House, 77 Oxcord Street London W1R 1RB Tel: 0181 500 8141 Fax: 0181 5014818 Email: 70624.557@compuserve.com

Bibliography

Digital Business – Surviving and Thriving in an Online World   Date: 1996
Source: Hodder & Staughton Ref: ISBN 0–340–66659–5

Digital Money – the New Era of Internet Commerce   Date: 1996
Authors: Daniel C. Lynch and Leslie Lundqvist
Source: John Wiley & sons Inc. Ref: ISBN 0–471–14178–X

Internet Business to Business Directory   Date: 1996
Authors: Sandra Eddy, Michael M. Swertfager, Margaret M.E. Cusick
Source: Sybex Ref: ISBN 0–7821–1751–1

The New Internet Business Book   Date: 1996
Authors: Jill H. Ellsworth and Matthew V. Ellsworth
Source: John Wiley & Sons Ref: ISBN 0–471–14160–7

Contacts

BT's Internet service, aimed at small businesses and home users, costs £20 inc VAT to join (although this fee is waived for subscribers joining before August 1996), followed by £15/month inc VAT thereafter. Tel: 0800 800 001

CompuServe Information Service (CIS) 1 Redcliff Street, PO Box 676 Bristol BS99 1YN Tel: Freefone 0800 289378 or 0272 760680.

Demon Systems Limited (commercial Internet access) 42 Hendon Lane, London N3 1TT. Tel: 081 349 0063 Fax: 081 349 0309.

Pipex (commercial Internet access) 216 Cambridge Science Park, Cambridge CB4 4WA Tel: 0500 4-PIPEX (474739) Fax: 01438 311100 Email: sales@dial.pipex.com

Ireland On-line (commercial Internet access) 87 Amiens Street, Dublin 1 Tel: 01 855 1739 Email: info@iol.ie

Internet Services Ireland (incorporating Ieunet) 35a Westland Square, Pearse St, Dublin 2 Tel: +353 1 679 0832 Fax: +353 1 670 8118 Email: info@isi.ie

Teleworking Europa Forum: GO TWEURO on CompuServe. The Wizop for the forum is TCA board member Paddy Moindrot. Tel and Fax: 0691 648887. CompuServe: 100145,3363. Also on the Internet at http://www.tweuro.com

European Electronic Messaging Association (association for large organizations involved in messaging) Pastoral House, Inkberrow, Worcestershire WR7 4EL. Tel: 0386 793 028 Email: eemaoffice@attmail.com Web: http://www.eema.org/eemahq

Greenet (Internet access specialising in community groups) 23 Bevenden Street, London N1 6BH. Tel: 071 608 3040 Fax: 071 253 0801.Email: support@gn.apc.org

Dow Jones News Service, Winchmore House 12–15 Fetter Lane London EC4A 1BR Tel: 071 832 9575 Fax: 071 832 9861

For the total technophobe, it is possible to have an email address which you don't have to bother logging into. A company called AWS will receive your email for you and fax it to wherever you are. 34 Filey Road, Reading RG1 3QG Tel: 0118 962 2123 Fax: 0118 962 2230 Email: admin@awsl.compulink.co.uk. Some telecottages also provide similar services.

http://www.RACE.analysys.co.uk This is the excellent server operated by British telecoms consultancy Analysys. It contains information on the EU's RACE and ACTS programmes. Do not miss the SONAH section which gives succinct, practical useful summaries of the findings of several EU projects.

http://www.teleadapt.com is the address of a company which supplies adaptors and kits for linking up to collect your email or browse the web anywhere in the world.

http://www.volksware.com/mobilis is the address for Mobilis: the mobile computing lifestyle magazine.

http://www.netcreations.com/postmaster is a good, free way to register your Web Pages at a dozen or more of the most popular search engines.

Quality for Teleworkers

Why do I need quality management?

Quality management, if implemented well, should make your company more efficient and also more responsive to customers, leading to greater customer satisfaction and increased sales. Many large companies will no longer deal with small suppliers who do not have a quality standard, so obtaining one can give you more sales opportunities.

However, teleworking companies should heed the words of Jacques McMillan, head of the European Commission department in charge of quality policy and certification for telematics networks and systems: "There are many enterprises going bust where the last flag as they go under is their [quality] certificate. I am trying to put it back in perspective so those companies that actually need it should go for it and those that don't shouldn't. It should not be thrust down the throats of small and medium-sized companies." Other critics say quality certification is expensive, bureaucratic and difficult to set up and maintain, and that companies mistakenly see certification as an end in itself, rather than as a step towards improving quality. Poorly implemented systems often consist of documenting the existing procedures of a company, and then checking that those procedures are adhered to – a uniform process leading to uniformly awful products.

Indeed, Stephen Simmons of consultancy Cornix believes that for small businesses, quality is simply a marketing issue – you need to demonstrate the will and ability to comply with customer requirements – a process that only rarely involves third party certification. Stephen also thinks quality consultancy is often "damagingly expensive". However, Lesley Carr of People, Processes and Systems disagrees: "If you work with a consultant who has the right attitude towards minimising bureaucracy, achieving certification does not have to be painful".

Either way, improving internal procedures should result in better efficiency, improved customer service and improved customer satisfaction. Using a documented quality system helps the different functions of your business to work together, and often results in considerable savings through preventing inadvertent mistakes. Bear in mind that an inappropriate system can become a bureaucratic overload that is particularly expensive for small businesses to maintain. Such systems stifle flexibility and innovation, so it is important to monitor the effectiveness of the system itself.

What is quality management?

Lesley Carr gives the following advice: "Quality management is consistently good business practice, and should be an integral part of working practices, not something 'bolted on'."

- a quality product or service is one that consistently satisfies the customer's requirements
- quality is right first time, on time, every time
- quality is achieving fitness for purpose at an economic cost.

While quality is a means of making sure your product or service is right for your customer, the term "total quality" describes a management philosophy that harnesses everyone's efforts to achieve continuous improvement and cost reductions.

What are the quality standards?

Achieving a quality standard involves producing a documented quality system that provides a consistent way of controlling working procedures. The internationally accepted quality standards, known as the ISO9000 series, were issued in 1994 and replace the previous British Standard (BS) 5750 standard. The ISO standards comprise a number of model quality systems together with guidance notes indicating which quality system is applicable to what situation. Most teleworking businesses will fall under ISO9002 except for those involving design activities that will need to take note of the design control requirements of ISO 9001:1994.

What's involved in registration?

Establishing a quality sytem

The steps needed to begin a quality system are fairly straight forward:

- decide that you have the motivation to improve your internal work procedures and customer service levels. Think about whether to involve a consultant now or later...
- obtain a copy of the standard (ISO9002 in most cases)
- analyse your current working procedures and document them
- identify which aspects of your service are most important to your customers (e.g. timeliness, accuracy, responsiveness)
- check the written procedures with all concerned for consistency
- get feedback and look at where improvements can be made
- work out ways of measuring how you are performing
- Formulate improvement objectives and targets
- Check that everyone is using the written procedures, and continue to ask for contributions towards improvement

At this stage you will probably need some consultancy help or advice in interpreting the standard and producing a formal documented quality system to meet the requirements, because the standards are extremely complex and hard to interpret.

Obtaining registration

When the quality system is in place to the consultant's satisfaction and has been working for a month or two, contact the appropriate certification body. It is a good idea to contact two or three and compare their costs and registration processes. They will visit your business and assess your quality system. Be aware that it is usually expected that you will operate the quality system for about four months before any certification is offered. If the certification body is satisfied both that the quality system complies with the standard, and that it is being used comprehensively within your business, you will be awarded a certificate. You can then use the certificate and the registered company logo in marketing activities. After registration, the certification body returns periodically (usually once a year) to ensure the quality system is up to date and in use. There is normally an annual fee to be paid for continued registration.

Is quality management different for teleworkers?

In a standard industrial quality system, a company controls its subcontractors or suppliers by insisting that they stick to specified contracts. Teleworking is usually a much closer and more delicate relationship than that between an off-site supplier and purchaser, so the teleworker needs to put a lot more effort into integrating with the client company's quality system.

Simon Burke of ISO9001 registered company Intermec Ireland agrees that ISO9000 is probably inapplicable to individual teleworkers or very small businesses of less than five people. "The effort involved and the corresponding documentation of the business processes could be enough to kill the business." Instead, Simon recommends making sure you can comply with your client's vendor assessment procedures. "A company like ours divides its purchases of goods and services into "primary" items that can affect the quality of our own products and services, such as software developments. Other purchases are "secondary", such as office stationery and consumables. All primary goods and services must be purchased from other companies that are listed on an internal "Qualified Vendor List". This list is compiled by the company, usually on the basis of a quality related questionnaire, sometimes called a "Vendor Appraisal Form". This must be completed prior to trade between the two companies. If the vendor is ISO9000 registered then there is no problem. If not, samples of goods or services will be tested, or they will be accepted through a reputable third party recommendation. A vendor is normally on the list only for a given product or service. If a vendor is qualified to supply one item, it does not qualify them to supply everything. So for small teleworking businesses, the best advice may be to be aware of your client's vendor assessment forms and make sure you can comply with their quality system."

Teleworking consultancy Cornix has prepared a code of conduct for Devon & Cornwall TEC that gives a good starting point for teleworkers:

The Telnet code of conduct

(© Devon & Cornwall TEC)

1. To carry out the assignment which the teleworker has undertaken diligently, conscientiously and with proper regard for the client's interests.
2. To apply good management and quality assurance practices to all teleworking assignments.
3. To agree with the client a written statement which clearly defines the objectives and scope of the proposed work, the timescale and fee basis, and also where necessary to agree in writing any subsequent revision.
4. To respect all information concerning the client's business as strictly confidential and not to disclose or permit the disclosure of any such information without the client's specific prior permission.
5. To ensure that all property, data, text and other materials belonging to the client and held by the teleworker are stored in a secure location when not in use and handled appropriately when in use.
6. To only accept such assignments for which the teleworker is suitably qualified and/or experienced to carry out to a high standard.
7. To refrain from undertaking any assignment which would result in a conflict of interest and to disclose to the client any financial or personal interest which may influence the work carried out for the client in any way.
8. To ensure that all hardware and software used by the teleworker is used only in connection with the teleworker's professional activities, is properly maintained and that all reasonable care is taken to ensure that it is free from defects.

9. To ensure that the teleworker's knowledge and skills are kept up-to-date, where necessary through obtaining appropriate training and professional development.

What activities do the standards cover?

Contractual relationships
(© Devon & Cornwall TEC)

Agreed terms and conditions for sales should be implemented. There should be a process for defining the customer's requirements, and dealing with any conflicts or changes to the requirements. Ensure that your business can satisfy its contractual obligations for each sale. Cornix makes the following recommendations for a minimum teleworking contract:

1. Include identities and contact addresses of both purchaser and supplier, and if either is a corporate body, the names of the individuals concerned.
2. Describe in general terms the work to be carried out, its purpose and scope.
3. Specify the payment for the work, and whether VAT will be applicable.
4. Specify a timetable for both the work, and payment for the work.
5. Describe clearly the proposals for confidentiality and security of the work and its Data Protection Act status.
6. Define the ownership of any resulting copyright and intellectual property rights, if appropriate.
7. Arrangements for loan or supply of equipment, where applicable, including insurance arrangements, should be listed.
8. Specify arrangements in the event of illness, incapacity, holidays etc. and for any consequent subcontracting, if permitted.
9. If the workload exceeds 21 hours per week, and is an exclusive use of the teleworker full time, then arrangements for PAYE and NI deductions should be made as in these circumstances, the teleworker may be classified as an employee for the duration of the work.
10. Refer to the quality assurance system to be used, if any.
11. Where group working is involved, the identity of the individual responsible for quality within the group should be specified.

Lesley Carr lists other areas covered by quality standards:

Suppliers and purchases
All your suppliers should be vetted for the quality of the product or service which they supply to you. Suppliers with bad track records should be dropped. Purchase requirements need to be clearly laid out to avoid misunderstandings.

Production and process control
You will need a method of checking, inspecting and rectifying the product or service while it is being produced to ensure it meets customer requirements. At the end of the production, any goods or services that are not up to scratch must be identified and dealt with accordingly. The quality system should allow the status of individual products or jobs to be easily traced or identified.

Handling and storage
Any items handled by your business should be stored, packaged and delivered to the customer in a way which protects them from damage, deterioration, loss or misuse.

Keeping records
The precise records needed for every business transaction or procedure should be specified. They should be identified, comprehensive, secure and accessible to all who need them. The records should be retained for an agreed time period and then archived or destroyed.

Financial affairs
There should be adequate control over aspects of finance that relate to the customer, such as invoice production.

Training and competency
Each member of staff should get the correct level of training, and should have the appropriate qualifications for the tasks they carry out. Records of training given should be kept.

Coping with complaints
A recognised procedure for dealing with complaints should be implemented to resolve problems.

Malcolm Lake of Effective Quality Management adds:

Management reviews and audits
A regular and systematic review by the management of the business to check whether the quality system is working well, and to monitor business performance, training needs etc.

Statements of responsibilities
A clearly defined statement of management/job responsibilities. Even if the business is operated very flexibly, the owner/manager will have different responsibilities from his or her assistants.

Corrective actions
A procedure for determining what to do when a problem occurs: ways of enabling the problem to be sorted out quickly and effectively, and of ensuring that it does not happen again.

Case studies

Antur Teifi – solving a quality problem

Mike Jones, Quality Officer for Antur Teifi, an organization located on 6 sites with 30 staff that includes a well-equipped Telematics Centre, sums up the quality process: "It should be a bottom up process – you need to keep your existing good practices. You have to ensure everybody owns the quality process – i.e. involve those who have to use it. Then write it down. I think anyone who is thinking about going for a quality standard needs to ask themselves the following questions:

1. Do we really need quality control?
2. Can we afford its costs?
3. Are we really committed to the work needed to maintain the system?
4. Do our customers expect us to operate to an ISO9000 standard?

If you decide to go ahead, the next step is to decide whether you are going to use a consultant, or whether you will try to "DIY" your quality system. Either way, the golden rules are:

1. Document what you do
2. Do what you have documented
3. Check that you are doing it

It took Antur Teifi 18 months to become certificated, but smaller organisations should be able to do it on a much shorter timescale. During our certification, we encountered a problem with a contract we had taken on from the Employment Department. The contract involved training for long-term unemployed people that culminated in each participant having their CV typed by our Telematics Centre. Within 4 days of the end of the course, the Jobcentre should receive ten correct copies of each CV. For months there were problems, ranging from late delivery of CVs to incorrect CVs, and inconsistencies in the CV format. When I initially investigated the problem, everyone involved blamed everyone else for the errors. The tutors thought the typists were incapable of the work. The typists believed the tutors did not care about their work because of the poor quality of the manuscript CVs.

We sat down and discussed the problem without apportioning blame, and the problem was tracked back to the lack of a procedure that everyone understood, that could be owned by everyone, checked independently, and where if anyone did not adhere to the procedure, non-conformance would be evident. The next step was to write down the problems and examine their causes rather than their symptoms. The tables and flow chart below show how we solved the problem and documented it for our quality system."

Problem	Reason/cause	Answer
Late delivery of CVs	• Scripts not arriving at Telematics Centre on time for typing	Scripts to be posted 1st class to Telematics Centre on same evening as course is held
	• No-one available to do the typing	A minimum of 3 days notice to be given to the Telematics Centre of the arrival of scripts
	• Some scripts unreadable	CV details to be printed by trainees and checked by the tutor for accuracy
Incorrect CVs	• Scripts unreadable	All CVs to be checked by a second person after typing and only typists with good skills to be used
		Trainees to print rather than write details
		Tutor to check script prior to despatch to Telematics Centre
		All CVs to be checked by another person before leaving Telematics Centre
Inconsistencies in format	• No trainee or tutor had a format by which a standard could be set	Each trainee to fill a standard form with CV details

This analysis was used to draw up the following quality system documentation.

Using form 116 Jobsearch participant prints CV during the course, or presents a typed version if preferred. Form 116 is attached [not shown in this factsheet]

▼

Completed form 116 or typed version checked by Jobsearch Course Leader by end of course and passed by end of Day 2 to Telematics Centre for typing

▼

Information from form 116 to be typed in CV fashion and despatched by end of Day 4
(2 working days from receipt). Prior to despatch, typed CV to be checked for accuracy against original by person other than typist

▼

Person who checks the accuracy signs and dates at item 5, page 6 of form 116 and passes copy and original through to the Training Department

▼

In cases where complete form 116 is unreadable or obscure, the Course Leader is contacted by Telematics Centre staff. If the day 4 deadline cannot be met the relevant Job Centre is informed by Telematics Centre staff

▼

Intermec Ireland – picking a teleworker

Margaret Burke, quality officer at Intermec Ireland, an ISO9001-registered company that specialises in barcode readers, printers and consumables, spells out what she is looking for in a teleworker:

"ISO9000 purchasing requirements list three questions that must be answered.

1. How can we control the quality of what we buy from subcontractors or suppliers such as teleworkers

2. How should we assess our subcontractors/suppliers

3. How do we control the quality of products given to us by subcontractors to include in our processes?

Let's look at how we might deal with this for two teleworking examples, one simple and one complex. First, Intermec have recently developed a new software package called 'Asset Tracking', which is a generic product for the barcoding market, and will be sold worldwide. We might need a teleworker to translate our user documentation into French or German. This is a specialised job, so just as though we were hiring a new employee, we would look carefully at the teleworker's qualifications and experience. We would hope to see a sample of work, but if we couldn't, perhaps because of confidentiality agreements, then we would ask for a referee, so we can assess the teleworker's basic ability to carry out the required work. We would then transmit our documentation electronically to the teleworker, who could retransmit the translated document. We might ask for the initial few pages of the document to review for quality of translation, correct use of terminology for the target industry etc. Our contract would contain confidentiality agreements if necessary.

The second example is more complex, and one where we intend to incorporate the product of the teleworking into our own products. Let's say we are overloaded in the software area and we need to contract out some development work on a once-off basis. As in the first case, we would look at qualification and experience, but we would also have to insist that the teleworker conform to our Development Standards Manual, which forms part of our quality system. The appropriate sections and samples would be provided to the teleworker, and we would also provide the teleworker with the functional specification from which the technical specification will be developed. From there on, the teleworker must conform to our standards. Development work would be reviewed by our team leaders at Intermec, beginning at the Technical Specification stage and progressing to testing of the software. Acceptance of the review could be authorised by electronic signatures, which can be used as a form of proof for an auditor. We would not accept a teleworker who did not wish to conform to these standards."

Somerset Computer Services – quality for microenterprises

Somerset Computer Services is a "1.5 man" operation run by Kieron McGrath and his wife. Kieron has three specialities – computer consultancy for small businesses, training for the local enterprise centre in the small business area, and a desktop publishing service. Kieron decided to go for a quality system with independent certification for two reasons. Firstly he felt that it would open doors in larger companies that he wanted to sell to by giving greater credibility. "Teleworkers already have a credibility problem because they tend to be microbusinesses, and because of the roses-round-the-door media image that has been promoted. Therefore it's actually more important to have a quality certificate than for other sectors," he comments. Secondly, he felt his business, like most small businesses was disorganized and too dependent on one person – himself. "After installing the quality system, when I went into hospital for a knee replacement, my wife was able to run the business quite happily for three weeks using the documented systems."

Kieron was fortunate in being able to join a subsidised quality course that was run at his local TEC, occupying one day a month for six months,

Dealing with enquiries, quotations and orders

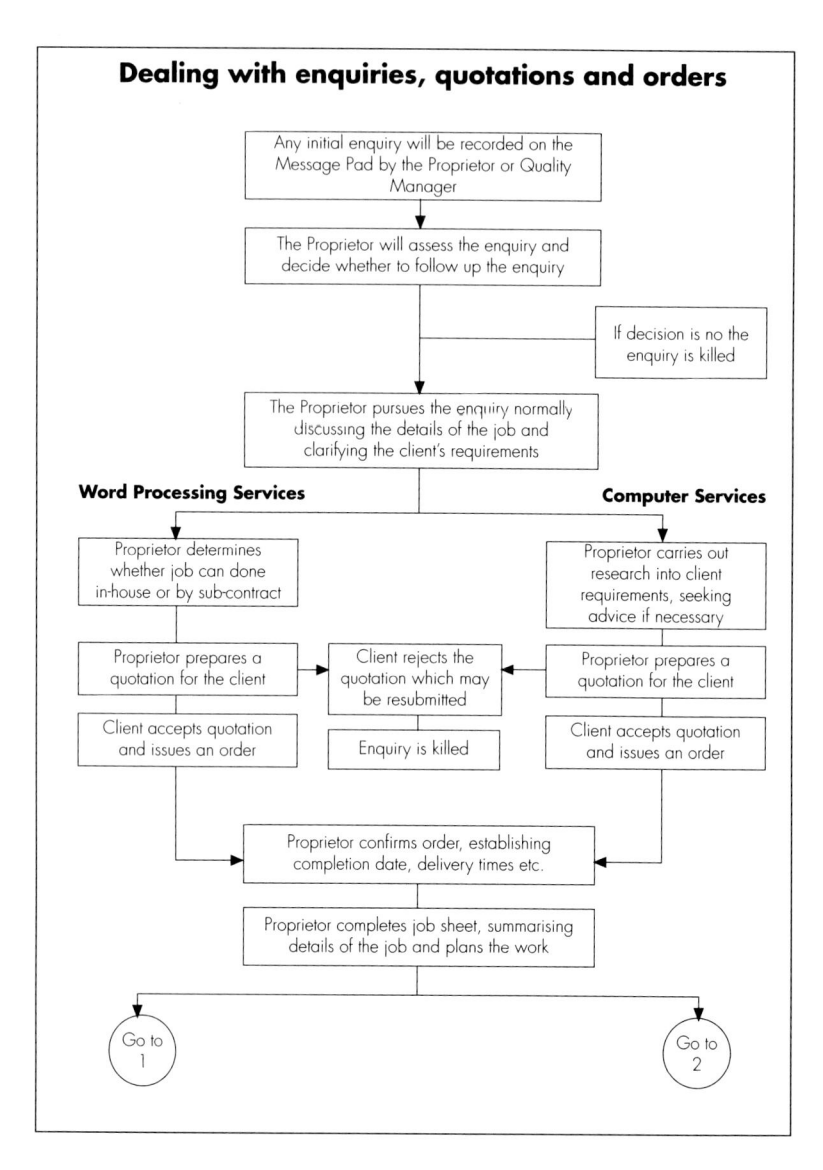

```
┌─────────────────────────────────────┐
│ Any initial enquiry will be recorded │
│ on the Message Pad by the Proprietor │
│ or Quality Manager                   │
└─────────────────────────────────────┘
                 ↓
┌─────────────────────────────────────┐
│ The Proprietor will assess the       │
│ enquiry and decide whether to follow │
│ up the enquiry                       │
└─────────────────────────────────────┘
                 ↓           → If decision is no the
                                enquiry is killed
┌─────────────────────────────────────┐
│ The Proprietor pursues the enquiry   │
│ normally discussing the details of   │
│ the job and clarifying the client's  │
│ requirements                         │
└─────────────────────────────────────┘
```

Word Processing Services | **Computer Services**

- Proprietor determines whether job can be done in-house or by sub-contract
- Proprietor carries out research into client requirements, seeking advice if necessary
- Proprietor prepares a quotation for the client
- Client rejects the quotation which may be resubmitted
- Proprietor prepares a quotation for the client
- Client accepts quotation and issues an order
- Enquiry is killed
- Client accepts quotation and issues an order

Proprietor confirms order, establishing completion date, delivery times etc.

Proprietor completes job sheet, summarising details of the job and plans the work

Go to 1   Go to 2

which reduced his consultancy costs considerably. "I think that the standard is incomprehensible, and that means you can't write your own quality manual – you have to get a consultant to explain things and to look at how your existing system conforms to the standard."

Some requirements are straightforward and sensible practice for all businesses, such as the logging of all incoming and outgoing mail. But being such a small business has caused a few absurdities. Kieron has to hold monthly quality audits taking about 2 hours, and quarterly management review meetings, which are attended by himself and his wife.

Size had its advantages when it came to cost, however. Kieron was able to negotiate with an organisation offering certification. "I said £2,850 for three years just wasn't on for a two person business that was going to take them half a day to assess, not one and a half days. I was about to go for a body specialising in small business certification instead, but then the original organisation came back and offered me £450 a year over three years". Another tip Kieron gives is to double check that your consultant and certifying organisation themselves have achieved quality standards. Kieron's advice on picking consultants and certifiers is to use word of mouth, and talk to other similar small businesses that have achieved quality standards. "It has definitely been worthwhile for us. Companies that wouldn't have looked at us are now letting us quote, and the business is run much more efficiently." The flow chart on the previous page gives an example of one of Kieron's quality procedures.

How much does it cost?

- staff time estimates are hard to make. However, if you contact a quality consultant at the beginning of your quality programme, they may be able to help you make an estimate before you embark on major expenditure. Stephen Simmons cautions that even the smallest group's scheme will involve at least 100 hours of effort: "the point is that the real cost is in own time expended, which is likely to be more expensive than the money cost".

- consultancy costs vary and you should obtain competing quotes. The NAT's scheme costs about £1,000 but does not lead to any third party certification. Kieron McGrath got his consultancy 50% paid for by his local TEC, reducing the cost to £1,250. Pat McCarthy of Quality Systems International recommends that companies in the same type of business should group together to save money on courses because the process is similar for each business. In Ireland, approved courses can qualify for grant aid under the FÁS training support scheme.

- certification costs (these are sometimes included in consultant's costs). Kieron McGrath got his certification at the bargain rate of £450/year for three years, but he was originally asked for £2850. Lesley Carr compiled the following information on total certification fees over three years. Check the details of each scheme – for example, some figures given here only apply to businesses with no design element to their work.

Certification body		Fees
National Quality Assurance (up to 25 employees)		
Chris Rhymer 01582 866766		£2550
SGS Yarsley (5 or less employees) 01342 305328		£2620
£100 application fee then £70/month		
BSI Quality Assurance (small business) Gary Sutton 01908 220908		
£990 application fee then £710/year		£3,120
Lloyds Register Quality Assurance (up to 10 employees) 01203 882790		£3,400
PECS (up to 10 employees – used by Kieron McGrath) 01268 770135		£1,700

In updating this list, during May 1996 there was a considerable variation in the quality of enquiry handling between these bodies, which may or may not reflect on their efficiency at certification. Some gave comprehensive, clear and immediate information. Others necessitated up to 4 separate calls to different units to extract information. The two companies providing clear, fast answers with schemes suitable for very small businesses of 2-3 people were PECS and BSI Quality Assurance.

Margaret Burke gives an estimate of costs for Intermec's certification: "We have over forty employees. My salary is an obvious overhead, and I would guess that over the eighteen months we have been working on ISO, each employee has probably spent 15 days on quality issues – a significant hidden cost. But there were hidden benefits. We saved money because of the stringent procedures, and looked at all aspects of our business. We have 105 procedures in place, and three manuals – Development Standards, Quality and Procedures. I feel the other major problem with certification is the amount of paperwork created. Intermec was relatively paper-free, despite operating from four different sites. All main communication and documentation was completed on our IBM AS400. All ISO9000 proof of approval, acceptance etc. requires sign-offs, which involve paper. I don't feel it's paperwork with a purpose – ISO does not support rainforests! " If you decide that certification is too expensive for your business, other options are:

- use an independent scheme such as that operated by the National Association of Teleworkers (this will not entitle you to use ISO9000 in your literature)

- discuss with your clients their vendor assessment and quality procedures. Make sure you are complying with their quality system, even if you don't have certification

- develop a consistent quality system for your business that is compatible with ISO9000, but do not apply for certification and its extra costs.

One of Malcolm Lake's clients commented on quality: "I can now see that twelve months ago we merely "muddled along". Now we are well organised, we know where everything is, we all know what our jobs are and we have doubled our turnover with the same number of office staff. I do not need to go for external certification but I know that if I do I will easily obtain it." Malcolm Lake of Effective Quality Management provides a free telephone advice service to any teleworking organisation that would like to know more about ISO9000 and its organisational implications. "Previously it could have been argued that quality standards represented a heavy industry, top-down approach. Now the ISO9000 models allow each organisation to be free to operate top-down or bottom-up and to choose whether or not to see certification."

Contacts

Many local TECs (Training and Enterprise Councils) in Britain or FÁS in Ireland keep information on quality systems, and some run subsidised workshops for companies going for ISO9000. Local offices of the DTI can also provide UK information.

Copies of the ISO9000 standard are available from: BSI Standards, Linford Wood, Milton Keynes MK14 6LE Tel: 01908 220022 Fax: 01908 320856

A list of quality certification bodies can be obtained from: National Accreditation Council for Certification Bodies (NACCB) Audley House, 13 Palace Street, London SW1E 5HS. Tel: 0171 233 7111 Fax: 0171 233 5115.

Antur Teifi, Business Park, Aberad, Newcastle Emlyn, Dyfed SA38 9DB. Tel: 01239 710238 Fax: 01239 710358 Contact: Mike Jones

Cornix teleworking consultancy, 64 Morrab Road, Penzance, Cornwall TR18 2QT Tel: 01736 69477 Fax: 01736 69477 Email: 100021,2563@compuserve.com or srs@cornix.co.uk Contact: Stephen Simmons

Effective Quality Management (EQM), Lake House, Wythop Mill, Cockermouth, Cumbria CA13 9YP. Tel: 01768 776687 Fax: 01768 77629 Contact: Malcolm Lake. This is the company that designed and developed Kieron McGrath's system.

Intermec Ireland, 19/20 York Road, Dun Laoghaire, Co. Dublin, Ireland. Tel: +353 1 280 0899 E-mail: iewfdprd@ibmmail.com. Contact Margaret Burke.

People, Process and Systems, 87 Waterloo Road, Wokingham, Berks RG11 2JG Tel/Fax: 01734 775892 E-mail lcarr@attmail.com Contact: Lesley Carr.

Quality Management for Teleworking, QMT Secretariat, The Island House, Midsomer Norton, Bath BA3 2HL (This is the uncertificated quality system recommended by the National Association of Teleworkers) Tel: 01761 413869 Fax: 01761 419438

Quality Services International Ltd, Shanballymore, Mallow, Co. Cork, Ireland. Tel/Fax: +353 22 25450 Contact: Pat McCarthy or Billy Nyhan, lead assessors.

Somerset Computer Services, South View, Runnington, Wellington, Somerset TA21 0QW Tel: 01823 661544 Fax: 01823 661544 Email: 100111.3412@Compuserve.com

Disability and teleworking

Teleworking has the potential to offer some disabled people new employment opportunities. People with mobility, visual or hearing impairments can work from their own homes, or from a centre adapted for disabled teleworkers. The work carried out encompasses the whole range of teleworking, from word processing to software programming. However, some of the problems of teleworking can be more acute for those with disabilities – such as social isolation – while the implications for those receiving state benefits need careful consideration.

Access to the technology

It is important to get a proper assessment of a disabled computer user's needs so that they can get the best access possible to the technology. The Computability Centre, based in Warwick, is a national charity that offers professional computer expertise to people with all kinds of disabilities. The Centre runs an advice and information service including a phone helpline, as well as an assessment service, training courses and consultancy.

As well as helping those who are already disabled to get better access to computers, the Centre helps those who already use computers but suffer from progressive problems due to disability. In the case of British Gas payroll supervisor Eileen Knowles, who has Parkinson's Disease, Computability "saved her job". Eileen's hand tremors were affecting her keyboarding accuracy and she was having difficulty holding a pen. Computability provided Eileen with a keyguard (a template with holes for each key) and recommended moving the keyboard down to a tray below her desk. Eileen was amazed at the effectiveness of these simple adaptations.

For Jane Thurlow, a biologist at the Imperial Cancer Research Fund, severe back injury meant she could not sit down at all, and could stand for only 20 minutes in an hour. Writing and typing was causing her considerable pain. Computability helped Jane to experiment with different techniques for using the computer while lying down. Jane now has a computer with voice input, and the screen is tilted through 90 degrees so that she can read it lying down.

The Disabled Living Foundation holds information on 1,600 technical aids online. However, their database is only available on subscription so most people would access the information via Disabled Living Centres or local authorities who are subscribers. There is also a CD-ROM produced by the EU HANDYNET project which details 35,000 aids and adaptations available in Europe and can be accessed through the Disabled Living Foundation. In Ireland, the Central Remedial Clinic in Dublin can offer a similar service to that offered by Computability.

Technical aids for teleworkers

- latch keys allow users who can only press one key at once, or those who use a stick on the keyboard, to use modifier keys such as shift, alt and control on PCs, or command and option on the Macintosh
- for users with visual disabilities, brightly coloured keytops, or those with big or bold characters can help
- keyguards are rigid plates above keyboard keys that can take the weight of hands or arms, and have holes above each key for accurate key depression
- personalised keyboards can be very effective for people with hand/arm difficulties e.g. smaller size keyboards, programmable keypads, switches that can be used with keyboard emulation software, and keyboards for those who only have the use of one hand
- for anyone who has difficulty with data entry, word processors that predict word endings, and most likely next words (keystroke savers) are a boon
- computer mice alternatives include tracker balls, which are fixed in position but you roll a ball to move the pointer, touch-sensitive pads and joy sticks. Alternative shapes and sizes are available. Highly specialised devices such as the "twiddler" operate on delicate tilting movements of the hand, while others can be operated by the head, or operated by biometrics from vestigial movements. Mouse movements can also be emulated using the keyboard cursors keys in some situations
- help for the visually impaired ranges from replacing old fashioned poor quality screens, to altering colour combinations, and installing larger screens. Another approach is to enlarge the image, but when this is done the whole screen contents cannot be viewed at once. In some systems an enlarged image from part of the computer's main screen is displayed on a second screen (usually a closed circuit TV system that can also be used to enlarge printed material for reading)
- voice recognition software for blind and physically disabled users can act as a keyboard replacement and is available from a limited "command level" to "free text". The development of laptop computers in conjunction with speech synthesisers and voice recognition can now provide some disabled people with an easily portable communications tool. Another alternative is "screen reading" using braille output, where whole or half lines from the screen are produced on an electro mechanical strip close to the keyboard
- OCR (optical character reading) text scanning can be used to "read" text into a computer, producing text on the computer screen, or a synthesized voice, or both
- text telephones can help those with hearing disabilities to communicate

by displaying conversations on a small screen connected to a normal telephone line. The most commonly used system is the Minicom. Text telephones are great for communications between the hearing impaired, but need an interpretation service to aid communication with other telephone users. The RNID offers a "TypeTalk" service where an interpreter "translates" between the spoken word and the Minicom messages

- many items not related to computers can help disabled teleworkers, such as page turners for books and journals, lights to indicate ringing telephones, talking calculators and specially adapted work furniture

- BT has recently introduced a series of text payphones for the deaf and speech-impaired sited at UK airports. The phones can be used to link up to other text phone users, or to the BT funded Typetalk system, which provides operator mediated relay services between textphones and voice phone users. The text payphones look like standard payphones but have a drawer from which a keyboard slides out when callers using a special phonecard are connected.

- Cheshire Deaf Society has set up videophone terminals allowing users to link remotely to social services.

Certain items of equipment for disabled people are exempt from VAT, but rules vary according to local VAT offices. A campaign to ensure equipment for disabled people is free of VAT is run by Dolphin Systems.

Access to work

The Department of Education and Employment in Britain runs the PACT scheme which can help disabled teleworkers and their employers. The budget for this successful scheme has, after pressure from disability organisations, been increased from £12m to £19m, but from June 1st 1996, the employer will be expected to pay the first £300 of any new claim made by a disabled person who is already employed. There is still a question mark over support for self-employed disabled people because the government has yet to decide whether self-employed people must pay the normal employer's contribution. Each applicant can get help to a maximum value of £21,000 over a period of five years. To qualify, you must be registered disabled, or able to register but have chosen not to do so. Examples of acceptable uses include:

- a communicator for the hearing impaired
- a part-time reader or assistance at work for someone who is blind
- equipment or adaptations to provide help at work
- transport into or assistance with adaptations to cars.

Job Centres now have Disability Employment Advisors (DEAs), who can provide help with the Access to Work scheme, the Job Introduction Scheme (a chance to try out a job for an introductory period) and work preparation (such as job trials with an employer). The Disability Information and Advice Line (DIAL) is another good starting point for information about a range of services. There is also the Disability Information Database DissBASE, which is used by about 170 providers of disability information in the UK. You can telephone DissBASE and ask them to make an enquiry free of charge. The database contains information on over 4,000 national and regional organisations and services related to disability. It is also often useful to consult specialist groups who deal in particular disabilities, such as MS, as they may well have disability-specific relevant information.

Access to training

The British government offers training through Training and Enterprise Councils (TECs). These organisations can offer information and support to people with disabilities who are thinking of starting their own business. For people who want to learn or update job skills, the Department of Education and Employment offers Career Development Loans which can provide 80% (and in some cases 100%) of training costs for up to two years. Loans are between £200 and £8,000 and the interest is paid by the Department of Education and Employment during training.

There are several schemes for training disabled people in their own homes, including the EDIT scheme (Employment for Disabled people using Information Technology) based in Derbyshire. EDIT provides courses in word processing, spreadsheets, databases and dtp. Courses are provided on an individual basis to suit the learning capabilities and physical limitations of each trainee. The training is conducted in an employer's premises, in a sheltered workplace or in the person's own home. Assessments are made regularly and trainees are expected to reach the NVQ level 2 standard and be awarded certificates. The courses are free. Confusingly, there is another scheme also called EDIT which operates from the University of Swansea in Wales. This is a European project which provides disabled people with the ability to access training telematically – using email and computer conferencing – from their own locations. Tutorials can be arranged through videoconferencing. The courses are free to people living in Wales and the Borders, are 40 weeks long, and consist of 640 hours of theory and practical work. EDIT is also working to train human resources staff within companies that employ disabled people to assist them in introducing teleworking.

The national charity Outset works to develop technology related employment opportunities for disabled people. Outset is working to create a national network of training centres, and is co-operating with telecottages where appropriate.

Another option is to take a distance learning or open learning course. To find out about suitable courses that can be completed in your own time at home, contact your local education authority in the UK, or the National Distance Education Centre in Ireland. Another useful starting point is the *Open Learning Directory*, which lists many courses, some of which are available on floppy disc or CD-ROM, to help you learn while using the computer. The directory is stocked in many libraries. Some distance learning courses are now provided "online" – you obtain and return your exercises by email.

European projects for the disabled

TIDE (Technology Intiatives for Disabled and Elderly People) is an EU initiative to develop new technological tools and applications for people with disabilities and elderly people to enable them to live independently and participate in the social and economic activities of the community. TIDE actions are intended to encourage innovative services and applications to meet the specific needs of the 60–80 million disabled and elderly people in Europe. The first round of TIDE projects is currently ending, to be replaced by a new set of projects which will be announced shortly.

The HYPIT project is one of the TIDE actions to help disabled people to telework. HYPIT studies the organisational and social factors that hinder telework, and is concerned that disabled teleworkers should be integrated into society and not excluded by home working. The project has produced:

- Telequest, a software assessment tool system that will support employers in assessing the suitability of tasks for telework, and the suitability of a particular disabled worker for that job (e.g. suitable assistive technology and training measures)
- a computerised telework management system to integrate the teleworker into the organisational workflow, helping the employing organization to manage teleworked employees and tasks
- a report on the human and organisational factors of telework, available on disk as a hypertext document.

A number of projects for disabled teleworkers have been funded under the HORIZON project including:

- The MERIT programme uses medical rehabilitiation to help disabled people get industrial training and employment. Dublin's Central Remedial Clinic is working with ten disabled teleworkers through MERIT. Two of the ten are homeworkers, one specialising in CAD and the other in data entry.
- The TWIN project is linking five existing European telecentres for disabled people and encouraging cross-border work such as translation and proofreading.

Teleworking networks for the disabled

Abilities Limited

Maiden Newton station in Dorset is the headquarters for Abilities Limited, which numbers among its major clients Excel Logistics, British Gas and P&O. Abilities carries out standard telecottage type services such as data processing and accounts, but their specialist services include industrial market research and tachograph analysis. Most of the workers are disabled, and Henry Llewellyn of Abilities comments: "I think that disabled people must form networks to telework successfully. There are two main problems to be overcome. The first is that many disabled people have a higher number of days sick in any given year, and they need to be able to pass on work to others if affected by health problems. The second is that it is very hard to get large firms to deal with individuals – a credible "network hub" like Abilities is vital." Henry also feels that a network can help those whose disability causes their work to be erratic: "Many organizations can cope with someone who can only manage 60% of the output. The big difficulty is when accuracy falls to 60%, and here you need an organization that recognises the problems and can use some form of quality system to filter out inaccurate work." Henry also encounters problems with the wide range of software packages that customers use, and that their services must encompass. On benefits, he says: "I strongly advise any disabled person considering teleworking to consult a benefits advisor first – for example, you can't operate a trading business and claim invalidity benefit. It is crucial to take benefits rulings into account before launching into telework training." Henry would like to see funding bodies offering work contracts rather than cash grants.

Network Personnel

Ann McBride of Network Personnel in Northern Ireland is part of an organisation that provides training for 16 disabled people to learn computer skills in their own homes, and which subsequently tries to provide computer based work for the trainees. Three of Ann's clients are now teleworking from home or at a local centre. She is very aware of the problems that people with disabilities face concerning their benefits when they wish to take up any form of employment, and suggests taking expert advice: "Earnings are deducted from income support, except for the first £15. Claiming the disabled working allowance can often mean that disabled people who work are no better off." But Ann believes teleworking opportunities are out there, and it is a matter of finding a niche in the market place both locally and further afield.

Ability Enterprises (Ireland)

Anne Dalkey (not her real name) suffered a car accident, and was left with little use of one hand and arm as well as problems with concentration. Previously Anne had worked as a bilingual executive secretary and personal assistant, and ran her own business supplying word processing services and temporary secretaries. One of Anne's customers, a pharmaceutical company, was extremely supportive and continued to send her secretarial work when she was well enough to start working from home, including correspondence, telephone dictation and production of bulk mailings. Anne also got help from the Irish organisation Ability (no relation to the Dorset-based Abilities), which keeps a register of disabled people who have teleworking skills. Anne has taken on several typing jobs for United Biscuits through Ability, but found that she could not get help with equipment or software from any organisation. She is critical of state rehabilitation services, which she feels did not assess her properly and sent her on an inappropriate high-level German course intended to train her as a translator. Another training course she was offered would have involved spending six weeks at the other end of the country which was impractical given her disability and personal situation. Instead, Anne borrowed money from her family to update her computer equipment and buy new software and a laser printer, which she is paying off. She has received some work for a Dublin insurance company through the HYPIT project, but to date technical difficulties with the remote access systems have delayed progress.

RNIB

Britain's Royal National Institute for the Blind has opened a telecottage in Darlington. Tom Boyd-Smith of the RNIB points out that 79% of visually impaired people of working age in the UK are unemployed, and says that the telecottage is part of the RNIB's interest in active job creation. He disagrees with Henry Llewellyn concerning sick days for disabled people, citing figures that show on average disabled people take less sick leave than the general population. The RNIB telecottage has two workstations, and a maximum of six are planned, though development has been restricted by a freeze on new job appointments caused by financial constraints. The telecottage has been founded with support from BT, the local TEC and the European Union. The Telecottage Manager is registered blind and uses a screen with enlarged characters and enhanced screen colouring. His computer monitor is on an arm so that he can swing it "to the end of his nose". Other modifications to the standard telecottage equipment include headset telephones, a talking calculator, large print dialling codes and liberal use of thick black felt pens. The telecottage also has a text scanner that can produce large characters on screen, or use a speech synthesizer to read out the scanned text. RNIB is also carrying out market research on opportunities for visually impaired teleworkers, but recently the project has been held up by funding problems within RNIB.

Outset

Outset is a UK national charity which works to promote technology based employment and training for disabled people, and is involved in two European funded projects, one to develop teletraining methodologies (ESPOIR), and the other to provide skills modules for people with disabilitites to train for teleworking (INNOVA). The INNOVA project is also planned to provide work for teleworkers and will include a European database of employers of teleworkers, as well as of disabled teleworkers. The plan is to create an employment agency for disabled teleworkers.

Employment opportunities

The Department of Education and Employment's employment service is the first port of call for disabled teleworkers. The employment service can assist with the funding of equipment, adaptations and transport. Normally you should call your local job centre and ask to speak to the local PACT (Placement, assessment and counselling team) manager.

Opportunities is a leading national charity working to place disabled people in employment, and staffed by secondees from commerce and industry. The charity maintains a register of disabled people who want to work, and matches these with local employers looking for particular skills. Jobseekers get help in identifying and developing skills, preparing CVs and interview technique.

For those already in work, but coping with a new or increasing disability, the Employers' Forum on Disability is the national employers' organisation dealing with disability and employment. It is non profit-making, and funded by members. It provides good publications, a regular journal, and a range of introductory literature. The Disability Discrimination Act which is currently being implemented will have the following effects:

- ■ from around the end of 1996, it will be against the law for an employer to treat a disabled person less favourably, without good reason, because of their disability. It will also be against the law to refuse to serve someone who is disabled

- from 1997 onwards, subject to consultation, it will be against the law to run a service or provide goods or facilities in such a way that it is impossible or unreasonably difficult for a disabled person to use the service or goods.

Electronic mail support groups

See the Electronic Mail and Online Services factsheet. CompuServe has several disabilities forums. The Internet has many mailing lists and newsgroups on disability issues. There is a listserv called the Able collaborative development group, run by the UK government's central computer and telecoms agency, which covers disability issues including telework. To subscribe send email to listserv@ccta.gov.uk with the message subscribe email address able. Once you are subscribed, send messages for discussion to able@ccta.gov.uk.

Contacts

Ability Enterprises, Ballindyne, Co. Mayo, Ireland Contact: Derek Farrell Tel: +353 94 65054.

Abilities, Station House, Maiden Newton, Dorchester, Dorset DT2 0AE Tel: 01300 321212 Fax: 0300 321270 Contact: Drew or Henry Llewellyn.

Central Remedial Clinic, Penny Ansley Building, Vernon Avenue, Clontarf, Dublin 3 Tel: +353 1 332206 Fax: +353 1 335496 Contact: Ger Craddock.

EDIT: University of Wales Jean Hough Tel: 01792 295679 Email: 100321.1620

EDIT: Employment for Disabled people using Information Technology, Derbyshire Tel: 01629 826285

National Distance Education Centre, Dublin City University, Dublin 9, Ireland Tel: +353 1 704 5481 Fax: +353 1 704 5494.

Network Personnel, 80–82 Rainy Street, Magherafelt, Co. Derry, Northern Ireland Contact: Ann McBride Tel: 01648 31032 Fax: 01648 31033

Open Learning Directory 1995 published by Butterworth-Heinemann, Jan 1995 ISBN 0750623055

Opportunities for People with Disabilities, 1 Bank Buildings, Prices Street, London EC2R 8EU Tel: 0171 726 4961

RNIB, 224 Great Portland Street, London W1N 6AA Tel: 0171 388 1266 The RNIB has specialist benefits advisors who can be contacted on 0171 388 1266, and produces a guide call Access Technology detailing available equipment for blind people and covering braille, large print and speech technology, available from 0181 968 8600

RNID, 105 Gower Street, London WC1E 6AH Tel: 0171 387 8033

The Computability Centre, PO Box 94, Warwick, Warwickshire CV34 5WS Tel: 01926 312847 Fax: 01926 311345

The Employment Service, Head of Disability Services Branch, Level 3, Steel City House, c/o Rockingham House, 123 West Street, Sheffield S1 4ER. Tel: 01742 739190

The **HYPIT** and **EDIT** projects: Toucan, 27 Ardwick Green North, Manchest M12 6FZ Tel: 0161 273 5122 Fax: 0161 273 5122 Email: 100321.1620@compuserve.com Contact Jean Hough

Outset: contact Jean Wiltshire Tel: 0181 692 7141 Fax: 0181 469 2532

DIAL – Disability Information and Advice Line Tel: 01302 310123 Fax: 01302 310404

DissBASE - the Disability Information Database Tel: 01306 742282

Dolphin Systems co-ordinates the fight to remove VAT from equipment for disabled people. Tel: 01905 754 577 Fax: 01905 754 559

Central Computer and Telecoms Agency (which runs the able CDG email listserv), Rosebery Court, St Andrew's Business Park, Norwich NR7 0HS – contact Richard West Tel: 01603 704791 Fax: 01603 704817 Email: rwest@ccta.gov.uk

Typetalk textphone services contact RNID Tel: 0151 709 9494 Fax: 0171 709 8119

Disability Discrimination Act: Tel: 0345 622633 for a copy.

Teleworking equipment

A note on prices

Technology changes dramatically, and prices with it. Sample prices are only given here where they are considerably higher or lower than you might expect.

Often the prices stated by equipment manufacturers in advertisements are slightly higher than the 'street prices' which you will actually have to pay. To get an idea of the likely street price, check a number of retailers' advertisements for the same product, and take an average. Remember that quoted prices for office products often don't include VAT.

How and where to buy

Different teleworking businesses require different equipment. When you are deciding what to buy, try to get quotes and advice from more than one source, and talk to other users of similar equipment. It may help to consult your local telecottage. The Consumers' Association magazine *Which?* is helpful for basic facts on computers, mobile phones and cheaper office equipment, and is often available from public libraries.

For PCs, *Personal Computer World*, *Computer Shopper*, *Computer Buyer* and *PC Direct* magazines are among the best for comparing advertised prices as well as useful information. *Computer Buyer* also does a 'faxback' service for its copies of reviews from back issues – most reviews are 3–4 pages, some as many as 10 pages, and calls cost 49p per minute. For Macs, *MacUser* and *MacWorld* both carry thorough product surveys. All are available nationally in newsagents, and some are kept in libraries. It can be well worthwhile to do some library research as most of the magazines regularly review the options for computers, printers, and so on. Use the index to the magazine (usually published annually) to find the last time that they reviewed the item you are interested in. Then look up the back number to find out more detail on the technology issues and product reviews. If the back number is missing, most of the magazines have a service for selling copies of back numbers.

Computers and office equipment are available from:

- independent local retailers, who can give you a personal service but may be relatively expensive;
- high-street chains such as Dixons
- computer superstores such as PC World
- direct mail order from companies such as Dell and Gateway.

If you buy by mail order, using a credit card may protect you against defective goods or suppliers going into liquidation, although interest charges can make this an expensive method of payment if you don't clear your balance quickly. Some magazines are members of the Mail Order Protection Scheme – look for the MOPS logo – which offers you limited protection against problems with advertisers. Bear in mind that, especially for complex items such as computers, a low purchase cost is no bargain if you are getting poor advice or limited after-sales service. Is on-site repair offered, or will you have to bear the expense of returning the equipment for repair? Is there a guaranteed response time? What is the service option beyond the standard guarantee period (usually 60 or 90 days)? Some computer dealers now offer access to technical support through premium rate telephone lines. This arrangement has the advantage that you only pay for what you use in terms of support, but you need to know that the dealer is technically competent and that you are not wasting expensive telephone time.

Another alternative is to insure your equipment against breakdown. Then if there is a problem you reclaim the cost of having it fixed. Be wary, however, of expensive service contracts where you pay a large sum even if no problems arise. High-tech electronics do not go wrong often and some dealers advertising low prices try to crank up their profits with exorbitant service contracts. You don't have to take one at all.

Also consider whether you should rent equipment or buy; the former is more expensive in total cash terms, but your accountant may decide it will save you more tax, and if money is tight at first it reduces your start-up costs. In essence, if you buy, then you pay upfront and you can only claim a percentage of that cost each year (around a quarter) against tax. If you buy you will probably also need to negotiate a loan with your bank to cover the purchase cost. If you rent or lease, the whole amount can be claimed against tax, and you do not have to stump up large amounts of money upfront. However, there are complexities – at the end of a lease, you don't actually own the equipment though there is usually a method of buying it. Leases do provide a degree of security – usually they can't be withdrawn or curtailed by credit squeezes or changes in economic conditions, and are not repayable on demand like an overdraft. Consult your financial advisor or bank manager to work out the best option for you.

Many equipment purchases have hidden costs. Computer printers require expenditure on toner and paper; mobile phones and portable PCs often require extra sets of batteries to maximise their usefulness; if you're travelling in Europe or North America, you'll need power and telecoms adapters for any portable equipment. These costs are often impossible to assess precisely as your use of the equipment will change over time, but an informed estimate will save you some unpleasant shocks.

ISDN (Integrated Services Digital Network)

ISDN lines are more expensive to install and rent than standard telephone lines, but the charges for connection time are the same and ISDN is about seven times faster – so it can prove more cost effective if you plan to send very large quantities of computer data. For example, a computer file one megabyte in size can be transferred in two minutes over ISDN, against 13 minutes over standard PSTN lines using 28.8K speed modems. Fax pages are similarly faster, and ISDN is also essential for videoconferencing. ISDN allows simultaneous use of a single connection for data, text, voice and image (up to six different devices can use one ISDN line), but for the teleworker who is mainly using the telephone for ordinary conversations and does not send many faxes or emails, ISDN may well be overkill. Remember that the person you are communicating with also has to have ISDN to make it useful – and not everyone uses this technology yet.

The fees for ISDN connection only supply you with a box on the wall. You still need to buy a terminal adapter or TA. For about £700 you can get a digital phone with an integral TA. Then you need a digital modem... another £700... and for a small extra sum you can get multiple subscriber numbering, which provides you with a block of numbers you can assign to the devices attached to your TA, including faxes (yes, you also need a special Group 4 digital fax and so does the person at the other end), spare voice lines, videoconferencing and so on.

ISDN is being used increasingly for connecting remote workers to office LANS cost-effectively. A technique known as spoofing allows both the local and remote computers to automatically disconnect during idle moments, saving call charges. When activity on either side requires the re-establishment of the connection this is easily done in a way which is transparent to the user – to the user it appears the machines are constantly connected. Your computer won't necessarily "plug in" to ISDN effectively without a suitable card or TA, and often the speed of systems is limited by your computer's serial port, not by the ISDN capability.

There are also pitfalls with incompatibility between some British and European ISDN systems, and there can be probems with transferring files from one kind of computer to another, such as Mac to PC, using different ISDN software packages.

Pricewise, there are two BT ISDN services. ISDN 2 is intended for small businesses and ISDN 30 is for larger businesses. ISDN 2 costs £400 for connection of two 64kbit/sec lines and £84.00 in quarterly rental. Each of the two lines can carry almost seven times as much information as an ordinary phone line. ISDN 30 provides 15 lines with 2mbit/sec capacity on each. Each of those 15 lines can carry more than 200 times as much as a standard phone line.

Telephones

A telephone is the only essential piece of equipment for a teleworker, and the choice of services is growing fast. First, check with your telephone company whether you are on a digital exchange (almost everyone in the UK and Ireland is), and whether ISDN services are available.

Whether you go for ISDN or not, you will probably want a separate telephone line so that you can easily distinguish business and personal calls and monitor business costs. Business lines are more expensive, but usually guarantee a faster fault-repair service and entitle you to a Yellow Pages entry.

You can also improve the flexibility of your telephone with some low-cost enhancements. Different phone companies offer slightly different services. From BT, for example, Call Waiting alerts you when a caller is trying to get through while you're using the phone; you can switch between calls. Call Diversion redirects incoming calls to any other number, so you can receive them at someone else's premises. Three Way Calling lets you talk to two other numbers simultaneously. Call Minder sets up a voice mailbox for you on BT's system. The mailbox works like an answering machine, recording messages when you're out or engaged, and playing them back to you through the phone. None of these services requires any extra equipment other than a standard touchtone telephone handset, and all currently cost less than £5 per quarter.

Featureline is a new BT system that can turn a collection of separate lines at one premises into a switchboard using facilities on the local digital exchange. Ordinary phones located within 200 metres of each other can be used as switchboard extensions, with facilities such as call diversion, call transfer between extensions, ring back when free, ring back when next used, call barring, five way call waiting and three way calling. Call answering can be set up in cyclical hunting to ensure even distribution of calls between a set of lines.

If you are looking at installing any kind of conventional switchboard, beware that the vast majority require professional installation and a pre-connection inspection by your telephone company, and have to be maintained by the installing company. Installation can take up to two days. The fee structure is usually arranged for larger businesses, and can be disadvantageous to small businesses needing only a couple of extensions and a very small switchboard. If you move house and want to take your switchboard with you, you could find that moving it will cost as much as installing a new system.

Computer telephony integration is a new set of tools which use the digital facilities now available for telephones in conjunction with computer databases and other tools to manage information for tasks such as telesales and telemarketing. Until recently these functions were only available via expensive call centre switchboards and mainframes, but a number of products have recently come on to the market. One is Callbox 200, suitable for an individual teleworker. Callbox will dial numbers stored in a database, or read the caller line identification (CLI) of an incoming caller and pop up associated information about the caller from a database.

For directory services, it is worth knowing that you can get the entire UK business subscriber phone catalogue in database format on CD-ROM for a mere £40.

Conferencing

Teleconferencing (also known as audioconferencing) allows you to hold full-scale meetings over the phone. Although large numbers of participants (over 15) can be difficult to handle in practical terms, the technology will support many more. If some only need to listen in without talking, you can have an audience of hundreds on a single call. Telephone companies and specialist teleconferencing firms will set these calls up for you on a one-off basis – the technological bells and whistles are at their end, and participants can use any normal phone.

There are two flavours of audioconference – dial-in and dial-out. For dial-in conferencing, the conference participants dial a special telephone number and are greeted by a receptionist who checks their identity before linking them to the conference. For dial-out conferencing, an operator dials each of the participants and links them together. Dial-out conferences are more expensive for the organiser (you) but free for the other participants. Some telecottages can help to set up teleconferences for you.

Videoconferencing

Paddy Moindrot of Telecottages Wales has wide experience of the use of videoconferencing systems. Here he describes a typical Picture Tel PCS100 system: "I've used this system several times for remote training, product development and demonstration to a variety of audiences. It runs under windows 3.1, requires an ISA or EISA bus on a 386 or 486 CPU, about 8 Mb of RAM and two free full length slots in the computer. It has an 'address book' which is badly needed – many videoconference facilities have at least two numbers so easy addressing is essential. It's H.320 compliant, the Euro-ISDN standard. The camera is a separate unit, with hinge and swivel for adjustment, and a privacy shutter, since the autoanswer facility means a caller can get an instant view of your office clutter or state or undress. The same camera can be used to film documents. Standard use of the system gives a sizeable screen from the remote camera, a small shot of what you look like, and a 'chalkboard' screen which can be used with a range of tools for sharing hand-drawn graphic information. These only work with other PictureTel systems. There's a separate conference phoneset with a loudspeaker or handset, and a headset phone is an optional extra."

Videoconferencing – using video images of participants as well as their voices – is voguish but expensive, although the growth of PC based videoconferencing systems is making this technology more accessible and more widely used. PC based systems are replacing expensive dedicated videoconferencing hardware for many applications. PC based videoconferencing uses a small camera on the top of each participant's PC and displays video images on the screen; the PCs are usually connected by ISDN lines. At the time this handbook went to press, PC-based videoconferencing systems were available for less than £1500 plus VAT. Older videophones are standalone telephone units with a video attachment, suitable for one-to-one videoconferencing.

Room or group videoconferencing systems are much more expensive, and best used where there are several people in each location. They can be used to link up international meetings, for example, capturing each meeting table on video. For simple presentations, one way videoconferencing allows an audience to see a speaker, but not vice-versa. If you are involved in a group or one-to-many videoconferences, experts advise having a separate audio (sound only) link as a backup, in case technical gremlins cause problems with the video transmission. Telephone companies and conferencing firms can provide bureau based facilities for videoconferencing, as can some telecottages; purchasing the equipment can cost several thousand pounds and it is not yet in widespread use for individual teleworkers.

Other technologies for electronic 'meetings' include electronic whiteboards which let participants in different locations work together on a document, with changes or additions made by one participant visible to all, so the group can quickly share and develop ideas. Electronic whiteboards can be used in conjunction with telephone conferencing or videoconferencing.

Portables, mobiles and pagers

Many teleworkers use radio or 'roaming' cordless telephones. Connected to ordinary lines, these portable handsets allow the user to roam around within about 60 metres of the base station. Roaming phones allow the telephone to be answered speedily even when you are not sitting at your desk.

Mobile telephones can be used anywhere there is signal available (although coverage in some rural and mountainous areas is still not great; if you live in an isolated place, do ask to borrow a phone and check the signal before buying). GSM (digital) phones can be used in a number of different countries, while the old-fashioned analogue phones can be extremely cost effective if you don't travel much abroad. However, the ubiquity and low cost of the phones themselves, which are sometimes even free when you pay for connection, disguise the fact that for everyday communications purposes they remain pricey compared with standard fixed phones.

Most major mobile phone services offer a choice of connection or 'airtime' contracts, ranging from a low basic charge with high charges for each individual call, to a high standing charge offset by lower call rates. This is one area too complex and fastmoving for detailed coverage in a book, but it pays to be more than usually suspicious of advertising. Try to imagine in advance how many hours per month you'll typically be using a mobile, and calculate costs of the different contracts on this basis.

Mobile batteries need recharging. This is easily done from the mains, but if you rely on a wireless modem and may spend long periods away from a convenient mains supply, check the cost of spare batteries. Some mobiles can also be powered by an adapter in your car.

Bear in mind, too, that some rural areas get poor reception; if you frequently visit remote valleys, a mobile service offering 100% coverage of major cities is of little use. Also think hard before signing service contracts, where the vendors of low-cost mobile phones often boost their profits. And consider whether you really need a mobile. If you spend time in clients' offices, call diversion services offer many of the same advantages at lower cost and with the advantage of a single contact number (answerphone messages giving several alternative numbers will probably just confuse and annoy your client). In the UK, it is also actually illegal to use a phone handset while driving. The magazine *What Mobile and Cellphone* is good for advice.

If you are moving around a lot but cannot justify the expense of a mobile phone, think about a pager. They are economical and have improved markedly over past years. Pagers store short messages and display them to you on a small screen. Some also offer a voicemail service, so the caller can leave a message which the pager owner receives by dialling into the pager service. Many pager systems do not cost the pager owner anything other than the initial purchase cost – instead, the person calling the pager is charged premium telephone rates – so it can be cost effective for the teleworker, if not for the caller.

Another item to think about if you travel around frequently is a telephone chargecard, offered by most major telephone companies. This can be used both in public cardphones and on any private telephones where you wish the call charge to be made to your own account rather than to that phone. International chargecards are also available though some transfer the bill to your credit-card account rather than your phone bill. Ordinary credit cards can also be used in many British and foreign payphones.

Answering machines

Answering machines, sometimes called ansafones, can be obtained for less than £50 and every teleworker should have one so that customers can leave a message if you are not available. If possible, buy an answering machine that uses the two-tape system, or holds the outgoing message on a chip.

Older (cheaper) single-tape systems are slow because they have to rewind between the outgoing message and the incoming message each time. Some also severely limit the length of message or the number of messages that can be left. One thing to watch out for is answering machines that do not reset themselves in the event of a short power failure. It is infuriating for you and for your customers if a momentary power blip puts the answering machine out of action for a whole day. Remote callback, often using a small bleeper to interrogate the answering machine by phone to see whether messages have been left, is very useful. On some models the same function can be achieved by dialling using a tone phone and entering a password code.

When using an answering machine, it is reassuring to your customers if you leave a daily message stating who you are, when the message was recorded, and when you will next be available, although this does involve more work on your part. If you are away for a long period, it is a good idea to be a little vague about this on the message to avoid arousing the interest of burglars. Some sophisticated machines can be programmed so that the caller can either leave a message, or press a code to be diverted to an alternative number. Similar systems, which amount to personal voicemail systems, can be installed on PCs to answer and redirect calls according to instructions received from the caller by pressing keypad tones. Many people also now take advantage of voicemail systems offered by telephone companies, which act like an answerphone, but store messages on computers at the local telephone exchange, to be picked up by the subscriber dialling in and using a PIN code to access their voicemail box.

Fax

Fax machines are now almost as essential as telephones to the small business. You do not need to have a separate telephone line installed for a fax machine, but if it is likely that you might use the fax extensively a second line should be considered for several reasons:

- faxes cannot be received while you are talking on the phone. Your telephone usage may expand considerably as you take up teleworking, and both voice and fax callers may not be able to get through if you opt to share a line
- if you are using Call Waiting, the second call on the line may well be a fax, which can be difficult to handle
- if you start off with one line and later decide to move the fax on to a separate line, for some time afterwards your customers may be faxing to the voice line causing irritation to both parties and lost business.

However, in case you do decide to stick to one line, many fax machines incorporate automatic line-switching devices which can detect whether an incoming call is fax or voice and act accordingly. Standalone line splitters are also available for older faxes.

Automatic paper feeders and guillotines are standard on faxes now, but consult consumer guides to decide what features you need and how much they will cost. There is a thriving secondhand fax market with the same advantages and pitfalls as any other used product. Some faxes now have preprogrammed cover sheets which save paper and time. Many of the more expensive machines output onto plain paper avoiding the fade and curl problems associated with thermal paper. (If your fax has thermal paper, don't leave the roll near a heater or it will blacken. It is possible to buy recycled thermal paper if you are environmentally minded.) Other fax machines can output to your laser printer and so provide plain paper printout.

Fax features to look out for include memories that allow you to feed in a document now but transmit it later (perhaps in the evening for an expensive international call), and polling, which allows your machine to collect messages from other fax machines. It is also possible to set up fax distribution lists, so that the same fax can be transmitted to several numbers without continually posting the piece of paper back into the fax for each number. Most faxes can also act as low quality, low volume photocopiers, although given that fax paper is more expensive than ordinary paper, this is a rather expensive means of doing more than the occasional copy. Remember to allow for the cost of fax paper in your budgets if you expect to receive many faxes.

One feature not to be swayed by is Group 3 compatibility, sometimes touted as a selling point in fax ads. All faxes sold today, and all but the most ancient secondhand models, are Group 3 compatible.

Faxback services

Faxback services are used for a variety of information services; Met Office Weather updates, theatre seat availability, magazine back issue reviews. Faxback involves ringing the information provider on your fax machine's phone, usually over a premium phone line, and following recorded instructions before the information is delivered to your fax machine. The effectiveness of the system relies on the information provider having successfully predicted what information is required and not forcing the user to spend too long going through a series of menus to get a response. Faxback can be rented from a number of providers or by purchasing a system such as the Andest Vantage VPA system which also incorporates voicemail, auto-attendant, fax and data features.

Faxing from your PC

You should consider whether a fax card or fax modem would suit you better than a standalone fax. A fax modem is a card that fits into a computer, and allows faxes to be received and sent. Fax cards are of particular value when sending the same message to a group of people, as the computer software can generate a new cover sheet for each recipient. They can also be scheduled to send faxes overnight when call charges are lower, to retry numbers that are engaged, and so on. If you keep details of your business contacts on a database, you can usually find a way to transfer fax numbers directly from this into fax software so you could easily send a 'fax mailshot' to your entire customer base. Fax modems also save time – instead of printing out the page and putting it into the fax machine, dialling the destination and setting it off, most fax software is installed as though it were another printer attached to your computer – you just select the fax modem and click the "print" button to send it.

Receiving faxes onto a PC is less useful as they can occupy a lot of disk space and you will often need to print them out anyway, or use OCR software (see below) to convert them into a text format which you can edit and incorporate into other documents. Also consider that if you use a fax card you may need some way of scanning in documents already on paper (as opposed to those typed into the computer) such as sketch drawings or maps. This can lead to extra expense.

If you want to fax to a very large group of people but don't think a fax card is viable, most telephone companies including BT provide fax bureau services. Here you set up a mailing list in advance with the bureau, then fax your document to them using a special password code, and it is automatically retransmitted to the entire fax mailing list.

Computers

Computers change so quickly that it is never the perfect time to buy the perfect machine, and there are two schools of thought that both claim to minimise the disadvantages. One is that you should buy the most powerful computer you can afford as you will always outstrip its capacity. The other is that if you require your computer to perform relatively simple tasks, it is not necessary to go for the latest technology, and secondhand or low specification computers provide a substantial cost saving. Part of the argument rests on the rapid depreciation of computer equipment – in accounting terms, a computer which is more than 3 years old is likely to be worthless. Even when you've only had the machine a year, and it is still useful to you, in monetary terms its value will have plummeted. This factor weighs towards the "buy expensive" option – an expensive computer may still be useful to you after three years, whereas a cheap computer not only has no financial value but becomes obsolete in practical terms more quickly because it is old and slow. But on the other hand, if your resources are limited, you probably have no choice but to go for the "buy cheap or secondhand" option.

In reality, the easiest way to buy a computer is first to consider not the computer itself, but the software you'll need – the programs with which you and your PC can actually accomplish something. Decide what task you want the computer to do, identify the software that does it, and then buy a suitable computer on which to run that software, at the same time making sure that it will be easy to add other software, extra memory and other enhancements to it. This is easy advice to follow if you are using specialist software such as CAD drafting packages, but if your needs are fairly general you will find the major software packages for word processing, DTP and so on are supported on almost all computers, so you may still find the choice confusing. Buying first hand also often means that you get some quite powerful software bundled in which would cost a lot to purchase individually.

The good news, though, is that over the past five years different computer systems have grown so similar that to a large extent choosing on the basis of price, on the basis of a very minor advantage or even because you like the colour of the case is unlikely to lead you to disaster.

The key questions to ask salespeople, or investigate in ads, concern:

- **the operating system or 'platform'**

This is the software supplied with the computer which manages its basic functions. Most likely, your choice will be between Windows 95 and the Apple Mac OS, though you might encounter Windows NT on a high-powered computer or Windows 3 on an older one; or OS/2, which is similar to Windows. (Computers which use the Mac OS are usually called Macs for short; those which use any variety of Windows, OS/2 or the now-outmoded DOS are termed PCs, although confusingly this latter term also applies to all personal computers generically.)

The difference between operating systems is a bit like that between regular and diesel fuel – though they do much the same things, they do them in entirely different manners and you can no more use a program written for the Mac OS operating system on a Windows PC than you can run a diesel car on unleaded.

As far as their actual functions go, there is increasingly little to choose between these operating systems, although many "newbie" teleworkers find the easy-to-use Mac OS more straightforward than Windows 95. In general Macs do come in at a slightly higher cost than the equivalent powered Windows 95 machine, however.

- **the processor type**

The central processing unit (CPU) chip is, to continue the motoring analogy, the engine of the computer. As with auto engines there's a multitude of models, but broadly if you are buying a Windows PC you want one with a Pentium processor or, at the least, a 486; if you are buying a Mac, you want one with a PowerPC processor, and the higher the number (for instance, 603) the better, generally. Computer magazines give in-depth advice on this complex issue.

- **the processor speed**

Often ignored, this is as important as the processor type. The processor speed, measured in megahertz or MHz, is usually quoted alongside the processor type and here a simple rule applies: the higher the speed, the faster and more efficient the computer will be. For example, a 166MHz

Pentium is considerably better (and more expensive) than a 75MHz Pentium, although they are the same type of processor.

■ the RAM or memory

Measured in megabytes (Mb), this along with the processor specification is the vital determinant of a computer's speed and its capability to run the latest software. You should not consider a computer with less than 8Mb of RAM, and the more the merrier – although more than 16Mb would be something of an indulgence, unnecessary for most office applications except advanced graphics.

■ the hard disk size

Again measured in Mb, this dictates how much information you can permanently store on your computer. If you expect mainly to be using word processing software, it is not a particularly important issue, as plain text takes up little disk space. However, if you are desktop publishing, you need much more and 500Mb would be a good baseline to work from. It is straightforward enough to add a larger hard disk, or additional hard disks or higher-capacity optical disks in the future if you need them. A gigabyte, abbreviated to Gb, is 1,000Mb.

Computers are such large investments that it's wise to try before you buy, talk to colleagues, and check that your chosen system will be compatible with clients' equipment when you need to send them disks or files. Often, such real-world experiences will tell you far more about a potential purchase than any number of reviews. In general, three useful rules do stand out:

- ■ Buy for your real needs, not to reach an abstract technological goal;
- ■ At the same time, beware of false economies, such as a cheap computer so slow that you will spend most of your working day waiting for it;
- ■ And if you have the cash, remember that it is usually cheaper to add extra memory or a more capacious hard disk at the time of purchase than later.

The BOON telecottage offers a service to specify, buy and set up computers for teleworkers. According to manager Drew Llewellyn, although teleworkers have to pay for the service, often they find that to do what they want they can buy a substantially cheaper computer than they had originally intended. Because the machine is ready to go from the moment it is plugged in, the time savings also mean that using the service can "save" money over what would have been paid without the advice. BOON's services also usually include relevant task-specific training.

Finally, once you have taken possession of the machine, set aside time to learn about it. Commercial training courses are good for coming to grips with specific software, and it's always advisable to curry favour with computer-knowledgeable friends; nearly all apparent problems can be sorted out that way without a repair bill!

Portable computing

Portables (laptops) are very convenient and can be used anywhere there is space to put them down, but tend to be less powerful than desktops, and more expensive if you want colour. IBM estimates that by the end of 1997, about 80% of its PC sales to business customers will be portables, or notebook computers (*Financial Times* 1/5/96). Recharging mobile batteries can become a chore; ask the salesperson how long the batteries will last between rechargers, and if you need to use a portable on long trips where you will have no opportunity to recharge, factor in the cost of additional batteries to tide you over.

As with mobile phones, portables are not worth having for their own sake – only if you will genuinely need a computer out of the office. Alternatively, it's worth considering a docking system, which lets you connect a laptop to a full-size keyboard and screen as well as additional devices such as disk drives for working in your office. The portable can then be easily removed, rather like a video casette from a video recorder, for use as a standalone laptop when you're on the road. Although this involves extra cost, it's still cheaper than having separate laptop and desktop computers – and easier, because you don't have to bother transferring data between two machines. It also means that when you're away, there is no computer in your office to attract thieves. For corporate teleworkers, docking stations and PCMCIA LAN cards are becoming increasingly popular for "hotdesking" applications where a mobile teleworker wants to "dock" with the office network for a short period. 3Com offers a card which holds both an ethernet connection and a modem, so that in the office, the laptop can be connected using ethernet, and at home via the modem. Wireless LAN cards are also under development for staff who have to move around an office building regularly.

Printers

Buying printers is comparatively simple, though installation is a common headache for first-time buyers (which is where those friends come in). The considerations are the obvious ones, such as paper size, colour versus black-and-white and the number of pages printed per minute.

If you are doing desktop publishing or graphics, you will need a PostScript-compatible laser printer and indeed laser printers are so cheap now that it can be argued no-one should look at anything else. But if you are on a very tight budget, consider dot-matrix and inkjet printers. Inkjet printers are very economical and provide good print quality, but are usually slower than laser printers. Dot-matrix printers are very cheap, but noisy, slow and lower in print quality than a good typewriter.

As for colour, if you just want basic coloured graphs, simple pen plotters or colour inkjets will do the trick. The best colour proofs come from dye-sublimation printers which can provide much finer variations in colour intensity but cost considerably more, both to purchase and in consumables.

The staple of colour printing for graphic designers is the thermal wax printer. It is now also possible to connect both Macs and PCs to expensive Canon full-colour photocopiers for excellent output. In any case, consider that for low-to-medium expenditure, you will get a much better black-and-white than colour printer – is colour essential to you, or could you just use a bureau service occasionally when you need it?

Printers of any kind involve ongoing cost as you need to replace consumables such as paper and toner. Most printer manufacturers quote a typical 'cost per page' of consumables for their models, but unfortunately there is no standard way of measuring this. A full-page sized laser print of a complex logo, for example, uses considerably more toner than a page of double-spaced text.

Consumable costs are most painfully felt with colour printers, which need multiple ink or colour sources as compared with a black-and-white printer's single colour, and may even require special paper. Some replacement cartridges are only sold in packs of the four colours, yet almost all real-life use wears out the black cartridge long before the others. If you are considering a dye-sublimation printer, for example, it is well worth establishing exactly the basis on which 'typical' consumable costs have been worked out; multiplying or dividing these costs to match your anticipated usage of the printer. You could well find that over a period of years the device will cost considerably more than you had expected. On the positive side, it is a joy to have access to a good colour printer when you are working from home, and it substantially increases your presentation standards and image with customers.

Another trend from equipment manufacturers is the addition of extra equipment to the basic printer to create a multi-functional device. For example Hewlett Packard's OfficeJet combines plain paper printing, faxing, copying and scanning. This allows incoming faxes to be received (up to 24 pages can be buffered) whilst printing.

For teleworkers operating remotely from a central office, it is possible to print over the telephone system. The Primrose Printback! software uses a pair of modems and a serial printer at the destination to output finished, printed pages.

Scanners

A scanner converts images on paper, including photos and logos, to images on the computer screen which can then be edited, manipulated or inserted into other documents such as a DTP publication. Anyone considering professional level DTP should invest at least in a cheap device; this is useful for 'positional' scans, which give an impression of the finished design, even if the final version is to be done by a bureau using a very expensive, very high quality scanner such as those used by colour magazines. Scanners can be greyscale, meaning that they will only create monochrome images on your PC, even if the original is colour, or they can be colour.

Greyscale scanners are fine for OCR (see below) but reasonable colour scanners are now so cheap, starting at under £300 and also doing greyscale, that there's little point in a publisher or designer going for greyscale alone. At the other end of the scale, where true colour separation of the scans for four colour printing is required, very few desktop scanners can produce acceptable results – instead the desktop scanner will be used for position scans only.

Scanner resolution is expressed in dots per inch, or dpi. Higher resolutions mean sharper and more accurate reproduction of the scanned image. 300dpi is acceptable for everyday greyscale use, or 600dpi for higher quality. Ask about the 'true' or 'optical' resolution of the scanner; many models use a software technique called interpolation to simulate a higher resolution than they actually offer. 300dpi interpolated to 600dpi is certainly better than plain 300dpi, but not as good as true 600dpi. For colour scanners, the 'bit depth' is also important; the higher this number, the more different shades of colour the scanner will be able to distinguish, giving more accurate reproduction of photographic images. 24-bit colour is a common standard. However, higher resolutions and bit depths do produce larger files; if you are planning to do much colour scanning, you will need to invest in optical media (see below), or at least a very large hard disk, to store the scanfiles.

Most desktop scanners are flatbed models: the original is placed on a flat glass surface for scanning, as with a photocopier. These usually cannot handle transparencies unless you buy an extra attachment. Alternatively, a few drum scanners (traditionally the preserve of the printing industry, with five-figure price tags to match) are now available in desktop models, but they are still pricey and only necessary for top-quality professional transparency scanning.

At the bottom end of the market, handheld scanners are fine for small images such as signatures, logos or passport photos, but inadequate for most publishers or designers. Specialist barcode scanners are also available.

Optical character recognition (OCR) software lets you scan printed material, such as a book or typescript, and turns it into text that you can edit in a word processor, by 'recognising' each character. This is useful if you have very large quantities of clearly printed text that you need in an editable form, but OCR is usually more trouble than it's worth for smaller quantities or for badly printed text which the software will find difficult to read. Impressive-sounding claims such as '99% accuracy' disguise the fact that 1% inaccuracy means one in a hundred characters will be wrong – at least one error every 20 words. The time saved on typing may be lost in proofreading the scanned text.

CD-ROM

Many computers sold today have CD-ROM players, also called CD-ROM drives, built in. These let you access information on CD-ROMs, which use a similar technology to audio CDs to store enormous quantities of data: one CD-ROM holds the equivalent of about 450 floppy disks. Software (especially multimedia software), games and reference works such as encyclopaediae are often sold on CD-ROM. You can also use CD-ROM drives to play audio CDs.

If your PC is not supplied with CD-ROM, you can easily buy an external player for around £150. The key thing to look out for is speed: recent CD-ROM players are 'quad-speed', ie four times the speed of the first ones, and some new CD-ROM titles will not function properly on slower players. Nowadays, a 'six-speed' is also available. Compatibility with Kodak's PhotoCD standard is also a slight bonus. Ordinary players don't let you store your own information on CD-ROM, however. To do that you need a CD-ROM recorder, costing around £2,000 for a quad-speed device (single-speed and double-speed are cheaper). Unless you need to publish information on CD-ROM, this is an expensive way of storing your data.

Multimedia

To benefit from the latest multimedia productions (hypertext documents containing audio and video clips) on CD-ROM and the Internet, your PC needs a sound card, some sort of speakers and support for motion video. It's possible to add these in after purchase but much easier, if you expect that work or leisure will lead you in this direction, to look at the machines advertised specifically as 'multimedia PCs'. Voice recording facilities, which are particularly advanced on the Apple computers, are sometimes used in business where people are exchanging computer based documents. You can record a voice message to comment on the document, which is then played back when the recipient opens it on their screen.

Optical and tape media

If you have great quantities of data to store – perhaps you are scanning and archiving colour photos, or you need to keep backups of a large database – consider an optical or tape drive. Optical drives store information on cartridges and work much like floppy disks, insofar as you insert the cartridge into the drive and can then save files onto it or open the files that are stored there, but they hold far more information, with some cartridges accepting 1.3 gigabytes of data, or the equivalent of more than 900 floppies. Tape drives are intended for long-term backup, rather than your working files. They can store even more data than optical cartridges – as much as 4 gigabytes, equivalent to almost 3,000 floppy disks – but putting files on tape and retrieving them off the tape can be slow. They are used for regular data security backups, run overnight when the computer is not in use.

External hard disks and cartridges

If you don't need the capacity of optical or tape media, you can simply add a second hard disk to your PC. These can be bought separately and are plugged into the PC as simply as any other device. They range in size from about 500Mb to 4 gigabytes. A further option, useful if you need to transport large files, is a cartridge based hard disk drive, often referred to as a SyQuest (after a well-known manufacturer). This lets you store data on as many cartridges as you like, simply putting one in the drive when you require it; the easily-portable cartridges commonly store 88Mb, sometimes more. SyQuests are available for Macs and PCs, but are more commonly used in conjunction with Macs.

Modems

The explosion of interest in the Internet, and the growing acceptance of electronic mail (email), are changing the status of the modem from an obscure peripheral to a central part of many people's computing activity. Yet modems have a reputation, not entirely undeserved, for being among the most arcane of PC accessories and the toughest to set up.

Fortunately, there is an easy way to buy a modem: ignore nearly all the technical specifications. There are only a few points you need to check:

■ **internal, external or PCMCIA**

Internal modems, usually the cheapest, are installed directly into a slot in the back of your PC. It's a slightly tricky job, but it only needs to be done once. External modems plug into your PC as easily as a printer does. This means that, unlike internal modems, they can be moved independently of the PC, for instance if you need a temporary modem connection on a client's computer; but they do require their own power supply. PCMCIA modems are intended for notebook computers and come on small cards which fit into the PCMCIA slot; unless there is one of these slots on your PC, a PCMCIA modem is useless. Also available for the widely-roaming teleworker with laptop are expensive GSM modems, usually in the PCMCIA format, which use the worldwide GSM mobile telephony system to let you make wireless modem calls from a portable computer – the modem equivalent of a mobile phone.

■ **modem speed**

Here, the truism that you should buy the fastest you can afford is more than ever true, because a slow modem translates into longer periods spent online and a higher telephone bill. Modem speed is measured in bits per second (bps) or baud, which are not strictly speaking the same thing but usually treated as such. Most modems sold today operate at either 14,400bps (sometimes called V.32bis) or 28,800bps (V.34); the price difference can be minimal but the V.34 models can, in some circumstances, be twice as fast, so a small extra cost is well worth bearing.

(A V.34 modem is not always twice as speedy as a V.32 modem, because any modem can only receive data as fast as the other end of the connection is sending it, or send it as fast as the other end is prepared to receive. So you will occasionally find even a V.34 modem slowing to a snail's pace of 300bps or less, particularly on busy World Wide Websites. In this circumstance the difference in speed rating is, sadly, no help to you, but at other times you will find the faster modem lives up to expectations.)

■ Hayes compatibility and BABT approval

Nearly all modems are marked as Hayes-compatible, which means they will work with communications software that employs the Hayes command set – and that means nearly all available packages. But it's worth double-checking, as a non-Hayes-compatible modem may be difficult to operate with your communications package. In the UK, all devices connected to the phone system must be approved by the BABT, a government board; it's illegal to connect a non-approved device, so check for the green BABT sticker on the modem box. (This is not to say that non-approved devices are not widely used.)

■ software

A modem is no help without the software which lets you control it, dial numbers, and send and receive text and files. At least a rudimentary software package should be sold with the modem (or you may have one already without knowing it; examine the software that was sold with your PC). Many modems let you send and receive faxes; see the section on fax above, but you will need the appropriate software package to do this.

Talking via modem: Internet phones

It's also worth keeping a weather eye on the the development of 'Internet phones'. Using microphones and speakers attached to PCs, these convert the spoken voice into a form which can be carried as data over the Internet, and then reconverted into audible voice at the destination. Theoretically, this lets you carry on an international conversation with acceptable voice quality for no more than the cost of a local phone call to your Internet access provider. However, many experts believe that Internet phones will never take off because, if widely used, they would bring the Net to a standstill by jamming up the available bandwidth. Several large American telecoms companies are attempting to have Internet phones banned by regulators. Demonstrations are available from companies offering this service; try a World Wide Web search for 'Internet phone'.

Software

Software is as, or more, important than the computers on which it is used, and it would be impossible to do such a complex subject justice here. There are thousands of software programs (often referred to as applications, or packages) in existence, and most are updated regularly. The British computer press covers software thoroughly, as do the specialised trade papers of particular industries.

However, a quick tour of the generic software categories will help you prepare a shopping list. Beyond these, there are many, many packages developed to fill particular niches such as computer-telephony integration (CTI), which are likely be well known to you if they are relevant to your particular field of business.

■ **word processors**

Word processors are probably the most widely used category of software, and the one that's essential to nearly every computer user. They allow you to write and edit text on the screen, providing facilities such as search-and-replace (for example, changing all references to 'USSR' to 'CIS' instead); style sheets (an easy way to ensure that all your subheadings, for instance, are in the same typeface and size); a running count of the number of words in a document; headers and footers (automatically placing predefined text at the top or bottom of each page); automatic page numbering and cut-and-paste (an easy way to move large blocks of text from one part of a document to another).

Those are just the common-or-garden features. Many word processing packages also approach the flexibility of desktop publishing, allowing you to mix text with graphics, divide the printed page into columns, and so on. The best known and most widely used word processing packages are Microsoft Word and WordPerfect.

Related to word processing is a new development - voice dictation systems. Teleworking translator Roger Fletcher, who works on Chinese to English medical translations, recently purchased an IBM VoiceType Dictation system. Although Roger can type at 80 wpm, his work often requires both hands free as the Chinese characters are small and detailed, sometimes needing magnification. Fletcher dictates at between 70 and 100 wpm with a slight gap between words. The system "learns" a particular user's voice. "Some perserverance is required at the beginning, but what takes your breath away is the speed at which the package learns. If you just want the odd letter typed, you're not going to invest in this software. But it's really of benefit to anyone who processes large quantities of text, for example authors and editors, so obviously it will put some WP operators out of work". The system was retailing at £829 when this guide went to press.

■ spreadsheets

Spreadsheets are specialised tools for the large-scale manipulation of numbers, usually, but not necessarily, financial. A spreadsheet document is divided into rows and columns, forming an array or table of 'cells'. In each cell, you can enter a number, or you can define the cell in terms of other cells: for example, the cell 'Profit' could be defined as equal to the cell 'Sales' minus the cell 'Costs'. Then, when you enter a new figure in the cell 'Sales', the number in the cell 'Profit' will change accordingly.

Very complex financial models, covering the operation of a large company, can be set up this way – and by changing a single figure, you can easily predict the effect that a change in one aspect of the company's operations would have on other areas. For example, if paper costs rose by 10% but rent fell by 5%, would your firm be more or less profitable? The best known spreadsheet packages are Lotus and Excel.

■ databases

Databases are used to store data in a structured way. Each database is composed of a large number of records, each made up of fields. For example, in a database of customers, one record would represent each customer; the fields might include name, address, credit limit, and so on. Once the information has been typed in or imported from another database you can then sort and analyse the data in many ways: what are the names of customers who spent more than £500 in 1995 and live in Guildford? Using some advanced database features takes great skill, so it's worth checking out comparative reviews to find a package that will meet your needs but not demand that you learn a complicated programming language. Popular packages include Microsoft Access, Dbase and Foxbase.

■ desktop publishing

DTP software is used to design pages of type and images, for newsletters, books, brochures, forms and any other kind of printed matter. There is great variation between the cheaper packages intended for home or casual use, and the powerful professional systems that can be used to produce a commercial magazine. Pick the right package for your level of expertise and presentation. Widely used professional packages include Quark Xpress, Adobe Pagemaker and Corel Ventura.

■ graphics

Graphics software is slightly different in that it's usually employed to create or manipulate single images, such as logos, rather than entire publications. Again, there is a vast gap between hobbyist and professional-level software, and knowledge of printing processes is required to get best final results. The best known professional packages are Corel Draw, Adobe Illustrator and Macromedia Freehand.

■ **presentations**

Presentation software is often similar to graphics software but is used to create presentations that you can display on your computer. Usually these combine text, graphics and images in a series of 'slides'. Microsoft Powerpoint and Adobe Persuasion are widely used.

■ **contact managers**

Contact managers are specialised databases used for storing personal contact details, often used in conjunction with PC-based fax software, email or telephone control systems.

■ **time or calendar managers**

Time managers, likewise, are databases set up to help you schedule your diary. Advanced time management packages, called project-management tools, can be used to plan and schedule ventures involving many people, such as the organisation of an exhibition.

■ **accounting**

Accounting packages ask you to type in financial data such as your daily expenditures and sales, and then produce summarised accounts for you, saving you the trouble of sorting out which information should go where and adding it all up. It's a good idea to ask your accountant's advice before buying one of these, as not all such packages produce information in a form that's acceptable to banks and tax authorities. American accounting packages, particularly, follow US norms which sometimes differ dramatically from British practice. The two most widely used by UK small businesses are Quicken and Sage.

■ **CSCW tools (groupware)**

Groupware tools are used to help work teams collaborate over a network or over the internet (see also Chapter 2, *Implementing teleworking*). Groupware facilities can include editing of documents by multiple authors, electronic diaries, email conferencing, access to networked databases and electronic forms (e.g. to record customer contacts). By far the best-known package in this area is Lotus Notes, now owned by IBM, which is used by many major corporations. A recent addition to the market is Microsoft Exchange, which acts as a message centre for fax and voicemail as well as email. Novell Groupwise has a substantial following too. For individual teleworkers, a number of Internet groupware products are being developed, where all that is required for access is an Internet subscription. Examples include Collage, which provides an electronic chalkboard, available via ftp from

I'm a freelance copy editor working from home. Last year I was working for a major international publisher, and the author's disks turned out to include the virus Stoned. To cure Stoned, the author's computer staff sent me a doctor disk that contained the much more lethal virus Flip, which put my machines out of action for months and cost me over £1,000.

The author's company at first refused compensation. "The responsibility is with the end user." The publisher offered a mean advance against future work of £400. Before I could respond they changed track and dropped me altogether - my chief source of copy-editing income for 15 years. When pressed, they said it wasn't due to the virus but because I'd upset an author three years earlier. There was nothing I could do despite support from my professional association, the Society of Freelance Editors and Proofreaders.

The Computer Crime Unit at Scotland yard says passing on viruses is illegal under the 1990 Computer misuses Act. They confirmed that Flip came from the author's company disks. I then received £500 compensation. The publisher still paid nothing. I subscribed to Dr Solomon's anti-virus toolkit, and the brilliant Pete Edgeler spent hours on the phone talking me through rescue procedures. I think the author's company, which had professional computer staff, should have helped more. Take my advice – don't put any visiting disks into your machine, wherever they come from. [Name and address withheld].

ftp.ncsa.uiuc.edu/UNIX/XCollage/Collage1.2, WebBoard from O'Reilly (http://www.ora.com) and CoSy, which includes email and conferencing systems (http://www.softwords.bc.ca). A useful site for information about this fast-moving area is http://www.collaborate.com.

When shopping for software, don't ignore shareware: a class of semi-commercial software which is distributed free, or at nominal cost, but for which you're expected to pay the author a small fee if you use it regularly. Shareware doesn't always have all the bells and whistles of the big commercial packages, but the best shareware certainly beats an indifferent commercial product, and often at a fraction of the cost. You'll often find it on the free disks with computer magazines; recommendations from friends, colleagues and user groups are also worth following up. Before buying software, be absolutely sure that it will run on your computer: that it's written for a compatible model (Mac software won't run on PCs or vice-versa), that you have enough RAM to run it, and that you have a compatible monitor. All the requirements should be printed on the box in which the software is sold.

Computer security

Most fears of computer crime and computer viruses are exaggerated – but then we buckle our seatbelts even though we're unlikely to crash. Here are some security issues you should consider, which are also covered in the Chapter 7, *Staying Safe and Legal.*

Do you have **virus-screening** software to ensure that the floppy disks you use or receive are virus-free? Such software is available free or at nominal cost from bulletin boards and user groups, as there are well known commercial packages such as Dr Solomon's AntiVirus tools, Symantec's Norton Utilities and utilities from McAfee Associates. Viruses are very rare, but a single occurrence could damage vital data and, if you passed it onto a client via a disk, cost you your good name.

Do you allow anyone to dial in to your computer by modem? Consider operating a **password/callback** system to prevent unauthorised access. With Internet access becoming commonplace, you are less likely to need to provide dial-in facilities; information can be exchanged relatively safely using the Net as an intermediary. However, there is a widespread virus which is spread through Word files sent across the Internet, and it is likely that in future hackers will turn their attention to viruses which can be spread across the Internet.

Are you worried that an employee might set up in **competition** to you? Use password protection systems on your computer or network. Keep a close eye on what is being taken in and out of the office.

Do you keep anything on your computer that you would lock up if it was on paper? Get an **access-control program** which can lock files and directories unless the correct password is given.

If you work at home, do **children** have access to your computer? Access-control software is needed again – it's easy for play to accidentally delete or alter files.

Do you keep **stationery** that could be misused? (For example, you might have a pharmaceutical company's headed paper that could be used to obtain samples of controlled substances.) Keep a check on paper stocks. Lock them up if necessary.

Have you **backup systems** in place in case your computer or network crashes? Institute a regular backup system. Consider storing some of the backups elsewhere in case fire, theft or flood destroys both computers and backups.

Are you at risk from **theft?** Computers, being portable, anonymous and high-value, are favoured targets of thieves. Protect them physically as you would anything else worth thousands of pounds yet so easily pinchable.

Other equipment

There are a number of items of non-computer and telecoms equipment that you may need depending on the teleworking services you are offering. If you cannot justify purchasing the equipment outright, consider using it at a telecottage, or a printshop. It is a good idea to try out equipment at these facilities so that you can work out what you require before you purchase.

Photocopiers

The best advice here is to consult consumer guides on the machine best suited to your needs. Estimate how many copies you make a month and check out maintenance contracts carefully. If you are entering into a service agreement, check what breakdown guarantees are being given and how quickly your photocopier will be returned to working order. Bear in mind that in the computer age, fewer photocopies are needed. The new buzz word is mopying – multiple original copying – using sophisticated laser printers. You may alternatively be better off using a local photocopying bureau. However, there are some bargains to be had on the secondhand market because many older photocopiers are physically bulky despite their good quality and so are being replaced. Look into charge cards if you are running a photocopying bureau service. You sell a prepaid card to the customer which entitles them to a number of copies. There are now a number of peripherals which combine fax, scanning, printing and photocopying such as the HP OfficeJet, and colour photocopiers have come down substantially in price recently.

Tape recorders

Tape recorders fulfil several purposes. Pocket memo machines can be used for recording thoughts or verbal 'notes' when you're away from the office, perhaps for transcribing later by an audio typist. Telephone recording devices are often used by journalists to record phone interviews and can be useful to others; even where a recording is not needed as a legal precaution, preserving a complicated, technical conversation this way can be more reliable than using hastily scrawled notes. Small acoustic devices which connect a handset to an ordinary tape recorder cost a few pounds from specialist electronics shops, though they are not high-fidelity.

Be aware that the legal position surrounding telephone recording is complex; generally, attaching a device to the innards of the telephone (as opposed to an acoustic microphone affixed to the outside) is not allowed, but ask the phone company if you are in any doubt.

Transcribing machines are vital for audio-typing services. There are three main tape sizes, and each has different transcribers, so be sure that you know what size tapes you will be sent and that you have the correct transcriber size. The sizes are: C-size standard audio cassettes, Philips minicassettes and Dictaphone minicassettes. Transcribers usually have a pedal which controls the tape, and headphones, although if you are working alone it is great to be able to switch the transcriber on to its loudspeaker and dispense with those infuriating headphones.

Postal equipment and services

If you expect to send a large volume of mail, ask at your post office about franking machines, which save you the trouble of buying and licking stamps. Post offices will also frank bulk mailings for you by prior arrangement, without the need for investing in a franking machine, and can give you details of Freepost or Reply Paid services to increase reply rates to your mailings.

Other useful services include:

- **Special Delivery** (Mon–Fri) guarantees delivery by 12.30 pm next working day to "virtually anywhere in the UK", no signature required.Cost £2.70 on top of normal postage. An enquiry line is available to check on whether delivery has been achieved.

- **Registered Post** (Mon–Fri) guarantees delivery by 12.30 pm and does require a signature on receipt. £500 compensation is paid if the item is lost or damaged. Cost £3.00. An enquiry line is available to check on whether delivery has been received.

- **Recorded Delivery** ensures delivery only if a signature can be taken from the delivery address. Items are not tracked by an enquiry line.

- **Swiftair** provides fast express airmail to overseas destinations. The service costs £2.70 on top of normal airmail postage, but the delivery times cannot be guaranteed. On average they are:
  Germany 2.3 days
  Ireland 2.6 days
  Belgium 2.3 days
  US 5.1 days
  NZ 5.5 days

- **Parcelforce** provides deliveries for larger packages where cost depends on the service chosen. Eg for a 10 kg package, delivery by 10 am next working day costs £20.65, but for delivery within 48 hours, you only pay £7.30 for the same package.

- **Datapost** provides a courier service with delivery by 12.00 next day, but you have to take the item to the post office – it is not collected.

Whichever service you are selecting, check with your local post office about cut-off times. Often services such as Datapost are collected earlier – say 4.30 pm – than normal last collection times.

Binding and print-finishing equipment

If you think you will be preparing reports and prospectuses and manuals, look into binding equipment such as guillotines, large staplers, large hole-punchers, comb binders, and laminators, which provide a protective plastic covering for covers and certificates.

Fittings and furniture

You can be almost certain that you will run out of electric sockets by the time you have equipped your home office. It is safer and more effective to have the home office rewired to provide extra sockets. If this is not possible, buy proper 4-way multisockets, available at any hardware or DIY shop. Do not use "towers" of 2-way adaptors plugged together and powered from one socket. This is a serious fire risk.

If you can afford it, have a surge-suppressed socket fitted for the computer to prevent the computer crashing in the event of fluctuations in the mains electricity, or voltage spikes caused by lightning.

Don't neglect the mundane: do you have suitable desks, and chairs? You will need a proper typist's chair if you are going to sit for long hours at the computer. Some people find kneeling chairs great for back pain. Have you got filing cabinets? Drawers and shelves? Can you reach everything easily? People in information-oriented jobs, such as editors and market researchers, usually find they run out of space for papers and reference materials.

Make sure that the office lighting is good, and that you have your eyes tested if you are not used to working with computers. Computers can produce considerable heat in a small room. Do you need fans or air conditioning?

Try to avoid pets near computers – pet hair does not agree with disk drives, and air intakes for fans can also become clogged with fur. Think about security. If everyone outside can see your expensive computer equipment, do you need to do something about preventing vandals and burglars?

Smoke alarms are always a good idea, especially if you are a smoker. A fire extinguisher may be required by local regulations in some business premises, as may a basic first-aid kit. Water and foam extinguishers are suitable for different fire risks; the fire safety office at your local fire station will be happy to advise. In larger premises, or if you store many valuable paper documents, a sprinkler system could be considered. All these investments, particularly fire extinguishers, need to be regularly checked and regulations or insurers may require you to have them checked by an outside service firm.

Contacts

BT Featureline 0800 400 400

BT telephone sales and services information   152 (Toll free UK only)

Voice dictation systems IBM VoiceType 01705 492249

Callbox 200 CTI system Contact John Chapman at Singleton Corporation Tel: 01600 714478 Fax: 01600 716451.

MultiMedia and TeleConferencing Solutions Ltd (MaTS) are suppliers of a number of videoconferencing products Tel: 01628 771027.

Telephone directory on CD-ROM - contact TDS 01345 697630.

Printback remote printing software: Primrose computers Tel: 01203 694 996

Andest Vantage VPA combines voicemail, auto-attendant (computerised instructions to caller) fax, fax back, and data features Tel: 01280 821841

For those considering a PC security device, a good starting point is the Loss Prevention Certification Board's list of Approved Fire and Security Products and Services Tel: 0181 236 9600.

Videoconferencing

Picturephone direct (vendors of videoconferencing systems) have pages at http://www.picturephone.com

RSI systems provides its videoconferencing via a separate box attached using a SCSI interface, rather than inserting a card into the computer. http://www.rsisystems.com

A cheap and cheerful system is Connectix QuickCam for about £150. http://www.connectix.com

At http://goliath.wpine.com/cudownload.htm you can find out about the CU-SeeMe software which can be downloaded from the Internet.

The Vivo Telework-5 comes recommended by the European TeleConferencing federation. It's H.320 standards compatible and uses an IBM WaveRunner ISDN card, a Logitec video Xcaputre card with microphone and speaker, all for about £1500. Collaborative computing software for use with the system costs about £100, and your computer will need to be something like a Pentium 133Mhz or similar for really good results.

Internet phones

Quarterdeck £49.95 plus VAT Tel: 01245 496 699 Email: info@qdeck.co.uk

Digiphone (not yet released in UK) http://www.planeteers.com

Training for teleworkers

As a teleworker, you must take responsibility for your own knowledge and skills. In planning training, focus on the goal of the learning – to make your services more saleable – and feel free to use any method to get the information you need, including online references, exchanges of information with colleagues, bought in technical support services etc. At the moment, you don't know enough to enable your business to survive for the next five years. You have to get that knowledge while continuing to run a business. There are gaps in your knowledge, skills and understanding; you may be able to identify some of those gaps now, but others won't become apparent for some time to come. This chapter aims to help you:

- identify gaps in your learning
- plan to plug those gaps
- look forward, manage and anticipate your learning needs

It is contributed by Brian Goggin of Wordwrights, a virtual company which works to prepare training courses including distance and open learning material.

Who are you?

The amount you need to learn depends to some extent on your role:

- employee in telecottage or telecentre
- employed telecommuter
- self-employed service provider
- manager or employer of others.

If you're an employee, you may be able to depend on your employer to provide all the training you need for your present job. You probably won't have to worry about any gaps in your portfolio of knowledge and skills – at least until the next round of redundancies comes along. You might, however, think it wise to take an active role in managing your own learning and increasing your knowledge and skills; that way, you'll be better prepared for:

- changing demands in your existing job
- promotional opportunities in your current employment
- changing to other employers
- becoming self-employed
- employing others.

Thus the material below should be as important to you as it is to others, but you can choose to be a passive rather than an active learner if you wish.

If you're responsible for managing a business (self-employed, employing others or managing others), you don't really have a choice: you have to learn and keep on learning.

At this stage, you can choose what you want to do with this chapter:

- put it away until you need to think seriously about training
- put it away forever
- skim through it
- work through it.

Working through it means getting a pen and some paper and making some notes; those notes should help you to draw up a realistic training plan. If you want to try that, here's your first assignment:

- Divide your piece of paper into two columns. In the first, write a list of the main work-related things you've learned in the past year. In the second, say where and how you learned each of those things.

Learning things

Look back on your list of where and how you learned. How much of your learning occurred on formal courses? And how much occurred outside them? Where and how did you learn:

- how to use WinZip?
- how to attach files to your e-mails?
- how to install an internal modem?
- how to embed CorelDRAW graphics in Word 6 files?
- how your best customer likes to receive finished work?
- what your bank manager considers a reasonable overdraft limit?
- how to reduce your tax?
- where you can find a cheap, reliable graphic designer?

The point is that you learn a lot outside of formal training or educational courses. So there's no point in confining this discussion to formal training and education – or in getting hung up on formal definitions. For teleworkers, training means learning stuff, irrespective of how you learn it.

Useful knowledge

It's 11.00pm on Sunday night. You've completed a major job for an important new client whom you're keen to impress. It's due to be on the client's desk at 9.00am on Monday and, for one reason or another, it's a last minute job. (Of course that never happens to you, but just pretend for the moment.)

You've finished the work; the file is ready for transmission. You dial your Internet service provider... and suddenly your modem starts making funny noises. One hour later, it's still doing the same thing; you've finished the whiskey and you're tempted to use the empty bottle to smash the computer.

At that moment, the clouds roll back and a Voice speaks. It offers you a choice: you can have free enrolment on a two year full-time MBA programme at a leading management college or you can have a five minute conversation with someone who knows how to fix modems. Which do you choose?

You may be tempted to say that MBA-holders don't have last minute problems with faulty modems and that good management would have avoided the difficulty, but an MBA-holder is more likely to be the Voice than the humble mortal struggling with the modem. For many small businesses (teleworking or other), especially those starting up, there's such a huge amount to be learned that you have to ration the time and money allocated to learning.

In general, that means a preference for relevance. It's no doubt very worthy to invest in Developing Human Potential by enrolling (or helping employees to enrol) on degree courses in Sanskrit, Sociology or Psychology, but you've got to be sure there will be an immediate return to the business. Furthermore, you've got to remember the opportunity cost: if you're funding a BA(Sanskrit), you may not be able to afford to send someone on a course on fixing modems.

There are two further lessons from the modem story. First, qualifications and awards are not, in themselves, important. It's better to go on a non-accredited course that teaches exactly what you want than to take an NVQ, SVQ or National Certificate that doesn't really meet your needs. Remember, the fact that a course is accredited doesn't necessarily mean that the content is exactly what you want – or that the teaching is any good.

Second, some knowledge is time-bounded. Before 11.00pm on that Sunday night, you didn't need to know about the class of modem problem you encountered; once you'd fixed the problem, you probably wouldn't ever need to know about it again.

Need to know?

There's a lot of knowledge and skills that you might need to have available. Take five or six sheets of paper; start writing down as many things as you can think of – things you don't yet know. You might like to use a separate sheet for whichever of these subject areas is relevant to you:

- your own specialism (accountancy, design, sales consultancy or whatever it is)
- entrepreneurship, business and management
- computers (hardware and software)
- communications technology (modems, Internet, phones, faxes etc.)
- the management of virtual organisations (including working with others, project teams etc).

Add a sheet for any other area you can think of. The first time you try this, you won't be able to think of everything. So keep the sheets somewhere convenient (maybe stick them on the wall) and carry on adding stuff to them. Ask friends, colleagues, customers, employees or contractors for suggestions and ideas.

Look ahead. Think about how your business is going to go; think how your customers' demands will change. What about the technology? What will you have to do to keep up? And how about your competitors? How will you counter their devious plots? Think about the little things. It's all very well knowing how to develop an ongoing corporate finance strategy, but you also need some basic information like:

- which customers are likely to pay on time
- which suppliers you can squeeze by delaying payment
- what new industries (potential clients?) are moving into the area
- how your customers' purchasing procedures work
- where you can order cheap stationery by phone for overnight delivery.

That sort of thing isn't usually covered in training courses, so you may not think of it as training. But that's no reason to ignore it: you need to know. Training providers may not be able to help you, but you should still make a deliberate effort to learn these things.

Keep your lists; keep reviewing them, adding to them and crossing things off when you've provided for them.

Delegate some learning

You've categorised your learning needs in one way, by grouping them in five or six subject areas. Now it's time to do a bit more sorting. At this stage, transfer to a separate list anything that you can get other people to know for you. Dr Johnson said:

"Knowledge is of two kinds. We know a subject ourselves, or we know where we can find information upon it."

For instance, how much do you really need to know about taxation? It's important, sure, but (unless you're offering tax-related services to your customers) you can get by with

- a system for ensuring you obey the law
- expert advice on call whenever you need it.

Professional advisers and consultants

You can get the system and the advice from your accountant. Using consultants or professional advisers means paying somebody else to know things for you. This handbook will have shown you many of the areas in which there are things to be known.

Go through your lists and remove (to separate lists) anything you can delegate to professional advisers or consultants. As well as tax and

> **Reclassifying your learning**
>
> One way of reducing the learning load is to reclassify some tasks. For instance, rather than learning the basics of double-entry bookkeeping, you might reclassify the task as "Get and learn accounts software." If you use a cheap package like Quicken for simple accounts, you won't have to learn much accounting at all. You may have to argue with your accountant (because Quicken won't really do a trial balance), but you'll have a simpler task and the benefit of Quicken's excellent built-in training.

accounting, you might include planning, law, the drawing up of documents and so on.

Obviously you'll have to go through the lists of delegated items and decide what you can afford. But remember, you pay someone else so that you can save your own time. Your accountant may, in five minutes, give you an answer that you'd otherwise spend a day finding. If you have a lot of time on your hands, you may be able to investigate everything for yourself. If you have lucrative work to do, get on with it, and pay other people for professional advice.

Colleagues and staff

In their early days, many self-employed people do have to learn a lot of things themselves, because they can't afford to pay the professionals. Later, if their businesses grow and they take on colleagues or employees, they may feel they should still be omniscient. That's a mistake.

In large organisations, the Chief Executive isn't expected to know everything. A squad of accountants is employed to know about accounting; a squad of designers knows about designing; a squad of cleaners knows about cleaning. The same should apply in small businesses. If you take on a partner or colleague, there's no point in getting someone who knows exactly the same things that you do. Instead, you want someone who knows what you don't know; you want division of the labour of learning.

As well as colleagues or partners, you may have junior employees or contractors. They know things too – things that you don't know. And they have the capacity to learn more. As you'll see below, you don't have to send them on expensive training courses to get them learning. At the very least, they can learn from their everyday experience and from the materials around them, but you'll probably be able to go further. If you are working in a virtual company or network of teleworkers, it may be worth discussing barter arrangements on training costs. For example, Jane wants Sally to improve her HTML authoring skills, but Sally is a part-time worker with young children and no funds available for training. Jane might offer to pay for the training course on the understanding that Sally will do free work to the value of half the training course over a period of months. That way, the expense is made manageable for Sally, while Jane gets access to the skill she needs. And Sally has an incentive to put her new knowledge to work.

So go back through your lists again. This time, remove (to separate lists) anything that your colleagues or staff already know or could be encouraged to learn.

Your network

By this stage, your list of things to be learned should be getting shorter. Your next step is to find things that members of your network know and can help you with. In practice, your network is anyone you know. So when your modem breaks down at 11.00pm on Sunday night, you start thinking who might be able to help:

- that affable person you met at the TCA conference
- your friendly computer-supplier
- the village nerd
- your sixteen-year-old nephew who knows how to program the video
- the woman you worked with on that project last year; the one who seemed to know everything about modems and the Internet and stuff
- your competitor in the next town
- the wild-eyed nutter in your customer's computer department (the one who said "Call me anytime")
- the entire population of the Telework Europa Forum on CompuServe (if you can access it)
- the supplier's web page... if only the modem was working!

You probably have many more sources of help available to you than most small businesses have. And it's likely that at least some of them will be working on Sunday night. OK, they may not be delighted to hear from you, but they'll probably help.

Of course if you keep ringing people up at 11.00pm on Sunday night, they're going to get a bit fed up with you. So maybe you should think about an agreement of some kind, formal or informal: you promise to provide expertise on printers in return for help on modems, or a commercial arrangement with a competent computer dealer.

For many teleworkers, such arrangements are both helpful and unthreatening. This week, you and the telecottage in the next village may be competing for a contract; next week they may be employing you; the week after you may be employing them. You do them a favour this week; they reciprocate next week. With shifting alliances and temporary project teams, cooperation is sensible and non-threatening.

So go through your lists again; remove (to separate lists) anything for which you already have a knowledge-sharing arrangement. Then mark anything for which you might be able to set up such an arrangement. Remember, there has to be something in it for the others as well as for you.

When do you need to know it?

Now that you're dealing with a shorter list, you can do some more categorisation. This time, think about when you'll need to know each remaining item on your lists. For instance, you might find some items like these:

What you need to know about	When you need to know it
Using email	Next week
Selling your services to large corporations	Three months' time
Interviewing applicants for jobs	Next month
Fixing modems	In an emergency
Windows 95	Immediately a client asks for it
Ratio analysis	When the end-of-year accounts are ready
Delegating	As soon as possible
Drawing up a web page	Whenever there's time

Your list will no doubt be longer, but you get the general idea. The important thing is to avoid classifying everything as "Immediately" or "Next week". You just can't do it all at once, so don't even try. You've got to categorise your learning needs. Postpone anything that can be postponed: yes, it would be nice to know all about Windows 95, but if your customers don't care, why should you? And rank the rest in order of importance: maybe you should learn how to take on (and train) the new staff member first and then learn about delegating afterwards.

Certified courses

Certified courses are those which provide you with a certificate at their conclusion. They are not always the most appropriate for the fast-changing world of the teleworker, but it is always worth considering what is on offer.

RSA, City & Guilds, BTEC

These bodies award certification for further education vocational courses. RSA has a largely secretarial bias and is well-respected by employers for its insistence on high levels of accuracy. City & Guilds has a wider remit, covering subjects from photography to IT. BTEC is aimed at 16+ full time education normally to intermediate GNVQ level (one year courses equivalent to GCSE) or advanced GNVQ (two year course equivalent to A-levels).

NVQs

NVQs are not the same as GNVQs. They are vocational training courses which emphasise on-the-job training, taking into account existing skills plus some classroom and private study. NVQ students normally build up a portfolio of documentary evidence of their skills in order to achieve certification. The TCA has drawn up a Teleworking VQ, which may be developed to become a full NVQ (see separate box).

Degree courses and extramural studies

Degrees in themselves may or may not be useful to a teleworker – it depends on the individual's skills and profession, though few would doubt the value of an MBA for any business owner if you have the time, intellect and money to obtain one. Many universities and colleges also offer shorter, non-degree courses. On these courses, students do not become full members of the institution and therefore may not have to meet normally stringent entrance requirements. Extramural courses, like NVQs, often award credits for existing skills. They are also modularised, like NVQs, with modules building towards the final certificate, and can often be "moved" from one college to another if the student needs to move.

Flexible or open learning

This is learning at your own pace, often using a workbook or taskbook. You complete an assignment and hand it in for assessment. Increasingly, such courses also make use of CD-ROM and computer-based training, as well as of the Internet and email.

Commercial courses

These are normally required for software or hardware skills. They are unregulated, but many manufacturers, including Microsoft, Adobe and Hewlett Packard, run accredited trainer programmes. Use accredited trainers wherever possible.

Rough guide to teleworker training needs

• **training in specialisms**
A wide variety of skills can be teleworked; many, such as accounting and graphic design, have existing, well established training routes. Information on courses is normally available from professional bodies.

• **training in small business management and entrepreneurship**
There are many courses available, both state and commercially run. One of the hardest areas in practice for startup teleworkers seems to be producing viable business ideas; this can be seen in the survival struggles of some of the rural telecottages. Here workshops with business and marketing advisors are probably the best approach – if such an initiative is not available in your area, contact other local teleworkers and approach local authorities as a group to request help.

• **training in basic computer skills**
There is substantial provision in existing training structures for computer skills – the problem is finding it. Information about the available courses is often widespread – consult local training bodies, the Yellow Pages, colleges and schools to check provisions in your area. One topic is currently poorly served by existing courses – the area of "housekeeping" and administration of computers, such as correct use of data backup, installation of software and conversion of data from one format to another. Teleworkers often receive data in one software package and then need to convert it to another package, add value and information and perhaps export it back to the client in a third file format. Many of these problems need to be handled as they are encountered and fall into the area of provision of technical support to teleworkers. This area is often avoided on conventional training courses delivered via low-specification educational PC networks because the last thing the average educational computer suite needs is twenty students messing with its internal workings.

• **training in communications technology e.g. use of the Internet**
Internet training is generally only available from the commercial sector. An approach which mixes conventional basic "hands on" training with technical support/mentoring is likely to be most successful. Related to the technical use of communications technology is the area of communications (interpersonal) skills, such as listening techniques. Such skills are best imparted via workshop sessions.

• **training in the management of virtual organisations**
This need is is clearly recognised by those who have been teleworking for a number of years. The subjects that need to be covered include project management, effective use of email, videoconferencing, CSCW tools, file transfer, recruitment and management of staff at distant locations and the conduct of face-to-face meetings between teleworking teams. This area can be productively tackled through workshop based programmes.

You will have to provide for some emergency items. Even if you intend to rely on someone else for expertise on modems, you may need to know some of the basics yourself, just in case there's nobody available on Sunday night.

For some items, you may find it best to prepare now to learn later. You may not need to know, right now, how to fix your modem or how to use Windows 95, but you may be able to prepare so that you can learn the moment the need arises. So, for instance, you might buy some learning materials (see below) about modems or Windows. You then know where you can find information on the subject; you have a resource to hand. When your modem crashes, you can start learning straight away. And, at 11.00pm on Sunday, it may be easier to find your book than someone to help.

Training needs analysis

By this stage, you've done a training needs analysis, not just for yourself but for your whole organisation (if any). You've set out what you, your colleagues and your staff are going to learn and when they're going to learn it. You've also identified some things that you're not going to learn because you'll rely on other people; in other words, you're going to make good use of your scarce resources of time and money. The next step is to work out how you're going to learn the things you need to know about. Now jot down every learning opportunity you can think of.

Learning opportunities

The phrase learning opportunities is used here because it encourages you to think of a wide range of ways of learning. You may have done your own list by this stage; here are some possibilities.

Experience

Much of your success will depend on your work skills (honed through experience) and your knowledge of your market (gained through experience). It's possible to get better value from experience by managing it. Imagine the scene once more. It's 11.00pm on Sunday night – but you remember the story… only this time, you want to hit yourself with the bottle, because this is the second time this has happened. You got the problem fixed last time, but how? Nervously you lift the phone and start looking for someone to help. Finally, you get a disgruntled mate who says "Not again! I fixed that for you six months ago."

You, your colleagues and your staff and your contractors need to keep logs, recording significant events and what you learned from them. You might include:

- computer problems and how they were fixed
- stroppy clients and how you dealt with them

- financing problems and how they were overcome
- designers, good and bad, you've worked with
- safety problems, their causes and their cures

and anything else of interest. Yes, you might be able to remember some of this stuff, but a lot of useful knowledge will be lost unless you record it on paper, card or computer.

Planned experience

While the last category covered learning from ordinary everyday happenings, planned experience means arranging something from which you (or someone else) can learn. Some examples:

- getting two of your staff to swap jobs for a week so each can learn about the other's work (and thus be better able to provide cover for absences)
- going on a round of visits to potential clients to learn what they want (before going back to sell your services to them)
- trying the beta version of a new software package to see whether it would suit your business
- visiting your competitors to see what you can learn
- assigning someone to a different business in a different location to pick up new ideas.

Those are just a few possibilities; there are lots more. Apart from the planning, the essential point is that you have to extract the learning afterwards. That may mean a debriefing session, a written report or a seminar, but in some way you record whatever (good or bad) has been learned. This sort of activity is very cheap and can be very productive.

Magazines

There is a huge number of magazines, most of them quite cheap, on a vast range of topics. Several of the computer magazines come with demo disks so you can learn about new software; there are also reviews, ads and feature articles.

Treat such magazines as part of your learning provision. Don't just put them in the reception area; read them yourself and circulate them to everybody else. The cost is small (much cheaper than training courses) so you'll be able to keep up with developments with very little trouble.

Books

Books are amongst the cheapest learning resources available. There's a huge number available, on practically any subject you care to mention, covering topics to any depth you care to mention. They're much easier to read than anything comparably detailed on the World Wide Web.

Go and buy books. Set up a basic library: books on computers, accounting, marketing, employment and so on. Add to your library every

The KITE approach: a pyramid and a circle

At the KITE telecottage in Enniskillen, four years of experience in teleworker training has given Managing Director Sheila McCaffrey a clear idea of how training and telecentre operations work hand in hand.

KITE's original mission was to use a virtuous circle of training, childcare and commercial work to provide employment in rural Co. Fermanagh. The telecottage received funds from the European Social Fund amongst other sources to provide a comprehensive initial training period for 8 teleworkers, including software skills, personal development and business administration. A number of modules were run on site at KITE by the local Fermanagh College. Because most of the teleworkers were women, they could not have attended the rigorous full time course without access to KITE's registered childcare facility. And from the start, Sheila was determined to ensure the KITE workers were trained not just in the skills, but in the practical application of the skills, doing real work for real commercial customers, so that they could understand and reinforce the training they were receiving.

Sheila believes that it takes around two years of full-time training and work experience to train a teleworker with no previous experience, but who had previously received second level education to age 18. The problem is, this is a very long lead-time for a growing business like KITE. Also some of the students will, through natural wastage or discovering teleworking isn't for them, drop out of the training process. So now Sheila is adding in the idea of the training pyramid.

At the bottom of the pyramid, KITE is offering personal development and assertiveness training as a prerequisite to basic computer training in word processing and spreadsheets for around 180 people in the local area, funded through the European Social Fund. From this broad base, she expects about 30 people to move up a level and show sufficient interest and aptitude to go forward to the teleworking VQ qualification. Of these, perhaps 8–10 will reach the top of the pyramid and go on to work at the telecottage or other local hi-tech businesses. Sheila hopes to repeat these activities, constantly feeding in to the bottom of the pyramid, and at the top offering employment to those who "make the grade".

Unfortunately, such a forward-looking approach is difficult for funding authorities to understand, and grants for the pyramid are proving problematic. Sheila emphasises the importance of personal development modules to ensure students understand why they are doing a course and what they want to get out of it, right down to how many hours a week they are prepared to work if they do get a job. Analysing and building up motivation are crucial for the teleworker training to succeed in the long run. Because the KITE students also see and assist with the commercial operation of the telecottage from an early stage, they understand the goal of their training, which gives the KITE course a special hands-on flavour and also ensures that no irrelevant training is given.

year; keep it up to date. If you have a local library, borrow other stuff when you need it. Encourage staff to consult the books. And read them yourself!

Libraries

Some libraries are starting to include CD-ROM and other sources of electronic documentation such as WWW sites in their collections. Even if your library does not offer this level of sophistication, talk to your local librarians about your information needs – they may well be able to help you access a wealth of relevant documents. In the UK, well over half of all public libraries provide online searching and CD-ROM facilities. A 1995 British Library R&D report by Monica Blake identified four functions of public libraries relevant to teleworkers:

- reference services with expert reference librarians available to help enquirers find information
- a means of access to knowledge and culture
- resources and skills that enable enquirers to obtain information on vital issues
- information and intelligence for business, trade, employment and training.

Seminars and conferences

In this sense, a seminar is a drink after work on Friday. Try to meet people in other businesses. Swap experiences and insights . Learn from them. Build your network. Go to relevant conferences – good ones will reinvigorate you, teach you new things and increase your network of contacts.

Working with others

If you can, try to work on projects with other teleworkers. Every time you do that (no matter who leads the project), you'll learn more. And you'll have more people you can talk to, more networkers you can ring when you have a problem.

Customers

Your customers possess a lot of information. Some of it could help you to gain more business: if you knew their needs better, you could develop products to meet those needs. But there's also information about operational procedures, standards, equipment and so on, information that may not translate immediately into sales but that could help to improve your business.

It's also worth remembering that most people are glad to help if they can – try ringing other organisations that you think may have had a similar problem and asking for advice or information on how they coped.

See what you can learn from your clients. Pick up information during your visits and discussions. Ask about their vendor assessment (before they ask you – see Chapter 9, *Quality for Teleworkers* for more information on vendor assessment). Show a willingness to adapt to what you learn. And make sure you document your learning.

Funding the training

Higher education courses of two years or more qualify for grants to cover fees and living expenses for anyone who has not already taken a degree or HND.

Unfortunately, this only applies to full time study. No grants are available for part-time study. However, a number of telework-related courses are funded through the European Social Fund (see Chapter 1, Overview). Usually to qualify for these you have to fall into a category of disadvantage (unemployed, women returner, rural dweller). Your local TEC will probably have free courses for anyone starting a small business, regardless of their status.

Vocational courses can qualify for Career Development Loans. These are available from certain banks and are guaranteed by the Department for Education and Employment. They are interest-free during the course itself.

Training and Enterprise Councils can give you information on any funding in your local area, as well as on the range of courses available.

If you are attending adult education or college of further education courses, you will normally receive a discount on fees if you are unemployed, a pensioner or a student.

For self-employed teleworkers, fees paid on training courses can be claimed as a business expense. The situation for employed workers is slightly more complex. According to Mark Dyer of Accountants thru' Internet, the cost of a "qualifying course of vocational training" can be set against taxable income (assuming that you paid for the course, not your employer). Such courses include those which count towards National or Scottish Vocational Qualifications, and it may be possible to obtain basic rate tax relief "at source" by paying a lower amount to the training provider. Higher rate tax relief has to be reclaimed through your tax return. The expenses must be incurred "wholly, exclusively and necessarily" in conjunction with your employment. Generally it is difficult to convince the Inland Revenue that the costs were "necessarily" incurred unless there is a clause in your contract of employment or other contractual arrangement for you to undertake the specified training.

In Ireland, only courses run by certain publicly-funded colleges with a duration of over two years can be claimed by employed teleworkers. The situation for the self-employed is the same as for Britain – training courses can be claimed as a business expense. The state training agency, FÁS, provides a number of free training courses for the registered unemployed.

Daytime courses

Much of the education system is based on ancient technology: put students in one end of a room and a lecturer in the other; get the lecturer to talk to the students. As Adam Smith said in 1776:

"The discipline of colleges and universities is in general contrived, not for the benefit of the students, but for the interest, or more properly speaking, for the ease of the masters."

Despite those wise words, there are still plenty of institutions that force you to attend lectures or training sessions at 9.00am on wet February mornings, when you'd prefer to be in bed. You probably don't have time for full-time education courses. It's likely, therefore, that any daytime courses you attend will be short training courses. But before you sign up, ask yourself whether there's a better way of covering the course content.

There's no doubt that interpersonal skills and similar topics require work with a trainer and with other participants. Thus, for courses in training skills, management, selling and such topics, a good conventional course is almost essential. But for learning about such subjects as marketing, software and accounting, you may be better off with a distance learning course, perhaps supplemented by some classroom tutorials and telephone support.

It's also worth remembering that the vocational qualification (VQ) approach, although widespread, is controversial within the training sector. On the one hand, courses such as the TCA's teleworking VQ fit well with the British government's funding structure and offer the only training designed for teleworking skills. The modular nature and practical approach of VQs are often much easier to handle for those who do not enjoy conventional courses or who have been out of the jobs market for a period of time. On the other hand other European countries are suspicious of the (N)VQ "competence based" approach where students collect a portfolio of

The TCA Teleworking Vocational Qualification

The Teleworking VQ is certified by City and Guilds, and was developed under the Teleworking for Europe project, a partnership between Staffordshire TEC, Leek College and Staffordshire County Council. It was part funded by the EU under the Euroform programme, and developed at the Moorlands Telecottage. Like most vocational qualifications, it is competence based. This means students can supply evidence to show their previous experience proves they are already capable of performing skills required by a particular module, and also that the tutor is free to design modules however they like, as long as the result is that the students can perform the required elements for certification. Students create a portfolio of evidence on their skills and competence.

The VQ is the only nationally available accredited course aimed at teleworking skills and gives a good basic grounding in relevant skills. It should be recognised that the VQ, reflecting the fact that teleworking is not in itself a skill or profession, but rather a way of working, is intended to equip the candidate with a platform of competence on which a service or skill can be overlaid. The competence acquired may be put to use in a conventional job, as well as for teleworking. On this basis, the Moorlands Telecottage has claimed that 95% of its trainees get some form of work or placement after completing their course.

For many unemployed or low-skilled returners to the workforce, the VQ offers one of the few opportunities for grant aided training relevant to telework. It is hoped that the existing qualification will be updated shortly and converted into a National Vocational Qualification (NVQ).

Existing teleworkers may find it interesting to read the course outline and check which units they think they could "pass" with their current knowledge.

Unit 1: Set up and configure computer system
Install hardware ready for use. Reconfigure or upgrade system.

Unit 2: Look after and operate computer system
Ensure equipment is maintained in good working order. Ensure data integrity is maintained. Oversee third party system maintenance. Diagnose and respond to problems.

Unit 3: Control media usage and security
Ensure all data storage media are stored correctly and securely. Control and record use of data storage media.

Unit 4: Telecommunications and data transmission
Process incoming and outgoing telephone calls using a multiline or switchboard system. Transmit and transcribe recorded messages. Transmit and receive copies of documents electronically.

Unit 5: Communicating information
Process incoming and outgoing business telephone calls. Receive and relay oral and written messages. Supply information for a specific

purpose. Draft routine business communications.

Unit 6: Data processing
Produce alphanumerical information in typewritten form. Identify and mark errors on scripted material for correction. Update records in a computerised database.

Unit 7: Mail handling
Receive, sort and distribute incoming/internal mail. Prepare for despatch outgoing/internal mail.

Unit 8: Health and safety
Operate safely in the workplace.

Unit 9: Storing and supplying information
Maintain an established filing system. Supply information for a specific purpose.

Unit 10: Information processing
Process records in a database. Process information in spreadsheets. Access and print hard copy reports, summaries and documents.

Unit 11: Text processing
Produce a variety of business documents from handwritten or typewritten drafts.

Unit 12. Self management
Identify personal aspirations and needs. Time management.

Unit 13: Project/team working
Project management. Team working.

Unit 14: Teleworking
Teleworking development

Unit 15: Business development
Compile a profile of personal strengths and weaknesses. Identify and determine business resources. Establish marketing and financial viability. Establish legal entity of a proposed business venture.

Unit 16: Obtain finance for a small business
Develop and produce a business plan for a start up business. Identify and access sources of finance.

Unit 17: Set up small business
Produce a marketing plan. Produce a sale activity plan. Plan operational running of a small business. Establish commercial and administrative procedures. Set up a financial record keeping system. Establish business relationship network.

Unit 18: Audiotranscription
Produce a variety of business documents from recorded speech.

Unit 19: Shorthand transcription
Produce a variety of business documents from dictated material.

Unit 20: Desktop publishing
Initiate software and create/edit file. Publish documents. Print and distribute job output.

Units 1–17 are mandatory while units 18–20 are optional. However, units 15–17 are optional for the basic teleworker, and units 12–14 are optional for the freelance, or self-employed teleworker.

evidence of their skills. Surveys of British employers also show many feel the (N)VQ approach is limited because it only demonstrates the ability to handle a particular task at a point in time to carry out a task, and not that the trainee has fully understood the background to the task or committed the task to memory. As with all courses, potential trainees should consider course content and teaching quality, as well as how the course will equip them for subsequent work. One of the best ways to find out about a course is to talk to former trainees.

Your time is precious. For taking in basic information, reading is more efficient than listening to a lecture: reading makes better use of your time. Keep classroom time for subjects that really need it. But do give some time for the management and interpersonal subjects; such courses are valuable even if you get nothing more than an opportunity to reflect on your practices.

Evening courses

Traditionally, evening classes have been devoted to adult education and to study for professional qualifications, degrees and other awards. Practical training-type courses in business-related subjects were confined to the daytime. However, several providers now run such courses in the evenings because that's what suits their customers. It's worth checking out what's available in your area: get as many brochures and prospectuses as you can. Start by ringing your local Business Link or TEC (in the UK) or the adult education officer of your VEC (in Ireland).

For both daytime and evening courses, you can take what's on offer from education and training providers or you can commission your own course. You might be able to get together with others in the same area, draw up a list of things you want to learn on a particular subject and get proposals from several local providers.

Distance learning courses

There is an ever-increasing range of distance learning courses in work-related subjects. You can do anything from a two hour course on Lotus to a full four-year professional accounting qualification or an MBA. The courses may use printed workbooks, audio, video, computer disks or multimedia CD-ROMs.

For work-related courses, consult the Open Learning Directory (Butterworth-Heinemann, annual). You should also get the brochures of the Open University and the National Extension College. Several professional, trade, educational and training bodies have their own courses, which may not be in the Directory; contact any bodies relevant to your needs and ask what they offer themselves and what they know about.

A good distance learning course is likely to structure your learning (see below): there may be starting and finishing points, help from tutors, get-togethers (tutorials or seminars) with other learners, assignments to check your learning and other helpful arrangements.

> **LISTED – finding learning resources online**
>
> The LISTED project is an EU Libraries scheme funded by the Telematics Applications Programme. It will provide an interactive online catalogue of flexible and distance resources, and plans to include information on:
>
> - *Information handling*
> - *Computing and IT*
> - *Health and safety*
> - *Business and finance*
> - *Quality and customer care*
> - *Personal development*.
>
> The programme has selected teleworkers as one of its six user groups. As well as supplying information about courses, it will also provide access to a number of titles or sample units to give a "flavour" of the course in question, either through participating libraries, or direct to the user.
>
> In addition, there will be online ordering facilities. As well as offering information over the Internet, the project plans to use other access methods including cable, satellite, networked CD-ROM and CD-I.

The Internet

Some education and training courses and materials are provided or advertised on the Internet. You can spend many happy days searching for them. In May 1996, a search for "training" reported over 87,000 finds; by the time you've searched through that lot, and then checked the quality of what you find, you'll probably be ready for retirement. Happy surfing!

That's not to say that there's no good stuff out there. But you'll have to know in advance that it exists – and be sure you know where it is.

Who's in charge?

The earlier suggestions in this section were about growing and cooking your own stuff; the later ideas were about the table d'hôte menu. But there are other approaches. Unless you're more interested in a qualification than in the content of the learning, there's no reason why you shouldn't pick and mix from several providers and add your home-grown goodies as well.

If you had a lot of time and money you could, for instance, plan a year's learning that included:

- a single module of an evening course on marketing at the local university
- a series of briefings from your customers on their future needs

- a two day training course on time management
- a distance learning module on management from the Open University
- a two week assignment to a telecottage offering services complementary to your own
- a reading programme on project management, finishing up with a short training course on MS Project.

If you're taking learning seriously, you have to be in charge of it yourself. You decide what you need to learn; you arrange to learn precisely what you need, when you need it. You don't have to take a package holiday, just because your local TEC or college offers it; it's better to get what you want, even if it's more expensive, than to end up wasting your time on a cheap, but unsuitable, course on (say) computers or entrepreneurship. Learning is worthwhile if it helps your business. Choose your learning experiences based on their quality (fitness for your purposes) rather than on the availability of qualifications or grants.

Structure

A course may be defined as a structured learning experience. At one level, the difference between (say) reading a textbook and studying a distance learning text is that the text may be better structured: you're shown the map of the whole course; you get an introduction and a summary of each unit (chapter) as well as of the whole module; there are various features along the way that are designed to help you to learn.

These days, the distinction between textbooks and distance learning texts is increasingly blurred. Many modern college textbooks, especially the American ones, look very like distance learning texts and use similar learning features.

A properly-run distance learning course is more than just a text (or other materials). A course provides managed learning: there are events of various types to help you to get started, to tell you what's expected of you, to monitor your progress along the way and to assess your performance at the end. Much of the cost of distance learning is in this management rather than in the materials. In general, courses that provide a lot of support to learners will have greater success: a higher proportion of learners will stick with the course and complete it successfully.

If you're choosing a long course, look for one that provides significant support, in many different ways, to help the learners. That applies as much to classroom based courses (are there tutorials? study-group sessions? individual discussions with lecturers?) as it does to distance learning courses.

If you decide to plan some learning from materials like books, videos, magazines or computer based packages, you should try to provide yourself with structure and support. Just as you plan your work (and perhaps that of employees or contractors), so you should plan your learning. Set goals, monitor progress, assess performance.

Build in some supports. One of the best forms of support is to work with someone else, in your own organisation or elsewhere. Discuss what you've learned. Share your insights. Question each other – and encourage each other too.

The year as a whole

What's true of individual courses applies to the year's learning as well. This chapter has encouraged you to plan for training as for any other aspect of your work. Your solutions don't have to be costly but, if they're to work, they must be organised.

By all means find out what grants and other support you can get. But don't sign on for an unsuitable course just because it's cheap or it's grant-supported. Instead, get your customers to pay for your training. Every time you bid for a contract, include an element to cover anything new you'll have to learn for that contract — and some extra learning as well. Put that money aside; don't spend it on anything but learning.

Focus on what you need. Nobody knows your business as well as you do; the views and recommendations of course providers are their sales spiels and should be treated as such: not dismissed, but not given too much weight either.

Don't sign up for a course just because there's a qualification attached. It may be useful; it may help you to land your next contract or the one after. However, the content and delivery of the course are more important than the qualification.

Keep managing the learning. Note new needs as you come across them; check and revise your lists of needs every week. Work out how best to meet each need, then arrange to do it. And remember to learn from experience; record what happened to the modem and how you fixed it.

Don't try to learn everything yourself, by yourself. Delegate some learning to professionals and more to your colleagues and your staff. Network with others; learn from them and let them learn from you. Make arrangements so you can call on them in time of need, but make sure you reciprocate.

Above all, keep learning.

Bibliography

Open Learning Directory 1995 published by Butterworth-Heinemann, Jan 1995 ISBN 0750623055

How on earth can a computer help my business? available free from Microsoft Tel: 0345 002000 (expect a wait before connection)

Information for Teleworkers *Date:* 1995
Author: Monica Blake

British Library R&D Report 6199, The British Library Document Supply Centre, Boston Spa, Wetherby, West Yorkshire LS23 7BQ

Contacts and URLs

National Council for Vocational Qualifications: 222 Euston Road, London NW1 2BZ Tel: 0171 728 1914

Information Technology Industry Training Organisation are keen to help train teleworkers and have some relevant literature Tel: 0171 580 6677

BTEC: Central House, Upper Woburn Place, London WC1H 0HH Tel: 0171 413 8400 WWW: http://www.demon.co.uk/btec

Making information work for you (Part of the *Managing in the 90s* series) available at http://www.bnet.co.uk

http://www-leland.stanford.edu/group/SLOW/ is the **Stanford Learning Organization** Web site covering information technologies and organization learning

http://www.icbl.hw.ac.uk/tet/usability-guide/ is a set of guidelines for producing easy to use computer based learning systems produced by Carmel Smith (carmel@icbl.hw.ac.uk).

City and Guilds of London Institute 1 Giltspur Street London EC1A 9DD

RSA Examinations Board (IT courses and exams including word processing and dtp, held in high regard by employers because of the level of accuracy required to achieve the qualification) Westwood Way, Coventry CV4 8HS Tel: 01203 470033

TCA Teleworking VQ Contact: Sarah Mcbrine Tel: 01538 386674 Fax: 01538 398445 Email: 100336.3353@compuserve.com

LISTED EU project for cataloguing distance and flexible learning resources Contact: Christ Robert Tel: +353 98 21885.

In Ireland, **Arthouse** offers training in multimedia and WWW related skills Tel: +353 1 605 6800 Email: training@arthouse.ie WWW: http://www.arthouse.ie/training/

In Britain, **ASLIB**, the association for Information Management, offers a number of Internet related courses from a library/information management perspective. Tel: 0171 294 3728 Fax: 0171 430 0514 EmaiL. pdg@aslib.co.uk

A WORD FROM OUR SPONSORS...

Lloyds Bank services for homeworkers

By Sue Keohane

As working patterns change, research suggests that this year alone approximately 100,000 "Homeworkers" will set up in business, representing 20% of all self-employed start-ups.

Lloyds Bank, which strives to provide practical start-up material and ongoing support for businesses, is now introducing an exclusive package of services for businesses run from home.

Those of us running a business from home have very different needs to those working in more traditional environments. Whilst we will usually have made the choice to work in this way, in reality some of us find the occasional sense of isolation and lack of available support a real challenge.

Lloyds Bank recognises these factors and has responded with a new service designed to offer practical and relevant support. The Homeworker Service will appeal particularly to professionals such as accountants, architects, computer consultants, graphic designers, osteopaths, physiotherapists and writers, but other businesses will also find that it meets their needs.

The following features are incorporated within the Homeworker service:

- Access to a free legal helpline, which will offer advice on a range of legal issues, including contractual disputes, health and safety and debt recovery. Both calls and the service are free of charge.

- 6 months' free subscription to "Home Run" magazine, a leading specialist magazine for Homeworkers.

- A copy of "Running a Home-Based Business" by Diane Baker, published by Kogan Page, at the reduced price of £4.00 (normally £9.99).

- Easy access to the Internet including access to Lloyds' bulletin board for Homeworkers and discounted hardware and free software for connection to the Internet.

Additionally, Lloyds are offering a 5% discount on their own Homeworker insurance policy, which was the first home contents insurance policy to be launched in the UK offering extra protection for business equipment, stock, business money and business interruption.

New customers may also call on the full range of services for new business customers, including the Sara Williams' Small Business Guide and the Lloyds Bank bookkeeping package.

And it doesn't stop there! Lloyds Bank Business Centres have staff experienced in business matters on hand to offer friendly help and guidance. Customers will benefit from a dedicated account manager who will take an interest in their business on a regular basis and who will be happy to visit them at home.

If you would like to find out more about the Homeworker service, or any other aspect of business banking with Lloyds Bank, please visit your nearest Lloyds Bank branch or telephone David Williams on 0117-943-4134.

(Sue Keohane is a mother of two young children and works from home).

Lloyds Bank

Office Solutions from Hewlett-Packard

Downsizing, redundancy, decentralising. Whatever labels you use, they don't disguise the fact that the business world is in turmoil. Out of this turmoil has come one of the growth industries - Teleworking. With a healthy proportion of the estimated 5 million small offices in the UK, and over 3.25 million self-employed (Federation of Small Businesses 1994), we are looking at a business sector with a significant need for technology to improve efficiency and presentation.

The right tools need not necessarily be the most expensive. Achieving the best price : performance ratio is the main priority, especially when equipping yourself technically for the core work that you do.

Hewlett-Packard knows this market. They've researched it and paid attention to what their customers really need. Now they believe they have got the equation right, with equipment where style and strength come together in a range which is competitively priced for the Small office/Home office (SoHo) market. Yet it still achieves the level of performance and efficiency that you, as business people, expect as of right and which your clients demand at all times.

Personal computers (PCs) in particular, have become virtually indispensable to the teleworker. Whether used for a database, as a word processor, for spreadsheets, accounts or charts - or all five - the HP Vectra 500 series of PCs has business and communications software ready to run. As many teleworkers work on their own without the benefit of on-site systems experts (albeit with the active support of organisations like the TCA) Hewlett-Packard has taken account of this and designed the Vectra 500 Series around three feature sets : ready-to-work capabilities; future-proof technologies; and reliability/support features.

Printer technology, too, has improved dramatically in recent years, with the dot matrix now rarely mentioned in the context of teleworking and the small office/home office environment. Inkjet (used in all HP DeskJet printers) has decisively taken over. In its 300, 400, 600 and 800 series DeskJet printers, HP caters for entry level, price-consciousness, the more sophisticated user and the need for mobility - yet they all have laser quality print output, as well as the capacity to print high quality colour using HP's ColorSmart software. Use of colour in business has been proved to increase awareness and retention of information.

With laser technology becoming increasingly affordable, another boon for the teleworker are the L and P categories of HP LaserJets. These two printers combine the superb quality associated with laser printing, yet at a price that makes them an excellent investment for teleworkers who may be working on their own, but as part of a co-operative scheme.

Increasingly, scanning is seen as an indispensable office tool, storing words and images which can then be reproduced, edited, printed, faxed, archived and even integrated into another application. The HP ScanJet range includes flatbed scanners which can cope with high volume scanning, while the HP sheetfeed version is ideal for black and white only, low volume work.

Space is always a factor for a small office, where separate items of equipment may become difficult to accommodate. Look no further than the Office in a Box. The logical solution.

Its official name is the HP OfficeJet LX - a printer, plain paper fax, a copier and a convenience scanner all in one! Multifunctionality doesn't make it complicated. Like the rest of the HP range all you have to do is plug and play. It couldn't be simpler.

The term teleworker doesn't just mean someone stuck on the end of a phone all day. Thousands spend much of their time on the road, and for them communications and information remain a priority, which is where the HP OmniGo personal organiser comes into its own. Light enough and small enough to slip into your pocket, in some instances the Omnigo might replace your notebook PC - even though the HP OmniBook, is a lightweight 3.8 pounds. With pen and keyboard the OmniGo combines diary and calculating functions, with a jotter application, financial analysis and spreadsheet capabilities and a host of others.

Latest information is that HP and Nokia are pooling knowledge and resources co-developing handheld voice, data and fax communications devices. After the office in a box, an office in your pocket?

For further information about Hewlett-Packard PCs and peripherals call 0990 474747.

HEWLETT® PACKARD

Teleworking – the inside story from BT

BT is a supplier well placed to talk to you about your teleworking needs, whether you are running a one-person home-based business or a teleworking project in a large company... BT had 130,000 people on the books as at March '96, and some 2000 of these could be found working from home full-time or part-time. The homeworkers range from BT managers or professionals working on the move or at home, to clerical and sales staff in carefully monitored pilot schemes like the Business Sales team in and around Southampton, and directory enquiries operators at Inverness.

"If the definition of a teleworker is anyone working away form a fixed base, full or part-time, then our 30,000 field engineers could also be included", says BT's Teleworking Manager, Nick Williams. To keep in contact with its field staff, BT makes productive use of 'off-the-shelf' technologies including mobile phone, laptops or personal organisers, pagers and Chargecards. Flexible working in BT is certain to keep growing well into the millennium. A project called Workstyle 2000 is being sponsored by the company's Group Property unit, keen to drive down the high costs of London accommodation.

Average accommodation costs in the UK run at around £4,700 per employee, so BT has condensed a substantial part of its Marketing Unit into purpose-built offices at Apsley, near Hemel Hempstead. Apsley has also become the hub for around 500 teleworkers, who use hot-desking facilities there for occasional use, and transact most of their day-to-day business from their homes through the Apsley LAN into other parts of BT, dialling in using normal telephone lines or ISDN2 access.

To support all this, BT's Health and Safety Advisers have been busy. But not too busy to share with BT's external customers, what the team have learned. A special helpdesk has been set up in Glasgow to advise and offer check lists, both to UK businesses as well as to BT's managers, helping each employer to meet his obligations under the Health and Safety at Work Act.

On the marketing front, 1996 has seen BT change its tack from promoting teleworking to the mass market as a 'good thing', towards promoting the financial benefits of teleworking to employers, focusing on increased productivity, cost control and extended customer service. Another change has been for increased interworking of BT products and services, rather than creating new products from scratch. 1996 has already seen the launch of MobileManager, the packaging of GSM Mobile phone, PCMCIA modem and software, and Fast File transfer – a packaging of ISDN2 service and BT's Ignition terminal adaptor. The benefits of packaging to BT are enormous, of course, in bringing end-solution to market much faster, but in addition the move will most certainly mean the ability for BT to offer highly competitive prices.

The year has seen BT develop sales agreements with Dell, with BT likely to offer Dell portable PCs to home-based businesses and teleworkers. At the upper end of the market, BT has also announced an agreement with Microsoft to jointly provide a complete solution for LAN interconnection. BT has also been strengthening a dealer network, particularly amongst retailers of ISDN2 equipment. The key difference between BT and other suppliers is that it can provide a complete communications solution containing both network services and terminal products. BT is keen to emphasise that a carefully considered package, tailored to the needs of the customer, is the way to ensure that businesses make the greatest productivity gains when changing to working at home or on the move (estimates of gains vary between 15% and 40%).

The range of solutions that BT has on offer is very wide starting at the very simple (e.g. a fax, answering machine and BT Chargecard) and ranging to the complex (e.g. access to a company LAN from home using ISDN2). Teleworking products on the drawing board at BT's Research Unit at Martlesham include: a video PBX, allowing dial-up video conferencing passing through company switchboards; a 'virtual' second line with distinctive ringing on a single telephone (depending on whether the call is a business one or a personal one); and the expansion of its exchange-based Featureline service to offer nationwide teleworking and switching.

Meanwhile, BT's call charges continue to tumble. The business choices schemes now offer savings of up to 21% off the regular business tariff, and this summer there will be further special offers on calls over ten minutes in duration – think of how much cheaper this makes long file-transfer or Internet calls!

In summary, most people find that BT is unique because it provides both a full communications solution and real experience of the human issues learnt from their own teleworking schemes. As BT's Nick Williams confirms, "For customers looking to pilot or roll-out teleworking schemes, we have made the communications issues a simple matter of choice. This frees up time for businesses to make sure that they have the human issues under control and gain the very most from changing the way that they work".

Useful numbers

For advice on BT's communication solutions for teleworking, including LAN access and BT MobileManager contact your BT Account Manager Tel: 0800 800 800

For advice on safety requirements for conducting business in the home environment (power, light, heat, space), drawing on BT's own experience contact BT Health and Safety Advice line Tel: 0141 220 1880.

Tolson Messenger Insurance Brokers

Whether you work from home as a self-employed person, or whether you participate in your employer's teleworking programme, there is a wide range of important issues which will require your careful consideration.

One such issue, where there appears to be a real lack of awareness and understanding, is that of insurance, which until recently has been greeted with little enthusiasm or urgency by the Insurers and their consumers alike.

Many people who work from home are unaware of what implications their activities have on their existing household insurance arrangements, and they are also largely unaware of the additional commercial insurance risks to which they may be exposed, by running a business from home.

Listed below are some of the points you need to consider, either in a self-employed or employed capacity.

- Is your existing Household Buildings and Contents policy affected in any way because you work from home? The vast majority of Insurers will specifically exclude cover for any item of business equipment, and others may go as far as refusing to insure you at all. (Check with your own insurers as they all treat this issue differently.) Failure to do so could mean your household policy being invalidated in the event of a claim.

Some Insurers are now beginning to offer some level of cover for business equipment under their Household Policies, typically up to £5,000. However many of these policies still fail to address the real insurance needs of those people who work from home. For example:

- Cover for portable business items such as laptops and mobile phones, taken outside the home.

- Business Interruption – you may incur additional expenses in running your business following loss or damage. For example, if your computer is lost or damaged, there may be costs involved in hiring a replacement machine, or in reinstating lost data.

- Public liability – If clients visit you in your home, or perhaps more commonly, you visit them, claims may arise where you are held legally liable for accidental damage to property or accidental bodily injury caused to a third party which arise out of your business activities. For example, a consultant working on a client site may spill coffee over a keyboard or may cause accidental damage during installation.

- Employer's liability – This insurance is compulsory by law, and you will require this if you operate as a limited company (and therefore technically an employee), or even if you are merely hiring staff on a casual cash-in-hand basis.

- If your business involves manufacturing and/or distributing stock, you will require cover for such stock held within the home and whilst in transit. You will also require Products Liability Insurance.

As an Employer, you will need to ensure that your existing commercial insurance arrangements are adequate to cover the employees who telework from home. All of the above insurances will need to be reviewed, particularly if, as is becoming increasingly common, such employees are no longer considered to be "employees" as such, but as self-employed contractors, in which case the "insurable interest" where responsibility for insurance will ultimately lie, may be passed on to the "employee" to make their own insurance arrangements.

Over the past 3 years, Tolson Messenger have pioneered and developed specific insurance schemes for the growing number of people who work from home. Our Home-Office Insurance Policy, underwritten by the Commercial Union, costs just £120.00 per year (£15 discount available to TCA members), for which cover is automatically provided for the following:

- Office contents and computers up to £7,500 (higher limits available)
- Portable equipment (laptops and mobile phones etc.) anywhere in the world up to £1,500 (higher limits available)
- Business Interruption (Increased Cost of Working) up to £10,000
- Stock cover up to £1,000 (higher limits available)
- Public and Employers Liability
- Business Money
- 24 hour legal helpline

Optional extensions in cover are also available to cover Personal Accident, Commercial Legal Expenses, Products Liability and Goods in Transit.

Tolson Messenger Limited are Insurance Brokers and Independent Financial Advisers. Members of the British Insurance and Investment Brokers Association, and regulated by the Insurance Brokers Registration Council, in the conduct of investment business.

For further advice and information call us free on 0800 37 42 46 or fax 0181 741 8361. 148 King Street, London, W6 0QU.

TOLSON
MESSENGER
INSURANCE · BROKERS

European experiences in telework

DG XIII of the European Commission has supported telework-related technology developments, analyses and trials since 1991. DG XIII is responsible for telecommunications, the European Information market development and exploitation of European research. Within these responsibilities, DG XIII manages the European Research programmes on Advanced Communications and telematics applications.

In 1993, a special set of exploratory actions were put in place for transEuropean stimulation of telework. Over 300 organisations participated. The following summary reports are available, free of charge, from DG XIII :

1. **Employment and economic impacts** of advanced communications, and social trends in use for communications services (PACE 1995) :
   - Results of the AD-EMPLOY project on Employment rends;
   - Results of the ACCORDE project on regional development impacts;
   - Results of analyses of changes in life styles and in use of electronic media;
   - Results of the METIER project on impacts on growth and trade.

2. **Legal, organisational and management issues** in telework :
   - Results of the COBRA analysis of constraints and opportunities in business restructuring;
   - Results of the PRACTICE survey of telework management practice in Europe;
   - Results of the ATTICA analysis of legal constraints to transborder telework in Europe.

3. **Telework and small business networking**: Results of six European collaborative trials and evaluations of telework and co-operative networking by small businesses.

4. **Telework, telecommuting and decentralisation**: Results of three European trials of telework in the context of urban planning, traffic reduction and business decentralisation.

5. **Transnational collaboration** from local telework centres; results of four European trials involving networks of telework and teleservice centres.

Results of these European analyses and trials are also summarised in the Proceedings of the 2nd European Assembly on New Ways to Work (Rome 1995), in commercial publication; notably "Business process re-engineering – Myth and reality" published by Kogan Press; and "Trends in the development of telework" published by IOS. Further information is available from:

DG XIII Directorate B, Advanced Communications Technologies and Services, 9 avenue de Beaulieu, 1160 Bruxelles Fax: +32.2.296.29.80, Email: pdg@postman.dg13.cec.be.

Glossary

ACD (automated call distribution): Computer systems used in call centres to distribute calls amongst operators and to monitor statistics such as average length of call, time before calls are answered and so on.

ASCII (American Standard Code for Information Interchange): Simple data format with no frills used as an "Esperanto" between different computer systems for the exchange of information.

Audioconferencing: using telephone systems to connect up to 20 people at different locations simultaneously for virtual meetings.

Baud rates: speed measurement for modems. Currently most modems purchased have a baud rate of 28,800 (also writtent as 28.8k)

Call centres: businesses for handling work carried out by telephone. The calls can be inbound (e.g. telereservations, technical support) or outbound calls (e.g. telemarketing, telesales). Generally call centres have sophisticated ACD computer systems to distribute calls between a number of operators and provide relevant information such as computerised customer records.

CompuServe: widely used American email and online services system.

CSCW (computer supported co-operative working): software tools and management methods which enable teams to work together from different locations by computer. Examples include electronic diaries, messaging systems, software for tracking updates on multi-authored documents, and videoconferencing tools such as electronic "whiteboards".

CTI (computer telephony integration): computer systems often used in call centres to integrate information between computers and telephones. For example, caller identification codes can be used by CTI systems to bring up the caller's customer record automatically for the operative answering the call.

Cyberspace: science fiction term used to describe the imaginative "space" where people communicate electronically using email and online services.

FAQs (frequently asked questions): files of information often held online for users of email and online services. Many newsgroups and listservs have FAQs which answer the most commonly-requested information on how to use a system, or specialist information related to the topic of the online resource. It is intended that new users should read the FAQs before asking typical "newbie" questions which may irritate more experienced users of the resource.

Fax card: card which inserts into a computer and connects to the telephone line to provide faxing facilities directfrom the PC.

Fax modem: modem which also includes relevant hardware and software for sending faxes. Almost all modems sold through retail outlets are fax modems.

Fax switches: electronic connectors which allow both a telephone and a fax to be connected to one telephone line. When a call comes in, the fax switch detects whether it is a voice or fax call and redirects it to the appropriate device.

Forum: term used to describe discussion areas of online services, particularly those on the CompuServe online service.

HTML (hypertext markup language): structured language developed from the ISO standard SGML markup language which is used to create hypertext pages for display on the World Wide Web.

Hypertext: computer text pages which contain active areas connected to other pages. By clicking on the active area with a mouse, the user is immediately transported to another page of hypertext. Thus documents can be read by subject of interest, rather than sequentially as when turning the pages of a book.

Internet: the global network of computer networks which is used to send computer messages and files. The internet has around 40 million subscribers worldwide.

Internet phones: development of the Internet to carry voice traffic at low cost. Internet phones have poor audio quality but can provide huge savings on standard international calls. The development is controversial because of its potential to "clog up" the data traffic on the Internet.

ISDN (integrated services digital network): new generation fibre optic telephone lines which allow fast file transfer, videoconferencing, high quality audio telephone lines and fast Group 4 faxing. Up to 8 different devices such as faxes can share one ISDN line.

ISO9000: the International Standards Organisation quality control standard. Companies which are certified to ISO9000 have shown that they have an internal quality system in place and that they can use the system effectively over a period of time. However, award of the ISO9000 standard does not indicate the complexity of the system that is in place – just that it is used as specified in its documentation.

LANs (local area networks): groups of computers connected together so that they can use common resources such as printers, file storage and software packages.

Listservs: mailing lists for specialist topics on the Internet. A message sent to a listserv is read by a human moderator to check the content is relevant and legal, and then redistributed to all those subscribed to that listserv for discussion.

Modem: abbreviation of modulator/demodulator. Electronic device for connecting a computer to a telephone line for the transfer of data.

Netiquette: contraction of two words, network and etiquette, and used to describe acceptable practice and behaviour in the use of online services.

OCR (optical character recognition): software used in conjunction with scanning devices to "read" typsecript into a revisable form on a computer.

OLR (offline readers): software packages used to automate connection to online services. Typically an OLR will log on to the online service, collect any waiting email, and check newsgroups or forums as instructed for new messages. The OLR will also send out any waiting messages from the user, before automatically logging off. OLRs can perform tasks faster and more reliably than human operators, leading to savings in telecoms and online charges.

Portable document format: a data format developed by Adobe which allows documents to be read on different computers regardless of their operating system or the fonts available on each computer.

Sysops and wizops: volunteers who manage forums and bulletin boards, particularly on the CompuServe online system. Sysops perform administrative tasks, answer questions and check files to ensure they are not infected with viruses or contain unsuitable or illegal material. A wizop is a chief sysop or teamleader.

Telecentres: centres where a number of people telework. They can range from small neighbourhood offices with basic computer equipment to sophisticated call centres employing hundreds of people.

Telecommuting: the practice of working at home and connecting to a central office using computers and telecommunications (commuting by telephone, or telecommuting).

Teleconferencing: see audioconferencing

Telecottage: a local centre providing access to low cost computer and telecommunications equiopment, which in turn gives access to information services and work. Some telecottages are community-run, others are commercial operations.

Teleworking: working at a distance from your client, customer or employer and keeping in touch using technology such as telephone, fax and computers.

URL (uniform resource locator): a unique identifier, analogous to a map grid reference, for a resource on the Internet. The most commonly used URLs are those for the World Wide Web, which always begin http://www.

Usenet News: global system of delivering information and discussion messages classified into specific areas via the Internet.

User-id: name which identifies a user to a computer system or online service when that user connects or logs in.

Videoconferencing: using video telephony to provide an image of the caller as well as audio communication. Videoconferencing can range from one-to-one calls using inexpensive ISDN equipment to high-level videoconference suites capable of connecting several rooms full of people together on high quality links.

World Wide Web: a user interface providing a consistent organisation to resources on the Internet, including HTML files. Using the World Wide Web, users can browse through different resources held anywhere on the Internet

without needing to see the "nuts and bolts" of Internet usage such as logging in and out of different computers.

Zipping files: using the widely-available PKZIP and PKUNZIP utilities to compress computer files before they are sent from one computer to another, and then to decompress them when they reach their destination.

Index

This index is arranged in word-by-word alphabetical order. The letter c following a page reference indicates a case study.

Abilities Limited	199
Ability Enterprises (Ireland)	200
abstracting	123-4
accountancy services	124
accounting software	224
ACD (automated call distribution) systems	47
advertising see also publicity	92, 93, 95-6
Allied Dunbar	39c
answering machines	210-11
Antur Tanat Cain Telebureau	103
Antur Teifi	7, 130c, 186-8
audio typing (see also transcribing machines)	124
audioconferencing	63, 125, 208
automated call distribution (ACD)	47
Barnham Telecottage	103-4
Bertelsmann/America Online	166
binding equipment	228-9
bookkeeping services	124
BOON (Business On Open Network)	104-5, 125, 215
box office services	129
Britannia Building Society	37c
Bronllys and Talgarth Telecentre	105
BT	237-8
BT Inverness directory enquiries	5-6, 12, 71
Burger King	7-8
business objectives	76-77
plans	78-9, 81
rates	138-40
call centres	126-7
Canada Life	9-10
Cape Clear Telecottage	105
Capital Gains Tax	137
cash flows	116-7
CD-ROMs	219
child care see also family life	10, 69-70
Cigna Benefits Processing	8
communications means, choice of	41, 60-66
communications software	161
CompuServe	65, 165-6, 168, 171
computer based faxes	64, 212-3
computer magazines	204
computer processors	214-5
computer programming	124-5
computers, purchasing	213-6
computer supported co-operative working see CSCW	
computer telephony integration see CTI	
consultants	114
contact managers (databases)	224
contracts	
employees	38-9
for service	140-43
of service	140-43
quality aspects	184
self-employed	53-4
copyright	151-3
Council Tax	137
couriers	66
covenants (restricting use of property)	137-8
Crossaig publishers	6, 124
CSCW (computer cupported co-operative working)	12, 47-8, 65, 224-5
CTI (computer telephony integration)	63, 127, 207-8
cyberspace	162-3
Daily Information	106
data	
conversion	125
input	125-6
processing	126-7
protection	149-50
security	13, 50, 155, 226
Data Protection Act	149-50
databases	223, 224
deadlines	59-60
debt finance	84-5
desktop publishing see DTP	
Digital	6-7, 45c
directories	92-4
disabled persons	
employment opportunities	201
European projects	198
networks	199-201, 202
state assistance	196-7
technical aids	194-6
training	197-8
disability see disabled persons	
Disability Discrimination Act	201

document formatting	124	forums, CompuServe	171-2
DTP (desktop publishing)	132, 223	fundraising	114-6
Dyer Partnership	125c	Grampian Regional Council	10
Eccles House Telebusiness Centre	106-7	graphics software	223-4
editing	123-4	groupware see CSCW	
electronic publishing	19	hard disks	215, 220
electronic village halls (EVHs)	110, 114c	health and safety	134-6
email		health insurance	148-9
addresses	169	Henley Management Centre 48	
advantages	163	Hewlett Packard	253-4
as communications means	42-3, 64-5	home office	
file transfer	163-5	insurance	155-8, 239-40
junk	170	planning implications	136
messaging formats	164	premises	38, 70-71
setting up	160-62	home shopping	128
endemic teleworking	34	Homeworker service	
environmental considerations	15-16	(Lloyds Bank)	255-6
equipment (see also under specific headings)		Hoskyns	10
		housekeeping	66-8
basic requirements	43-50	HTML (hypertext markup language)	175, 176
prices	44, 204		
rental of	205	indexing	123-4
renting out	127	information broking	128-9
security	43, 153-5	Information Society Initiative	22-3
where to buy	204-5	Instant Search	7, 93c
equity finance 82		insurance	148-9, 155-8, 239-40
EU		Integrated Services Digital Network see ISDN	
community actions	25		
funds	27, 115	intellectual property rights	151-3
projects for the disabled	198	Intermec	188-9, 192
research and development programmes	24-5	the Internet	172-5
		Internet phones	17, 221-2
telework programmes	23-6	Internet Relay Chat (IRC)	178
Europe Online	166	Internet service providers	162-3
European Social Fund	23-4	IRC (Internet Relay Chat)	178
EVHs (electronic village halls)	110, 114c	ISDN (Integrated Services Digital Network)	17, 45-6, 164-5, 206
expenses, allowable	143		
fair use see copyright		Isles Telecroft	107-8
family life (see also child care)	13, 20, 68-70	ISO standards	181
		isolation	11, 12, 13-14, 72-3
farm skills	127-8	job satisfaction	8-9
fax		journalism	36
cards 212-13		junk email	170
modems see cards		KITE (Kinawley Integrated Teleworking Enterprise)	8, 102, 108-9, 112
shots 92			
switches 64		LANs (local area networks)	163-4
faxback services 212		laptop computers see portable computers	
faxes	41-2, 44, 64, 211-13		
faxing services	128	learning opportunities see training	
feasibility studies	35	LETS (Local Enterprise Trading System)	129
finance, raising	80-85, 114-16		
First Class	167	LISTED project	249
fixtures and fittings	229	listservs	173

Lloyds Bank/TSB Group	52c, 255-6	pensions	145-8
local area networks (LANs)	163-4	personal health insurance see health insurance	
Local Enterprise Trading System (LETS)	129	personal pension plans	147-8
Lombard North Central	46c	photocopiers	227
mail order purchasing	205	photocopying services	128
mailing lists	89-92, 173	physical security	48, 153-5
market research	77-8, 113	pilot projects	36-7, 40
marketing	75-6, 86-7	planning, changes in use	136
Mere Telecottage	100c, 109-10	portable computers	216
Microsoft Network (MSN)	166-7	postal equipment	228
MIRAS mortgage tax relief	137	postal services	42, 66, 228
mobile phones	63, 209-10	presentations software	224
see also telephones		press releases	87-9, 95
modems	160-1, 220-21	pricing work	79-80
Moorlands Telecottage	112	printers	216-7, 253-4
motivation	11, 58-9	productivity	5-6, 11
MSF Union	14, 144, 145	proofreading	123-4
multimedia	219	Proto-type	123c, 142, 143
National Insurance	53	public relations	85-6
National Vocational Qualifications (NVQs) see VQs		public utilities charges	140
netiquette	167-8	interruptions	154
Network Personnel	199-200	publicity see	
networks	92-4, 199-201	also advertising	87-9, 95-6
NVQs (National Vocational Qualifications) see VQs		publishing services see also desktop publishing; electronic	
occupational pensions	146-7	publishing	129-30
OCR (optical character recognition) software see scanners		quality code of conduct, Telnet	183-4
office		management	180-93
furniture	44	standards	181, 184
overheads	6-7	system	181, 182, 191-3
services	129, 130	quotes see pricing work	
offline readers (OLRs)	168-9	rates, business	138-40
OLRs (offline readers)	168-9	Ratio (Rural Area Training and	
online		Information Opportunities)	121c
catalogues	177-8	remote support	19
etiquette see netiquette		remote typing see audio typing	
services	165-7	renting equipment	205
support	168	RNIB (Royal National Institute	
Open University	34	for the Blind)	200-1
optical character recognition (OCR) software see scanners		Rural Area Training and Information Opportunities (RATIO)	121c
optical drives	219	scanners	217-8, 253-4
Outset	197, 201	scanning	130
overwork	71	security	
Oxfordshire County Council	49c	data	13, 50, 155, 226
pagers	210	physical	48, 153-5
passwords	162	self-assessment taxation	143-4
PATRA report	9	self-employment	14-15, 140-43
pay	50-51, 53	Siemens Stockholm	42c
PCs see computers		skills registers	131

Small Claims Court	67c	audioconferencing; ISDN	
social policy	22	answering machines	210-11
social trends in teleworking	20-21	as communications means	41
software	222-5	enhancements	207-9
software support	124-5	equipment	44-6
Somerset Computer Services	189-91	mobile phones	63, 209-10
SPEC (Standon Parish Electronic		skill in usage	61-3
Centre)	110-11	recording devices	227
sponsorship	113	repairs	154-5
spreadsheets	223	telesales see telemarketing	
start up costs	81, 82	Telework Europa forum	172
State support	115-6	teleworkers	
stress	71	categories	5
support	40-41, 47, 73	numbers of	2-4
sysops	168	services	123-132
tacit teleworking	34, 35	teleworking	
tape drives	219	advantages	
tape recorders	227-8	for employee or self-employed	8-10
taxation see also capital gains tax;		for the employer	5-8
council tax	50-51, 53	and BT	237-8
technical aids for disabled persons	194-6	definition 1-2	
technical support	47, 73	disadvantages	
TECs (Training and Enterprise		for the employee	13-15
Councils)	115, 197	for the employer	11-13
telecentres see also telecottages	14	endemic	34
telecommuting	1	implementation of	34-54
teleconferencing see audioconferencing		networks for the disabled	199-201
telecottages		quality management	182-3
Antur Tanat Cain Telebureau	103	reasons for	4-5
Barnham Telecottage	103-4	staff suitability to	38
BOON	104-5, 125, 215	tacit	34
Bronllys and Talgarth		welfare benefits	21
Telecentre	105	Telnet code of conduct (quality)	183-4
Cape Clear Telecottage	105	time management	58-9
Daily Information, Oxford	106	Tolson Messenger insurance	
Eccles House Telebusiness Centre	106-7	services	239-40
Isles Telecroft, Shetland	107-8	tourist information	129
KITE	102, 108-9, 112, 242c	trade union, guidelines on	
Mere Telecottage	100c, 109-10	teleworking	144-5
Moorlands Telecottage	112	trade unions see also MSF Union	14
SPEC (Standon Parish		training	
Electronic Centre)	110-11	basic needs	239, 240, 246-7
WREN Telecottage	111	courses, certified	238
services	14, 100-1, 112	delegation of learning	234-6
setting up	111-114	disabled persons 197-8	
statistics	101-2	funds for	244
types	99	learning opportunities	240-45
in UK and Ireland 118-19		for managers	39-40
visiting	112	for new teleworkers	40, 72,
WREN	102, 111, 112, 128	plans	232
telemarketing	126, 127	prioritisation	237, 240
Telemart	94c	pyramid	242c
telephones see also		relevance	232-3